What's Wrong With Freud?

What's Wrong With Freud?

A Critical Study of Freudian Psychoanalysis

Originally titled
The Successful Error

Rudolf Allers, M.D., Ph.D.

$\mathcal{R}$oman $\mathcal{C}$atholic $\mathcal{B}$ooks

A Division of Catholic Media Apostolate
Distribution Center: Post Office I   2286, Fort Collins, CO 80522

First published November 1941

ISBN 0-912141-66-2

CONTENTS

PREFACE

THIS book is a critique. It is written by one who has studied psychoanalysis closely and is forced to deliver an adverse verdict. The author knows that he is far from being alone in this attitude. There are several who have criticized psychoanalysis, and more who have disapproved of it without troubling to criticize the idea. But the author of these pages believes that those critical studies of Freudian ideas have not been pushed far enough; they have not unveiled the background of the theory, or if they have, they have not pointed out with sufficient clarity how closely the several conceptions of Freud and of his school depend on the philosophy which is behind the whole system. Many adversaries of psychoanalysis have rejected its ideas because these were felt to be contradictory to morals, to generally accepted principles, to common-sense. But these reactions alone, however justified they might be, are not good arguments. They may spring from a vague notion that something is wrong with the facts and the ideas and the logic of the theory which is condemned; but unless these factors are made clearly visible, one's mere feeling on the subject is of no great value as an argument. Psychoanalysis prides itself on being a science. It has to be opposed by the means which science uses, that is, by logical analysis and critical examination of facts.

The intention in these pages is, however, not only to criticize psychoanalysis but also to look into the importance which this system is alleged to possess for psychology, for medicine, for education, sociology, ethnology and what not. And one more thing the author hopes to achieve. Psychoanalysis, after having been ignored and put aside for many years, has met a truly amazing success. It is not by psychoanalysts only that psychoanalysis has come to be considered the greatest achievement of psychology, the most important discovery in centuries. The nineteenth century, it is said, will be called the century of Freud. There is no field of human life and of human activity which has not in one way or the other come under the influence of the new "depth-psychology" or felt obliged to avail itself of the ideas offered by psychoanalysis. This success is itself a problem. Such developments are not frequent in the history of human thought. And because of their rarity they demand an explanation. I shall try to give one.

This book is written by a Catholic. Many people, especially the psychoanalysts, will immediately suspect a particular bias in the mind of the writer. It is because of this that I shall refrain as far as possible from contrasting the statements of psychoanalysis with those of the Faith or of Catholic philosophy. I shall endeavor to unmask the hidden self-contradictions of psychoanalysis and the inconsistency of many of its statements. I shall attempt to demonstrate that this theory is incompatible with any philosophy save the one whose spirit pervades the theory as well as the practice of psychoanalysis.

I believe indeed, and I want to make this clear from the very beginning, that theory and practice are so closely bound together in psychoanalysis as to be truly inseparable. One cannot accept the one without the other. Whoever desires to make use of the method cannot help adopting the philosophy. Since I believe this philosophy to be utterly and demonstrably wrong, I believe also that to apply the method is dangerous.

The manifold use which the ideas of Freud have found and their relations to so many sides of human life make it necessary that a critical study take account of all or, at least, of most of these sides. It is impossible today for one man to acquire competent knowledge in all these fields. He has to rely on others. In doing so he has to take care to choose trustworthy authorities. But where a man has been able to acquire knowledge of particular fields, by personal study and personal experience, he has to say what he has found to be the truth. I hope I shall not be accused of presumption in believing I possess reliable knowledge at least on the medical and the psychological side of our problem. I can indeed look back on thirty years of psychiatry and on twenty years of practice in psychotherapy; I may be pardoned for referring to the fact that I have been teaching medical and normal psychology for many years abroad and have been teaching psychology for the past two years in America. And I may be permitted to mention that I have in the last twenty years repeatedly written and talked on psychoanalysis and have followed its development for a very long time.

The result of my study of psychoanalysis, of comparing it with other psychological conceptions, of my personal experience of so many individuals, abnormal and normal, has been reported in several publications. Some statements contained in them I no longer maintain. They are mostly statements agreeing with this or that part cf Freudian psychology. My opinion has developed; the more intimate I have become with psychoanalysis and its problems the less favorable that opinion has become. The conclusions reached in this book are, therefore, mostly negative. It seems unnecessary to give here a lengthy exposition of psychoanalysis. It has become so well known that at least its essentials may be supposed to be in no need of further explanation. I shall, therefore, limit the report on the nature of psychoanalysis to a few pages, enough to give an indispensable basis to the critical analysis.

Freud is the true father of psychoanalysis, as everybody knows. He it was who developed what is generally comprised under this heading, though the first steps in this direction were taken together with Breuer, and, as it seems, partly under his leading influence. The latter deserted the work, shortly after it had been started, for reasons of which little is known and which are in any case without importance. Breuer was older than Freud and died several years ago. Freud died in London, the 24th of September, 1939, an exile from his country, 84 years old.

Some might feel, because of the biographical facts just mentioned, that to criticize Freud's life work so soon after his death means disregarding the old adage: *de mortuis nil nisi bonum.* But the living are more important than the dead. And to protect the living against falling prey to error is an important task, more important than all consideration of the dead. Voltaire somewhere in his writings very justly remarks: *"Aux vivants on doit des égards, aux morts rien que la verité."*

What then is the purpose of this study? Not so much to convince psychoanalysts that they are in error, but to make those who are as yet but interested see psychoanalysis in the light of truth. There are but few "conversions" of psychoanalysts. They are too sure of having laid hand on the deepest truths of man's nature. But one might hope to prevent the spreading of the contagion.

The psychoanalysts have seldom answered any criticism. They have, for dealing with such criticisms, a curious method. Instead of considering the objective arguments brought forth by their adversaries, they explain to themselves and to whosoever will believe it that the antagonism against Freudian psychology is due to the very factors Freud has declared to be active in human nature. Unless a man, they say, has been subjected to psychoanalysis himself, he is unable to understand and to evaluate this theory, let alone to make use of it for the study of the mind and the treatment of mental troubles. This way of reasoning is a unique phenomenon in the history of thought and of science. It will be dealt with in its appropriate place. But I must emphasize from the start that I hold this argument to be absolutely unjustified and to rest on certain fallacies which indeed are common to all parts of psychoanalytic teaching.

This book has three parts. The first part, comprising chapters I to V, is on the nature of psychoanalysis, its presuppositions and the philosophy on which the system rests. The second part, chapters VI to XII, deals with special questions and the relations of psychoanalysis to other sciences or fields. The third and concluding part studies the historical roots of psychoanalysis and attempts to give an idea of the reasons why this theory had such an astounding success. The last chapter summarizes the discussion of the foregoing parts and formulates definite questions which the psychoanalysts are called upon to answer. This book is in no sense a complete report on the facts which are available. It does not aspire to be exhaustive. It refers to literature only incidentally and for the sake of illustration. Nor do I here propose any other theory to replace Freud's which I criticize and hold to be unacceptable. Whatever my personal views on this point may be, they do not belong here. This book is a critique.

CHAPTER I

Basic Notions of Psychoanalysis

EVERY science rests on certain principles which do not belong to the science itself, but which precede it. In the primary sciences like logic and mathematics, such principles are called axioms. The principle of contradiction is one of these, as are also the basic laws of numbers. It does not matter here whether these first principles are such by nature and whether they are self-evident, or whether they are posited by the human mind. We are interested only in the fact that even the more fundamental sciences need some propositions from which to start their reasonings. The theoretical or ideal sciences are presupposed by those other sciences which deal with empirical facts. Physics presupposes measurement, and measurement rests on the principles of arithmetic and geometry. Biology presupposes physics and chemistry, and so on. Every science having a particular formal object adds to the principles which it takes from another science certain propositions of its own.

These fundamental propositions, however, are not proven by this science itself. They are taken for granted, and it is the task of a theory of science to disengage from the complex statements made by particular sciences the principles implied therein. Thus, biology assumes that living organisms are of another nature than dead matter. An extreme materialistic monism might like to disregard the essential differences of life and dead matter but it cannot fail to acknowledge that life as a phenomenon obeys laws other than those of physics and that it presents aspects which are not observable in inorganic matter. These differences of phenomena cannot be denied even by one who believes that "in reality" or "at bottom" no such differences exist. The fact has to be recognized, and the statement of this fact is not in the field of biology which deals only with organisms and cannot, as mere biology, make any statement about the nature of non-living things.

Psychology too rests on certain extra-psychological presuppositions. It is indeed the diversity of these "axioms" which causes the diversities of opinion among psychologists and brings it about that we have today not one psychology but several psychologies. One of these psychologies is psychoanalysis. To characterize its essence it will be necessary to go back to the very principles on which this particular psychology rests. We shall, however, look in vain for a clear statement of these principles in the writings of Freud and his followers, just as we shall fail to discover a satisfactory statement of the first principles of physics in one of the usual textbooks of physics or even in the more comprehensive treatises. It is not the task of a science, generally, to analyze its own principles; the principles are not discoverable by the science but are prior to it. Thus we must not wonder at the fact that psychoanalytic literature contains scarcely any remark on the basic ideas which precede the theory of psychoanalysis and its practical use. It is for the philosopher of science to discover these principles, to state them in an unequivocal manner, and to examine them in regard to their origin and their validity.

It is not necessary to delve into all the details of a theory to make sure of its principles. Such principles are necessarily implied in every general proposition and they are brought to light by considering the main lines, the framework, of the theory of which they are the foundation. We can, therefore, pass over many of the particular statements made by psychoanalysis and may limit our discussion to the more general aspects of the science. To give a full account of psychoanalysis, would be indeed impossible here. That is a task to be achieved only in a more or less bulky treatise. I shall, however, attempt a brief sketch of the psychoanalytic system in order to recall to the reader the main features of the Freudian conception and to introduce him to the propositions from which the "axioms" are to be developed. Any such sketch must be no more than a very brief outline; but I shall endeavor to include all that is really essential in Freud's theory. Envisioning this theory in its present state I do not take account here of its historical development. That aspect, insofar as its study contributes to the understanding of the whole problem, will be dealt with in chapter XI.

Psychoanalysis endeavors to discover the origin and the causes of mental states, taking this term in its widest sense. Why these states exist in a person and why at this very moment some impulse, some longing, some emotion exists, why he desires this and feels repelled by that, why he forgets a name or a purpose, why he commits this or that slip of the tongue, why he has developed an abnormal mood or some pathological so-called "nervous" symptom. These are the questions to which psychoanalysis claims to have found the answer. Its real scope is, however, still larger. Psychoanalysis aims at explaining not only individual mental life, but also the life of mankind, the evolution of culture, of religion, of social phenomena. We shall deal here only with psychoanalysis as a science of the individual mind; its further applications to the fields just mentioned will be studied in later chapters.

The main principle is that in order to unveil the causal connections and to ascertain by this procedure the true nature of the different mental phenomena, one has to go back into the remote past of the individual. The evolution of personality is conceived, if one is allowed to use this comparison, according to the pattern of geology. An early layer is covered by a newer one, and this is overlaid again by another and so on. Nothing is ever really destroyed; things disappear or become invisible by being covered; they are, as we shall see presently, rendered inaccessible to consciousness by being actively buried in deeper strata, but they do not cease to exist. The everlastingness of what has once been in the mind is one of Freud's basic ideas.

The statement that nothing is really forgotten in the com-

mon sense of the word, i.e., driven out of the mind so as never
to return again and not even to be capable of returning, was
suggested to Freud by the discovery of many apparently forgotten memories arising during analysis or, in a prior state of
Freudian psychology, in hypnosis. The facts, of course, justify
only the conclusion that things may apparently be forgotten
and nevertheless be brought back under certain conditions. The
statement that nothing is forgotten is a generalization, based
on induction and justified as much as, but no more than, an
induction of this kind generally is. On closer inspection, however, this generalization becomes somewhat doubtful. In the
average case of induction, which is indeed the common and
necessary tool of empirical science, the verification by experiment refers to causes having always the supposed same effect
or to effects being always reducible to the same causes. Both
terms of the relation are known, and both are susceptible or
experimental verification. It is not quite the same with the case
of "forgotten" memories. We can only prove, at the best, that
there are more memories preserved in the mind than one could
admit at first sight, but we can never prove that nothing has
been forgotten. To prove this we would have to know all the
impressions ever stored in memory or ever operative on the
mind, and we should have to try to make them return into consciousness. It is evident that this cannot be done. The proposition that nothing is ever forgotten may be very plausible if the
whole theory of psychoanalysis is once posited as true; but there
is no decisive proof for this proposition.

Since things remain "within" the mind—we must not forget
that all these expressions are metaphorical and have to be used
with a certain reserve—we have to ask for the reasons why
some of them disappear at all. Freud somewhere remarked,
quite in accordance with the main trend of his psychology, that
the problem is not why we remember but why we forget. This
is very much to the point. In the usual experiments on memoriz-
ing—for instance when learning nonsense-syllables or even

meaningful material—a certain amount of the stuff is remembered immediately, whereas a good part of it needs a number of repetitions. This may seem quite intelligible and not necessitating a particular explanation. But for the serious enquirer the question does remain why this part of the whole material is retained and the other is not. This is precisely the angle from which Freud envisioned the problem. His interest turned on the material content, not merely on the formal side of remembering and forgetting.

Things may be forgotten, merely for the time being, and may return to consciousness whenever we wish; if some effort is needed to bring them back, this effort is not hard and is generally efficacious. Sometimes we discover that it is not easy to recall things we are quite sure we know; but we usually lay hand on what we want to remember, either by continuous effort or by a spontaneous emergence of the thing. Certain memories may return on exceptional occasions without our desiring them or making any effort in the matter; they may surprise us, because we had not thought of them for so many years and had believed that they had slipped altogether from our mind. We feel that we had never known these things; if some one had asked us if we remembered we would have denied it absolutely. This common fact indicates certain differences in the nature of memory; there are at least some noteworthy differences in the relation of the things "stored" in memory and the readiness of their return to consciousness.

When Freud began the study of psychological questions, he had become acquainted with two facts which determined to a great extent the development of his ideas. One fact was Breuer's observation that in a certain clinical case facts which had been forgotten became conscious in a curious semi-hypnotic state or in true hypnosis; these things had therefore not been truly forgotten, though they had become, for some reason, inaccessible to consciousness. Freud had come across his second fact when studying hypnosis under Bernheim at Nancy, prior to his return to Vienna. The significance of this fact became clear to him, however, only much later. Bernheim had told a subject in hypnosis to attack him after a certain time—a so-called post-hypnotic suggestion. (We say "so-called" because the term is inaccurate, the suggestion is made during hypnosis, only the execution of the command is post-hypnotic.) Bernheim's subject carried out the order given to him in hypnosis, Bernheim then asked the subject why he behaved in this manner, and the man assured the doctor that he had no idea, but the doctor insisting and repeating that he had to know why, the subject suddenly said: "but you told me yourself a while ago to do this."

From this observation Freud concluded that post-hypnotic amnesia, that is, the incapacity to remember things experienced during hypnosis, if the return to memory has been barred by an adequate suggestion, is not as absolute as one might be inclined to believe at first sight. Things of which the individual apparently did not and could not know were known nevertheless, though evidently in a peculiar manner. To bring them back some effort was needed; it was as if a barrier had to be broken through before the return to consciousness became possible. In the Bernheim case this barrier consisted of the suggestion given to the subject that he was not to remember anything that had been said during the state of hypnosis. Freud thereupon drew two important conclusions. One was that there were in man's memory things not accessible to the average process of recall and that there were, so to say, degrees of accessibility. The other was that to reach down to these generally inaccessible depths of memory one did not need to employ hypnosis, since Bernheim had been able to overcome the difficulty by insistent questioning. The moment Freud abandoned hypnosis as the principal method of the study of neurotic troubles, psychoanalysis as we know it today was born.

Psychoanalysis was at first merely a method. Its very name denotes this. We have been accustomed to talk of psycho-

analysis as a definite kind of psychology and as a theory of
the nature and the functioning of the mind. But the name is
still only the name of a method. This fact is of particular
significance. There is hardly any other psychology—or, for that
matter, any other science—in which the importance of method
is as great as it is in the Freudian system; and nowhere is the
connection of method and theory as close as in psychoanalysis.
The facts mentioned and the observations Freud made afterwards suggested two questions. One had to form some idea of
the various kinds of memory or preservation of experience, and
one had to find a reason why some memories were easily recalled while others returned to consciousness only under exceptional conditions. The solution to this second difficulty involved
naturally an explanation of the particular conditions allowing
for the return of these reminiscences.

Speculation on the first question led to the conception of the
"unconscious"; the theory of the phenomena referred to in the
second question culminated in the introduction of notions like
repression, the censor, the unconscious, and the like.

The notion of the unconscious was, of course, not a new one.
For ages it had played a certain rôle in psychology and philosophy. It had been perhaps first conceived, though not explicitly
stated, by St. Augustine when he spoke of the existence of two
wills in man's mind. His explanation of the apparent weakness
of will implies that consciousness or conscious will is not aware
of the existence of a second will possessing what the first will
lacks. On the history of this idea we cannot expatiate here; it
has been studied by several authors, from the viewpoint both
of philosophy and of psychology.

Nor was the other notion, the one of resistance or of a complicated set of dynamisms at work within the mind, an unheard-
of one. The student of the history of psychology is struck by
the similarities between the Freudian and the Herbartian conceptions. Herbart, in his indeed speculative and not empirical
psychology, had introduced the idea of mental states acting on

each other according to laws fashioned very much on the pattern of physics. These historical antecedents of psychoanalysis will be one of the points to be discussed toward the end of this book; they contribute much to our understanding of the position of psychoanalysis in the history of psychology and, for that matter, of the theory of human nature in general, and they help to explain the amazing success achieved by Freudian psychology.

Even though these notions of the unconscious and of the dynamism in mental life were already known, they took on a new significance when used by Freud as fundamental elements of his theory. Freud combined his concepts of the unconscious and of memory with the notion that the mind consists of different "layers." This image was suggested to him probably by the work of the English neurologist Hughlings Jackson, from which he took also another notion, that of "regression," though here again the old term received a new and particular significance. Freud was, of course, well acquainted with Jackson's work. There might have been also some influence from the side of the French psychologist and philosopher, Ribot, who did much to make known in France the ideas of contemporary English and German psychology.

With the notion of "layers" in the human mind, the factors of spatiality entered psychoanalysis, which later on developed a "topological" point of view. The three basic ideas of topological, economic and dynamic consideration will occupy us presently. It is, however, better to explain first the special form the idea of "layers" assumed in Freud's mind.

There were at first but three of these layers. There was consciousness at one end and the "unconscious" at the other, and between these there was the subconscious. The last named was supposed to "contain" all memories not actually in consciousness but always ready to turn up there, either spontaneously or by being recalled at will or by following the connection of associations. The unconscious was conceived of as the "place" where those memories were stored which could not return spontaneously nor be made to return to consciousness. Freud had the idea from the very beginning that there are forces at work in the human mind which somehow influence the operations going on there and the single states which become conscious. This idea, as I have remarked, was not altogether new, since it had formed one of the basic notions in Herbart's psychology. The speculations of Herbart, however, had little in common with experience and observable facts. When Freud developed his conception he had to build it up along lines of his own.

The next question to be answered* had to be: which reasons condition the differences in the kind of memory or in the possibilities of recall? Why did some past experiences remain within reach of consciousness, whereas others seemed to elude it altogether and were capable of being brought back only by special methods? And why was it possible to break through the barrier which evidently kept those memories from returning to consciousness either by insistent questioning, as in the case of Bernheim's experiment, or by hypnosis, as in the patient studied by Breuer? This barrier, of course, could be conceived of only as being erected and maintained by some force. Here is the origin of the notion of repression and the notion of the censor. Repression is the name of the force or power which removes certain facts from consciousness into the unconscious and holds them there; the censor is the power which makes a spontaneous return to consciousness impossible.

This question leads to another. Why are certain facts repressed? Why do they not simply remain in the subconscious so as to be recalled whenever, by some association, they come "close to" consciousness, or to use another metaphor common with Herbart, ready to pass the "threshold of consciousness"? The answer given by psychoanalysis is that these memories are

* It may be well to state expressly that our description of psychoanalysis is mainly one of systemization and not one of history. Terms like "the next question" do not refer to factual development of Freudian ideas, but to systematic relations.

felt to be intolerable, because they contradict certain masterful tendencies of consciousness. This idea too was not quite new, though it had perhaps been but little recognized by the "official" psychology of those years. It had been known to popular psychology as well as to poets, and it had been very forcibly expressed by Frederick Nietzsche.

It is to be remarked, however, that Freud repeatedly denied having been acquainted with the writings of this author. (We shall have to discuss the possible influence of Nietzsche and of other writers on Freud in the chapter on the history of psychoanalysis.) The passage in Nietzsche reads: "You have done this, says memory. You cannot have done it, answers pride; and memory gives in." The memory "forgets" things at the command of pride, says Nietzsche. The forgetting is the outcome of a conflict between memory and pride. According to psychoanalysis also, it is a conflict, which becomes the reason of repression, though it is not a conflict between pride and memory, but between forces which are conceived very differently.

Breuer's observation and several other experiences had taught Freud that things which were felt by the subject to be incompatible with certain fundamental convictions or feelings or tendencies were apt to be "forgotten" so thoroughly that under normal conditions they could not be remembered any more. They were, as it was called, repressed, relegated to the unconscious and had become incapable of spontaneous return and inaccessible to voluntary recall. There is no doubt that conditions of this kind exist; it is doubtful whether the explanation Freud devised and made a pivotal point of his whole theory can be accepted.

Here it seems advisable to point out a circumstance to which great attention must be paid if one wants to understand and to criticize psychoanalysis, or, for that matter, certain other theories too. One must be careful in dealing with what such a theory calls a "fact." Many of the so-called facts really contain a good deal more than the facts. They are "findings" couched in the language or terminology of a definite theory. Repression is not a fact, but an explanation of a fact. The pure finding is that there are often memories which become inaccessible to consciousness and which evidently would cause, if they did return, some serious conflict. To say that these memories have become inaccessible by "repression" is already part of a definite theory. The danger of being misled by the word "fact" is particularly great in psychoanalysis, the followers of Freud having never been really capable of distinguishing between a mere "finding" and its statements in the language of their master. If the term "repression" is analyzed, it becomes apparent that it implies in truth, if not the whole of Freud's theory, at least a good part of it. The term ought therefore to be discarded by all those psychologists who feel that they cannot accept the Freudian interpretation of things psychological. The same remark applies to many other so-called "facts" which the psychoanalysts refer to as empirical proofs of their theory.

Memories which have been banished into the unconscious are held back there by the force of the censor. If the mind somehow, be it spontaneously or by some other memory or by "free associations," gets, so to say, near such a repressed memory, the force of the censor prevents this memory from arising. The strength of the censor becomes manifest by a certain behavior of a person analyzed. This behavior is called "resistance." The choice of these terms reveals the dynamic conception to which Freud, from the very beginning of his studies, adhered.

Resistance becomes particularly visible by the method which Freud adopted after he had abandoned hypnosis as a means of exploring the unconscious. We have already pointed out that Bernheim's experiment was one of Freud's strongest reasons for replacing hypnosis by another method. The psychoanalytic method—that which alone may be called analysis in the strict sense of the term—consists in having the person who is to be analyzed produce "free associations." The "basic rule of psychoanalysis" states that the subject, starting from some point, must produce all ideas, images, or whatever else might turn up in his mind, no matter whether these ideas and the rest be felt as pleasant or unpleasant, as important or unimportant, as being to the point or not.

The chain of free associations is suddenly broken; the subject declares that no further ideas will turn up; there is a blank in his mind; he cannot go on. If the analyst insists and assures the subject that ideas will come, that they are bound to come, that the subject simply has to produce some more, experience proves that memories turn up which were forgotten altogether and which have, generally, a definitely unpleasant and painful character. The behavior of the subject of analysis, his unwillingness to go on, his alleged incapacity to produce new ideas is called "resistance" and is attributed to the action of the censor-power which has first to be overcome, before the "repressed" memory is allowed to pass over the threshold of consciousness.

The name "resistance" is again not precisely one of a simple fact, but already implies some theoretical interpretation, or at most is a metaphorical expression. Resistance, in the strict and original sense of the term, is a phenomenon of the physical world. Its use as the name of a mental fact or of a feature of behavior is based on a likeness which does not necessarily indicate any essential similarity or analogy. We speak of a man making resistance not only when he resists by bodily strength, but also when he simply refuses to obey orders. This resistance may develop without any "feeling of effort" on the part of the reluctant person; he might simply do nothing, without any activity. In such a case it is clear that the name is a pure metaphor. It is a metaphor of the same kind as the one we use in saying that a thing we want to move and which is too heavy "will not" move. There is not only an "animistic" interpretation of dead matter, but also a "physicalistic" interpretation of mental facts. We may feel we are making an effort when we try to get the unwilling person to obey orders; but on his part he does not necessarily have to make any effort in order not to obey. Thus the fact that the analyst "makes an effort" in trying to make the subject take up again the chain of associations is no proof at all that any real force is at work in this situation. The "effort" of the analyst has however been referred to as a sign of the dynamism entering into play and as a proof of the power of resistance which really exists and which is due to censoring and repression. In many cases the analyzed person himself will tell of an effort he has to make, of his effort being fruitless, of his feeling a kind of resistance. Such impressions arise also outside of psychoanalysis; a person may feel it "impossible" to tell this or that; he has to "make an effort" to overcome, for instance, a feeling of shame, and the like. But this subjective impression is not in itself a convincing proof of some power really hindering the utterance. Resistance is therefore not a simple fact. The fact is limited to an interruption in the chain of association and to insistence on the part of the analyst and to the necessity of an "effort" on the part of the analyzed. Resistance as it is understood in psychoanalysis implies an interpretation, based on some of the essential presuppositions of this theory.

Two further questions arise. What is the origin of these powers and what are the conditions for their manifestation? With these questions we touch on one of the most important parts of the whole Freudian system. In regard to the origin and the operation of these forces, we are referred to the primitive instincts which form part of the organization of man. The notion of instinct or drive, as it has been developed by psychoanalysis, and the place it holds within Freud's theory will be examined more closely in the third chapter, dealing with the "axiomatic" premises of the whole conception. Here we limit our discussion to a mere report on the statements made by Freud and his school.

We are told that in the child there exist instincts which strive, as yet uninhibited by any other force, for immediate realization of their ends. Compliance with the instinctive urges causes the experience of satisfaction and pleasure. To gain this is the only aim of any activity whatsoever during the first period of life. Freud expressed this by describing this first period of life as being ruled by the "principle of pleasure." According to this principle, the individual strives only for pleasure and its realization by the shortest way; every instinctive desire which arises becomes immediately an action aimed at the satisfaction of this desire and at the pleasure ensuing therefrom. On the one hand the environmental influences of education and of society and, in a lesser degree, of development, and on the other hand personal experience gradually transform this principle of pleasure. The immediate satisfaction either has to be postponed, because the conditions of reality do not allow for it, or has to be given up altogether, because the laws of environment forbid it. The individual has to adjust himself to reality step by step. The ruling principle is no longer that of pleasure, but what Freud calls the "principle of reality."

We must note, however, that by adjustment to reality nothing is changed in the basic attitude of the person. The only aim is still the greatest possible amount of pleasure. It is the principle of pleasure itself which leads to the adoption of the principle of reality, because experience shows that the attempts at an immediate realization of primitive, unchanged instincts causes eventually more pain than pleasure. This fact is illustrated plainly by the punishment following indulgence in certain forbidden ways of behavior. The essential identity of these two principles must be remembered. The adaptation to reality does not imply any real change of attitude, not a turning from a purely subjectivistic and hedonistic attitude to an objective one. The acceptance of the reality-principle really amounts to a change of methods, not of ends.

The environmental forces thus do not modify the instinctive desires themselves, but merely condition the development of new ways for satisfying them. Whatever striving we may observe in the mature personality, it is basically the same as existed in a manifest form in the first period of early childhood.

Freud is fully convinced that human nature cannot be studied anywhere better than in primitive stages, be they those of an individual or those of mankind. Developmental psychology owes to him, if not many reliable statements, at least a potent incitement toward pursuing its researches.

Since the direct satisfaction of unaltered instinctive desires is no longer possible in later stages of development, the question arises: what becomes of these desires? The fact that the reality-principle does not introduce new ends, but only influences the choice of means, points to the answer. The instincts remain what they were. Their desires are the same in the mature as in the undeveloped organism, but they are veiled, hidden behind other goals. These other goals appear to be the real ones. There is nothing in their immediate aspect nor in the consciousness of the person himself to indicate that they only take the place of the instinct to which they owe their strength and the satisfaction their realization procures.

The instincts themselves are not part of mental life; they never become conscious as such. What appears in consciousness is but the idea or the image of a situation promising satisfaction. This idea, called the "representation" of instincts, possesses a compelling force. As soon as such an image arises in the mind, it is associated with an intense longing to make it become real and thus to get the satisfaction the image anticipates. The instincts belong to the physiological organization of man. They are "amoral"; that is, they do not take account of any rules of morality or of society. They are intensely egoistical, aiming at nothing but the pleasure of satisfaction.*

The notion of the instincts holds a central position in Freudian psychology. It has therefore to be explained in some detail.

---

* The fact that instincts serve for the preservation of the individual or of the race is not a psychological one. Nor does the mind become aware directly, without reflection, of these "ends" of the instincts. The mind knows only of craving and satisfaction, of unpleasantness conditioned by the first and of pleasantness ensuing from the second. The objective "purposes" of instincts may accordingly be discarded in a discussion of purely psychological intent.

It seems that, according to Freud, there is no behavior nor can there be any without its being based on some instinctual mechanism. Instincts are usually considered only as related to activity. But Freud evidently conceives—and not without a certain reason—of every behavior, however passive it may appear, as an activity. There is nothing purely passive in man, or for that matter in an animal. Even passive receptivity presupposes some active behavior. Perception implies at least a minimum of attention turned toward the object perceived; without such a turning toward the object there might be some vague impression but no perception in the true sense of the term. Objects are perceived, according to Freud, because they are, or the knowledge of them is, in a way an end of some instinctual desire. Thus one may safely assert that, according to psychoanalysis, the human personality or the human mind consists of instincts or their representations and the modifications wrought on them by the influences of the factors mentioned above.

The instincts are not all of one kind. Freud distinguished at first two great classes which he called the instincts of "libido" and those of the "ego." He later added to these two a third instinct, which he defined as the "instinct of death." The instincts of libido and those of the ego may be subdivided in various ways, though all these single instincts remain essentially either libidinous or directed towards the ego. Libido means sexuality. The Freudian conception of sexuality and of its place within the whole of human nature will be made the subject of a special analysis. Here, therefore, I shall simply set down the statements of psychoanalysis without expressing either approval or disapproval. Even here, however, it must be pointed out, to avoid certain common mistakes, that psychoanalysis undoubtedly acknowledges the existence of non-libidinous, non-sexual instincts. During the first period of its history psychoanalysis was occupied mainly with the libidinous instincts and rather neglected those of the ego. But it is not quite just to accuse psychoanalysis of indulging in a "pansexualistic" conception. It is true that psychoanalysis has exaggerated the range and the importance of sexuality, that it has applied this name to phenomena which are anything but sexual in nature. It is also true that it professes to discover traces of sexuality where there are none at all; but it is nevertheless untrue that sexuality summarizes the whole of Freudian psychology. It is but just to remark on this, particularly because I propose to criticize this theory severely. The theory itself is open to much graver objections than pansexualism is. The so-called pansexualistic attitude is merely the inevitable consequence of certain basic assumptions on which psychoanalysis rests and which prove to be utterly untenable.

To return to the notion of instincts. They belong to the organization of the human being; they are deeply rooted in its very depths and are as necessary elements of this organization as any organ or any physiological function. The organism cannot stop its instinctual activities any more than it can stop its heart beating or its metabolism functioning. The instincts cannot, accordingly, ever disappear. What disappears—only to return, as we shall see presently, in another form—is the mental representation of the instinct; that is, the original, crude, brutal image of a situation promising immediate satisfaction to the instinctual craving.

By nature the instincts are dynamic. They are not always active, but are released either by the environmental situation—as, for example, the non-Freudian psychology of instincts supposes the instinct of flight to operate—or by an internal alteration, as is the case with hunger or, partly at least, with sexual instinct. The dynamic nature of instincts necessitates a "discharge" whenever the instinctual tension has reached a certain degree. This discharge is an elementary need of the organism which somehow resents being denied it. The discharge conditions satisfaction, corresponding to a return to a lesser degree of tension or even to the zero of tension, and satisfaction of the instinct is equivalent to pleasure.

The idea of dynamism had been an essential part of the first conception contained in the *Studies on Hysteria* by Breuer and Freud. It had then been linked, not to the notion of instinct but to that of emotions. Emotions demand a discharge. They need to find utterance in the corresponding expression, and they may, if such an expression and "abreaction" is denied them, become the cause of mánifold troubles. An emotion which has not found its normal outlet in expression remains in the mind like a "strange body" and there causes an irritation, just as a strange body which had become embedded in some tissue may give rise to all kinds of disturbance. In his later development of psychoanalysis Freud conceived of the emotions as being secondary to the instincts; an emotion is but the sign or the manifestation of an instinctual process. It is not the emotion which is in need of discharge but the instinct, of which the emotion is but an epiphenomenon or an effect.

The discharge of the instinctual tension is brought about by indulgence in the instinctual desire. The realization of this desire may be delayed under the influence of the reality-principle; but sooner or later satisfaction will have to be attained. The delay is supposedly facilitated by a property of human organization which Freud called pre-pleasure (*Vorlust*), a peculiar kind of pleasure which is got out of anticipation and may contribute very much to increasing the total pleasure of instinctual satisfaction. Delay is possible and even, eventually, advantageous in regard to the total amount of pleasure, but total denial is impossible. Instincts have to find their satisfaction; otherwise the gradually increasing tension would become intolerable.

The environmental forces, however, are strong enough to enforce a denial; they create absolute obstacles which make satisfaction impossible. On the other hand, satisfaction cannot be dispensed with. The organism finds itself therefore in a painful dilemma the solution of which is not always easy and which, when not solved in a satisfactory manner, becomes the cause of many a pathological trouble. Here in fact we touch on the very roots of neurosis.

The solution of this dilemma lies in the instinct's turning from its original end to another which is in accordance with the laws of environment and therefore allows for instinctual satisfaction without any conflict taking place with these laws. The process by which a new goal is substituted for the original one is called "sublimation." (This term as well as the idea it covers is also found in Nietzsche.) Normal and healthy development of personality depends on this process of sublimation being carried through thoroughly and to a good end. Every goal a man may pursue, whether it be of business or of social life, of science or art, of philosophy or religion, is really the mask under which the original and unchanged instinct veils itself. Sublimation is a kind of trick, as it were, by which the instincts manage to deceive the principles active in consciousness and to bring about a compromise between these principles and their own needs. The instincts use, so to speak, the non-instinctual ends offered by reality for achieving, by a curious detour, their own satisfaction. We shall see that this notion is not without serious difficulties.

This "use" the blind and crude instinctual forces make of culture and its possibilities reminds one somewhat of a notion of which Freud probably had no knowledge at all. In Hegel's philosophy there is the interesting conception of the *List der Idee*; the "idea" which by its own nature and its own law moves onwards to ever new realizations, by the "dialectic process" of thesis, antithesis, synthesis, "uses" individuals as well as historical situations for its ends. Individual man believes he achieves his own ends, but really he serves the ends of the "idea," of the pre-ordained march of the Absolute toward being "in itself and with itself." This analogy, which perhaps is not so insignificant, deserves to be noticed. It throws a certain light on the general mentality underlying psychoanalysis; it reveals a certain "impersonalism" of which more will be said later on.

Thus every goal owes its attraction and the pleasure we may feel in its achievement to the instinctual force which is hidden behind it. The fact that the several goals are attractive in various degrees is accounted for in psychoanalysis by crediting each of them with a definite amount of instinctual energy. The goal or its idea in the mind is endowed with a greater or lesser quantity of mental energy. The strivings or attitudes regarding objects of the outer world—of things as well as of ideas— are, all of them, derived from "libido." The libidinous instincts refer to every possible end which is not of the ego itself. The "charge" of mental energy or libido attached to some object or idea is called "cathexis," meaning retention or retaining.

The fact that an original instinctual aim is replaced by some other object which when attained or realized causes the instinct to become satisfied, is expressed, in psychoanalysis, by calling the object substituted by sublimation the "symbol" of the original one. Symbolization thus becomes another of the basic categories of psychoanalysis. There are, however, other symbols which play a very great rôle in the theory as well as in the method of psychoanalysis.

The censor operates not always with the same intensity. There are times when its attention, to use the allegory of a "keeper of the threshold," relaxes and when the repressed material may re-enter the field of consciousness. But the attention of the censor does not relax so far as to allow these repressed and reproved things to break through undisguised. They too have to be clad in symbols so as not to be too easily recognized. Their entrance into consciousness in their true shape would renew the conflict which originally caused them to be repressed into the unconscious, and would be felt as intolerable. The contents of the original representations of instinctual longings have been repressed because they were absolutely incompatible with ideas, tendencies, attitudes acquired later, and because the co-existence of such incompatible things is simply not to be borne by the human mind. Thus, these things needs must become disguised to re-enter consciousness. The most common case is their becoming conscious in dreams.

Dreams consist of symbols representing in a veiled manner instinctual ends. It is because of this conception that Freud insists that every dream is the fulfillment of a wish. But since the figures and situations of a dream are symbols, that is, put in the place of what the instincts really demand and of the images which would appear if the censor were not active, the wishes contained in a dream are not manifest but hidden. The "manifest content" of a dream has to be analyzed and interpreted to unveil the "latent content" which still remains in the unconscious. There are other instances too of the censor's watchfulness relaxing; thus slips of the tongue or of the pen, misreading of written words, all kinds of clumsiness and mistakes are caused by some unconscious factor breaking into the sequence of a conscious function. These things, however, need not be discussed; they are but a special instance of a general theory which is better illustrated by the Freudian conception of dreams.

The analysis of dreams is in fact, according to Freud's own words, the *via regia*—the royal road—into the unconscious. Many of the statements of psychoanalysis are based on the discoveries Freud and his school believe they have made through the analysis of dreams. Freud himself has devoted a monographic study to dreams, the *Traumdeutung*, interpretation of dreams.

It is important to note the title of this book by Freud. It refers expressly to interpretation, which is indeed an essential part of the technique of psychoanalysis. At first, during his collaboration with Breuer and immediately afterwards, Freud made use, as has been related, of hypnosis. He then replaced this method by that of free associations. But as yet the only aim was to make disappear certain pathological phenomena, viz., neurotic symptoms. Their disappearance indicated also that the part of the total treatment referring to a certain symptom was ended.

Freud's conception had developed, however, in the meantime, from a theory of neurotic symptoms to a general psychology. He felt that there was no decisive difference between the mentality of a patient afflicted with neurosis and a normal person. The ideas of psychoanalysis had to be applied to the normal mind as well as to neurosis. But in normal psychology there was no possibility of making use of the one criterion which had been so helpful in treating neurotic patients, *for there were no symptoms which could disappear.* The relation between the unconscious material brought forth by free associations on the one hand and the facts of conscious mental life on the other, had to be established by another procedure. This procedure was found in interpretation.

The use of an art of interpretation, or—as the psychoanalysts would call it—of a science or technique of interpretation, became possible through the conception of symbol. A symbol has to be understood. It is understood either because it is generally known—as, for instance, the cross is understood as a symbol of Christianity or the flag as a symbol of one's country—or it had to be explained or interpreted to some one who is not yet acquainted with the symbol's signification. The symbols of the unconscious are not understood at first sight. They are not even recognized as what they are, namely as symbols. They are taken at their face value. A dream is, to the unsophisticated mind, just a dream and nothing else. It is for analysis to make the dreamer see that behind the apparent nonsense and lack of consistency in a dream there is hidden a definite meaning.

Analysis of dreams led to the introduction of several new notions. Some of these refer to the psychology of the dreams themselves, and also have certain analogies besides. They need not be expressly mentioned here. A closer study, for instance of the idea of "displacement" by which a certain sum of energy is shifted from one mental fact to another, or of the idea of the elaboration of dreams and all the pains the mind takes to hide the unconscious meaning, do not contribute to an understanding of the essentials of psychoanalysis.

There is, however, one notion which deserves special mention because it reveals something of the mental structure of the whole Freudian system, and because it is a remarkable manifestation of a basic attitude of Freud and his school. The dream analysis, as has been remarked, had no means at hand for knowing when the chain of association had reached a significant point; the criterion of therapy—i.e., the disappearance of a symptom—was missing. When a dream element is analyzed, and there is either no symptom which could disappear—in the case of a normal person—or no immediate relation existing between the dream-content and the symptoms, then the only way of making sure that the unconscious material hidden beneath has been made conscious is either the assent of the analyzed person, or the plausibility of the explanation, or the consistency of the interpretation of the whole dream. Even when such a point had been reached, the chain of associations may always proceed still farther. There is practically no end to it. The analysts are of the opinion that in following up this chain one digs deeper and deeper into the unconscious and, parallel to this, farther and farther into the past of the individual. The layers of the unconscious are, as we said, comparable to geological strata in which the newest deposits overlay the older ones. In pursuing the chain of associations, even after a satisfactory interpretation of some dream-element has been attained, one discovers a second, a third, or even more interpretations. Hence psychoanalysis concluded that every dream-element was "overdetermined," that is, depended not on one but on several unconscious factors which had been "condensed" into this one symbol.

The factors which serve as elements of interpretation were, accordingly, sought in an ever more distant past. Originally the idea had been that a neurotic symptom was conditioned by a

"psychic trauma" which, for instance, in the Breuer case, had occurred in the immediate past. Freud soon developed the idea
that this trauma had occurred in childhood; the "infantile
trauma" played a great rôle in his first conception. With the
introduction and development of the theoretical views ex-
pounded in the *Interpretation of Dreams* and with the alleged
discovery of multiple determination, the cause of some mental
fact, be it a symptom or a dream or anything else, could be
located in a still more remote past. The "trauma of birth" began
to be spoken of, birth being considered as the first shock the
human organism suffers—there is a moment of asphyxiation,
there is the presumably intense shock of the pressure exercised
on the body of the child during birth, there is the abrupt change
of the conditions of life and environment. These are all factors
which, according to psychoanalysis, cannot but make a deep
though quite unconscious impression on the mind of the newborn child.

There was even more. Some analysts professed to discover, in
the unconscious material they dug out by means of pushing on
the free associations indefinitely, traces of memories going back
to the prenatal period. There was, of course, no means of empirically proving any of these statements. No man ever remem-
bers the moment of his birth, and no one has the faintest idea
how it felt to be an unborn embryo. The only criterion the
analyst could rely upon was, evidently, the compatibility of these
assertions with the rest of the theory. This is the point where
psychoanalysis began more and more to become mere construction. Why this theory had to develop in this manner will become clear when we shall have studied its foundations and the
"axioms" on which it rests.

Even this brief sketch of psychoanalytical ideas cannot leave
unmentioned Freud's notions on what he termed "metapsychology." The name he gave to this part of his theory evidently expresses the idea that it is mere theory or speculation as opposed
to other parts which he believes to deal with facts. The "meta-

psychological" notions, however, are used by the psychoanalysts as if they were assured facts which observation may detect without any difficulty. This metapsychology refers to three ways of looking at mental phenomena and at the unconscious factors determining them.

Considered from the point of view of "dynamism," the mental phenomena appear as caused by and as expressive of the instinctual forces. The "economic" consideration deals with the distribution of mental energy among the various mental states and the levels to which they belong. These levels or strata are discussed in "topology." This notion deserves particular study.

Psychoanalysis distinguishes several layers or strata within man's nature. There is the "id," essentially unconscious and containing the instincts. The "ego" forms the next layer, and it is in a certain antagonism to the "id." Above the "ego" there is the "super-ego," the receptacle, as it were, of ideals, conscious aims, moral notions and the like.

It has been scarcely noticed, so far as we know, that this conception is faintly reminiscent of the one implied in the old "faculty-psychology." Scholastic psychology distinguishes in man vegetative, sensory and intellectual faculties. The first comprise all the purely organic functions, within which are listed the faculty of growth, of nutrition, and of reproduction. They are non-mental, though they depend on the soul which is the only vital principle and the substantial form of the whole body. The sensory faculties are those of the external and internal senses; the latter are: imagination, sensorial memory, the *sensus communis* and the *vis cogitativa*. It is important to note that the two last-named faculties are capable of rather high achievements. The *sensus communis* builds up, by its synthetic power, the images of objects and combines the impressions received by the different external senses into the sensory or perceptual idea of one object. The *vis cogitativa* enables man to become aware of certain relations between things, and between them and himself, which may be known without intellectual reasoning and the production of abstract, universal concepts. The sensory faculties are not only receptive; there are also principles of activity or reactivity, the sensitive appetites. These are of a higher nature than mere instincts or natural appetites, and more or less like what psychoanalysis understands by instinct or drive. There is finally the intellect and the intellectual will, immaterial in nature, concerned with the abstracted forms and the good as such.

This Scholastic conception sees the essential feature of human organization in the intellectual faculties. They depend indeed on the lower powers, because these have to supply the material from which the intellect abstracts its notions, and the dynamic strength of its volitional acts. But the higher powers are not determined in their operations by, nor do they originate from, the lower ones; their dependence is merely the result of the fact that the immaterial soul is linked to matter and reaches reality through the material organization of the body. The soul and those of her faculties which express her spiritual nature most, reign over the whole complex being that is man. The Scholastic way of considering human nature is exactly what we call—and shall explain more thoroughly later—the "way from above," whereas the way of Freud is one of the most characteristic instances of the "way from below."

However mistaken psychoanalysis may be in regard to the relations existing between these various layers of human nature and however wrongly the precise properties of these layers may have been stated by the Freudian school, there is a nucleus of truth in this conception. Yet it is impossible to take over this conception, because the truth in it is so deeply hidden among a tremendous mass of error.

The notion of economics has a particular meaning in psychoanalysis because it is very closely linked to one of the "axioms" of this psychology, of which the third chapter will treat at some length. If this notion is divested of its psychoanalytical garment and translated into the plain language of· common sense and average experience it states primarily the fact that man's mind may concentrate on various objects or interests, that this mind gets wrapped up with one thing and has then but little capacity for containing another at the same time, that the "amount" of interest may be shifted from one end to another. Such experiences are indeed one of the reasons why we use, also in pre-scientific considerations, terms like mental energy or mental power. We have an impression as if sometimes certain things would consume all our mental power and as if they would occupy all the space our mind disposes of; it is clear that the latter expression is purely figurative, and so in truth is the former.

Psychology is always threatened by the danger of getting caught in the traps of verbalism. Human language is frequently inept at expressing mental things. Its expressions and forms are molded on the pattern of the tangible world of bodies and of space. There are no other figures save those supplied by language as it has been handed down through so many generations. But we have to be aware of these snares. Their true nature was recognized by Francis Bacon, Lord Verulam, centuries ago when he warned against the dangers of the *idola fori*. The particular difficulties arising from these circumstances in psychology have been pointed out by Bergson. Others too have sounded this warning. But the seduction of taking for adequate description what in truth is but an inadequate similarity is so great that psychology ever and again falls a prey to it. Nor did psycho-analysis escape this danger.

The same seduction as by images of language may be exercised by spatial images or schemata. We illustrate by tracings something which is not spatial in itself and then argue from the properties of the graphic symbol to the properties of the thing symbolized. When Freud, in his book on dreams and later in his analysis of the super-ego drew a graphic schema to illustrate the mutual relations of the various layers, the image, it seems, soon replaced in his mind the reality it was meant to depict. Many statements made on the subject of topology and economics seem to apply more to the schema than to the mental reality itself.

Notwithstanding all these objections we have to acknowledge that in these notions there is hidden some truth, however distorted and masked. It does not matter that the idea of layers or strata of the mind is not originally Freud's; it is indeed older than psychoanalysis. But it is always meritorious to have applied an idea and to have shown its usefulness.

Another notion which has to be mentioned is that of "transference." This notion, which the psychoanalysts of course consider to be the name of a "fact," holds an important place in the theory, and especially in the theory of the therapeutic efficaciousness of psychoanalysis. But this is not the reason why it is to be discussed here. From the viewpoint of systematic structure this notion is less important because it is in fact merely an application of the general notion of libido as the driving force by which man gets in touch with reality. The importance of transference consists, in regard to our ends, in its revealing in a very striking manner one of the fundamental attitudes of psychoanalysis. The significance of this notion will be pointed out in the third chapter. Here we deal only with its content.

Transference means that libido is shifted from one object to another; it takes on, however, a very particular meaning; it is the name for the alleged fact that in mental treatment by psychoanalysis the libido of the patient, which has remained fixed on infantile objects, especially on the parents, is detached and redirected to a new object which is found in the person of the psychoanalyst. Transference thus becomes, according to the theory, the truly efficacious factor in therapy. This does not mean, as some rather mistaken critics of psychoanalysis apparently believe, that the analyst tries "to make his patient fall in love" with him. He does not try to do this, but he cannot prevent it—though he does not call it love but libidinous attachment—if the treatment is expected to be of any use. By transference the libidinous forces whose normal evolution had been inhibited and which stayed at a developmental phase corresponding to childhood, or at least to an early period—hence the statement that neurosis is a kind of mental infantilism—are liberated and the patient becomes able to let them find their normal aims. The psychoanalyst has accordingly to take care that transference becomes replaced, when the treatment has sufficiently advanced, by a more normal attitude, by the readiness to turn to real objects of love or, generally speaking, of libidinous activity.

The rôle played by the psychoanalyst in the therapeutical relation to his patient and the rôle of transference in the process of healing were once stated by two pupils of Freud in this way: The only task of the psychoanalyst is to accelerate by the natural process of transference the development of libido toward normality. Natural in this proposition means according to the laws of nature.*

It remains to be seen how psychoanalysis views the origin and the nature of the super-ego. This "part" of human personality is not preformed as is the *id*, which alone exists at first, or as the *ego* whose development is based on the activity of the preformed ego-instincts. The super-ego is, so to say, a late acquisition and it is that by which man is distinguished from animals. This distinction is, however, only one of degree, because the super-ego also results from the activity of the instinctual forces and owes its existence and its influence to them. The super-ego contains all the ideals, moral precepts, social conventions and the rest which rule over the life of the mature person; it is the super-ego by which man turns to abstract ideas, to ideal ends, to scientific research, to art and religion.

It is not quite clear how the super-ego can be regarded as being on the same plane with the id and the ego; it has no instinctual basis of its own. Nor is it easy to determine whether the super-ego is more than a certain complex of contents. In

* H. Sachs and O. Reik, *Die Entwicklungsziele der Psychoanalyse,* Vienna and Leipzig, 1925.

psychoanalytic literature the super-ego is spoken of as if it were a layer co-ordinated with the others. The question of its true nature is of secondary importance. More weight has to be attributed to the question of origin. The super-ego owes its existence to a process called "identification" which has a certain resemblance to transference. Identification means indeed that an individual places himself in imagination in the place of another whom he wants to be like or whose place he covets. The deeper reasons which make possible such an adoption of another's aims and libidinous objects remain somewhat mysterious. It is not easy to explain such a process by the principles of Freudian psychology. However this may be, the main thing is that the adoption of ideals, convictions and so on, is also considered by Freud as an effect of causes which go back ultimately to the instinctual organization.

It is surely not wrong to ascribe to psychoanalysis the idea that man's mind and personality derives from the id. The id is the very matrix out of which evolves the ego, and later, by this ego's co-operation, the super-ego.

These various *"loci"*—we might use this term, since the theory about them is called topology—stand in manifold relations to each other. They are partly antagonistic and partly co-operative. This would give rise to insurmountable difficulties in building up a comprehensive theory if Freud had not previously in an early stage of his constructive work, introduced a remarkable concept, that of the "ambivalence" of instincts.

Ambivalence means that the selfsame instinct may condition opposite ways of behavior. Libido is both attraction and repulsion. There is the desire of possession and the urge toward destruction. There is love and aggression. All these are essentially not distinct drives, but sides of one drive which may turn hither or thither. This idea is intended also to explain facts which have been observed before and independently of psychoanalysis. Thus, William James spoke of an instinct of isolation being associated with the social instinct. Poets and philosophers had remarked that love and hate dwell close together. We may refer to a pertinent word of La Rochefoucauld that the more a man loves his mistress, the readier he is to hate her; or to a similar idea expressed by Oscar Wilde.* There are scores more facts and quotations that might be listed. It is then, according to Freud, the property of instincts to be capable of turning in two opposite directions. The possibilities of conflict between the instincts is definitely increased, since nearly every instinct may become antagonistic to another, even to one with which it may go parallel on other occasions.

This sketch is far from giving an adequate idea, even a vague one, of psychoanalysis as it exists today. The student of psychoanalysis is at first bewildered by the many technical terms and the unusual notions he has to digest. He hears the initiated talking about the Oedipus-complex, the castration-complex, incestuous longings, archaic thinking, about regression, fixation, about many other strange things. But if he comes to know psychoanalysis better he begins to understand that the framework of this apparently so very complicated fabric is quite simple. There are some few basic notions from which the rest of the theory may be deduced, if the true meaning of the former is really grasped; and upon these enough has been said. Some complementary remarks will be added as we proceed with the critical analysis of Freudian psychology.

Several Freudian notions have not been mentioned here nor are they discussed in the following chapters, notwithstanding their importance as elements of the psychoanalytical system. This is true especially of the notion of the "unconscious." These notions do not necessitate any special analysis nor do they reveal much of the philosophical background of Freudism.

I realize that since the notion of the "unconscious" is regarded, by many psychoanalysts and their adversaries, as a keystone of the whole theory, the reader might expect to see this

* *The Ballad of Reading Gaol:* "Yet each man kills the thing he loves . . ."

notion explained and criticized. My intention to disregard this notion therefore needs justification.

The idea of "an unconscious mind" is not a peculiarity of psychoanalysis. Many authors have made use of it, before and after Freud. It is doubtless true that the "unconscious" as conceived by psychoanalysis is different from the conception bearing the same name in other systems. The characteristic features, however, that the unconscious is given in psychoanalysis result from the ideas on the nature and the rôle of the instincts and from the general conception of mental dynamism. Of these things. enough has been said to supply a basis for critique. A study of the notion of the unconscious would not reveal more of the fundamental attitudes of psychoanalysis than does the study of the notions of instincts, of mental energy, of causality, etc., all of which will be examined in the following chapters. The notion of the unconscious is secondary to the notion of instinct, of dynamism, etc. Being an important link in the chain of Freudian conceptions, it implies, of course, all the fundamental suppositions of psychoanalysis. But it does not imply more or others than do those notions which will be studied presently. To indulge in an inevitably lengthy analysis of the notion of the unconscious would necessitate useless repetition.

For the same reasons it has been considered needless to enter into a discussion of notions such as the "castration-complex" or the "compulsion of repetition" and several others.

CHAPTER II

The Logical Fallacies of Psychoanalysis

IF ONE looks at psychoanalysis it appears to be a wonderful building, in which each detail has its appropriate place, fitting in with every other, and thus evoking the impression of a well-planned and consistent edifice. Nor is this impression deceiving so long as one considers only the façade and the arrangement of the visible architectural elements. For indeed Freud's was an eminently constructive mind. But the impression undergoes a profound change if one turns from admiring the façade and the general plan of the building to a closer examination of its foundations. Neither the terrain on which this building is erected nor the way its foundations have been laid can satisfy the exigencies of material soundness and formal correctness. The first point will be dealt with in the chapters discussing the relation of psychoanalysis to psychology, philosophy, and ethnology. In this chapter the foundations themselves will be submitted to a close examination.

Anticipating the conclusion at which we shall arrive after such an examination we may state that psychoanalysis rests on several gross logical fallacies, all of which are of the kind known to logic as *petitio principii*. Psychoanalysis, in fact more than once, takes for granted what it claims to prove and surreptitiously introduces its preconceived ideas into its reasonings so as to give the impression that these ideas have resulted from facts and evident principles. The demonstration of these logical fallacies is of a particular importance for a critique of psychoanalysis. The analysts have repeatedly asserted that their critics lack competence and are unable to judge psychoanalysis as long as they do not make use of the same method by which the results of analysis have been obtained. They claim analysis to be an utterly new approach to the problems of mental life and to be therefore, in its results, incomparable with statements obtained by any other method.

The insistence that a special method has to be acquired and that only this one method is capable of yielding certain results is in itself rather remarkable. But even if we were willing to recognize this insistence as justified, the obligation of complying with it would exist only if there were no *a-priori* objections invalidating the method itself. Nobody indeed can be forced to apply a method he knows, for convincing reasons, to be wrong. To repeat a comparison used many years ago, in fact nearly twenty years ago:* suppose that a chemist is told that a certain substance contains chlorine and that this is news to him, news he is not ready to believe without convincing proof. He will, of course, ask his informant what method was used to demonstrate the presence of chlorine. If he is answered: "Well, I dissolved the thing in hydrochloric acid," he will refuse to take the experiment seriously; for as chlorine is present in hydrochloric acid, it would be bound to be present at the end of the experiment whether or not it were in the original substance. In other words the method is worthless: it gives no information either way.

This is just the situation of the critic of psychoanalysis. He is sure, and for very good reasons as we shall see presently, that the method is wrong, and wrong in such a way as to guarantee— so to speak—the presence of chlorine, that is to presuppose and to imply a good deal of what it is claiming to prove. Just as the chemist introduced in the course of his test the very substance whose original presence he thought he was proving, the psychoanalyst, when applying his method, has already accepted the very propositions he is going to deduce from the results.

---

* *Ueber Psychoanalyse,* Berlin, 1922; being a report by R. Allers and a lengthy discussion by many contributors.

The first of these fallacies may be called the fallacy of resistance. It was pointed out, in the foregoing chapter, that the term "resistance" is more than a mere description of an objective finding, that in truth it implies many of the theoretical views characteristic of Freud's system. No harm would be done if this referred only to the term as such. But calling the observed phenomena by this name means more than just choosing a more or less appropriate term. The observed phenomena—namely the interruptions occurring in the chain of free associations and the so-called efforts to be made by the person analyzed and the analyst—are viewed as a kind of ocular demonstration of resistance. Resistance itself, not the mere objective facts enumerated above, is what is "observed" according to the psychoanalysts. But all that they are observing is that no association occurs to the patient. The belief that they are actually observing resistance is founded on a previous acceptance of Freud's main conceptions. The psychoanalytic school might reply that they do not know of any other theory explaining the facts. This may be the case or not; it is not our task here to devise another theory capable of replacing Freud's. But the lack of a satisfactory explanation is not a sufficient reason for accepting one which, as I shall show, is evidently mistaken. It is definitely not the mark of a truly scientific mentality to content itself with a demonstrably wrong theory because no other is available for the present. It is better to have no theory at all than a wrong one.

The second *petitio principii* refers to the alleged causal connection between the conscious mental fact—part of a dream, idea, feeling, misspelling, symptom or the like—and the "unconscious" material brought forth by analysis. It has been remarked already that the idea of a causal relation existing between both these terms has some semblance of a proof only in the case of abnormal symptoms which disappear after the unconscious facts have been made conscious. This proof is missing altogether where there is no abnormal symptom to begin with. A dream does not disappear, nor does a mistake in spelling nor any other of the normal mental phenomena. The idea of these last-named being caused by the unconscious facts rests first on a generalization of the results obtained in the treatment of neurotic patients and, secondly, on the identification of causal relations on the one hand and those of meaning or signification on the other. Because the psychoanalyst, before he even starts an analysis, is previously convinced that all relations he will eventually be able to establish are of the nature of causation, he discovers only such relations.

It is, however, evident, that there are other relations existing between the contents of the mind. The relation of the premises of a syllogism to the conclusion are relations of meaning or signification, of sense—*Sinn,* as the German philosophers say—and can hardly be considered as being the efficient cause of the conclusion becoming a content of consciousness. In the syllogism: All men are mortal; Caesar is a man; Caesar is mortal, the truth expressed in the first sentence is not the cause of Caesar's death, nor of our thinking of Caesar's death. The relation is one of logic, but not one of causation. Some psychoanalysts seem, for that matter, to have felt that logical relations present a serious difficulty and they have accordingly attempted to supply a psychoanalytic interpretation or explanation of logical laws. These attempts were clumsy enough and were bound to fail; we shall mention them incidentally in the fourth chapter.

The identification of relations of meaning with those of causation becomes possible only if the theory of psychoanalysis is previously accepted. This identification has been made easier by the choice of a term introduced by Freud and destined to play a very prominent rôle in the whole system. We refer to the term "determination." This word is equivocal. It has many different connotations, which color its meaning differently according to the various uses the theory makes of it. Determination, the word itself, immediately suggests a definite kind of relation. If Freud had chosen a less definite term, if, for instance, he had spoken of mere connection, or of one thing being ordained toward another, certain of his conclusions would doubtless have been less impressive and less imposing.

Determination, so far as we can see, has several significations in psychoanalysis; it has more than four in common language. There is always some danger in taking over, for the sake of coining a scientific term, a word used by common language. At least such a word ought not to be used without being previously examined, and very carefully too, as regards its meanings. It is not enough to describe some phenomenon and to state that it is going to be called by this or that name, *e.g.* by that of determination. One has to state expressly the particular meaning given here, in science, to this word and to exclude all other meanings the word may have in common language or in another science. That such a precaution is indeed very necessary, may be gathered from the confusion due to the equivocation of a word like idea. It has indeed quite different significations, according as is used by Hume or by Hegel; the "regulative ideas" in Kant have nothing in common with the "pure ideas" in Husserl, and the "glorious idea" of doing this or that has no reference to the *idée claire et distincte* of Descartes.

Freud neglected to examine the various meanings of determination. He did not even bother to find out what meaning he himself attributed to this word. The word has, in fact, not one meaning in psychoanalysis but four which are never distinguished, though such a distinction is absolutely necessary.

Determination means, in psychoanalysis, first a connection pertaining to logic and semantic, that is the science of signification. We use—and the psychoanalysts use too—the term determination, in this sense, when we say that a particular grammatical form is determined by the thing we want to express. Our ignorance determines our making use of the syntactical form of question; or we know that a certain object we want to name belongs to a certain class which knowledge enables us to use the class-name for the particular object (*e.g.* "a dog").

Determination means secondly a connection between two

terms due to association. Association implies a temporal relation, since all associative relations may be reduced to the one of
contiguity. Contiguity means that the two terms have been
experienced together, that is, at the same time or in close temporal propinquity. Thus our remembering some fact determines
the appearance, in consciousness, of another fact "associated" to
the first. I remember, for instance, a visit to Nôtre Dame and
the image of the Sainte Chapelle arises in my mind, determined
by the temporal relation and by my having thought of these
two buildings often as belonging together, both being in Paris,
both having been seen during the same visit to Paris, etc. The
same applies to other associations which have become established by repeated experience, as, for instance, the word "white"
recalling the word "black."

There are, thirdly, emotional states which are determined by
certain contents of consciousness; these contents refer to—or, as
a certain school of psychology prefers to say: they "intend"—
certain objects which possess a definite emotional value. These
objects, or the awareness of these objects, accordingly determines a definite emotional behavior. Sometimes this relation is
spoken of as "association"; some emotion has become linked to
some object, an association between the two things has been
established. This is, however, a loose use of the term association.
Association, strictly speaking, means a relation between two
significant terms, between words or ideas or images. The awareness of some object given directly in perception or indirectly in
memory, and an emotion are terms of different nature. In the
case of emotion a subjective state is determined by the awareness of an object. It is therefore much better not to apply the
name of association to this process. But it is doubtless one of
determination.

Fourthly we have the causal determination. The effect is determined by its cause. The rise of the mercury in a thermometer
is determined by the caloric state of the surrounding medium.
The mental state of "feeling hungry" is determined by the

emptiness of the stomach and by the chemical alterations of the body conditioned by lack of food. A sense impression is determined by the influence the sensible object exercises on the sense-organs. An action is determined by our will, if it is a conscious and voluntary action, or by instincts, if it belongs to the level of instinctual behavior.

It is perhaps as well to point out expressly that the relation of association and the determination it conditions has not to be confused with the causal relation. Association exists between two terms or contents of the mind. The recall of the first is followed by the recall of the second. The original cause of this effect is the co-existence of the two terms in previous experience. The actual cause of the arising of the second term is a certain psychological law; but this law does not cause the second term as such, only its arising in consciousness. It is not the first term which causes the second; there is no causal relation between black and white, neither between the objects named by these words, nor between the words themselves. The cause is a certain habit of the mind, or—if this expression seems preferable —their being linked together so as to form a new unit. They have lost, so to say, independent and separate existence; they are found only together. This is, as one easily sees, a rather far-going simplification, because there are many instances in which only one of the terms becomes conscious without dragging the second with itself. One has never to forget, in psychology, that the notion of "sameness" of psychological situations has to be used with great precaution. Thinking of white is not the same state of consciousness simply because we are thinking of the same term. Much depends on the rest of the actual mental situation. It has, however, become clear that associative relations cannot be identified with causal relations.

The relation of symbol and thing symbolized is one of signification. It belongs to the first kind of determination. It is essentially the same as obtains between word and concept, or image and name. If this relation is sometimes referred to as one of causality, we have to be aware of the fact that this causality is definitely of another kind than the efficient causality considered by physics, by science in general, or also by common sense. That the term "cause" is itself equivocal and that one has to distinguish between several kinds of causal relation, is a truth which was quite evident to Aristotle and his medieval followers, and which has been almost totally forgotten by modern scientists and even by many modern philosophers. The oblivion into which the classic conception of causality has fallen is one of the main reasons for so many unacceptable and self-contradictory statements being made by the scientists and philosophers of today.

We cannot wonder at Freud having known only of efficient causality, since not even those who called themselves philosophers among his contemporaries knew better. The relation, however, of sign and thing signified, of symbol and thing symbolized cannot be reduced to efficient causality. The flag symbolizes, *e.g.,* the nation; but the nation is not the efficient cause of the flag. Nor can the relation between a word and the thing this word names be called a causal relation in the sense of efficient causality. Freud pretends that he can, by his method, discover the hidden meaning of some mental fact. A man dreams, for instance, of mounting a staircase, and he is told by the psychoanalysts that this dream symbolizes sexual relations. If we concede to Freud, for the sake of argument, that his method really enables him to discover the hidden meaning of a mental fact, and that he is able to prove this mental fact to be, besides what it appears to be, a symbol, we can never, nor could he, conclude that the discovery of this meaning is equivalent to the discovery of an efficient cause. The discovery is of the same nature as the discovery of the meaning of a word we never heard before, for instance a word of a foreign language; or as the understanding of a strange sign, for instance a Chinese sign or a hieroglyph. But the meaning of such a sign is not the cause of this sign and even less the cause of this sign becoming known to us. In a similar manner, the meaning of a symbol is not the cause of the symbol and not the cause of this symbol occurring at a given moment.

The last statement needs some further elucidation. The psychoanalysts tell us that a certain dream is conditioned by our desiring this or that, these desires having been repressed and longing for utterance. But the symbol does not symbolize the desire; it symbolizes the desired object. The object is the true meaning of the symbol. Let us suppose that some words were invented or came to be used by man, because there existed a desire for notification of certain things. It was, let us say, necessary to tell the members of the tribe that on a certain spot there were wild bees and that one could get honey there. This situation made necessary the introduction of words symbolizing, *e.g.*: go there, the nature of the spot, bees, honey. The adequate signs might have been invented on this occasion—we do not assert that this was the case—the cause for these words being introduced was, of course, the desire or need arising under these conditions. But the bees were not the cause of their name, and the same holds of all other words or any sign whatsoever.

But Freud sees no reason why the relation of signification ought not to be identified with the causal relation. This equation becomes possible only if certain principles of the theory are posited as true, previous to all empirical research. Research can never discover such an identity. The identity has to be presupposed, but the argumentation of psychoanalysis proceeds as if the causal nature of the relations revealed by analysis were demonstrated by empirical research. The identity of causal and significative relation is, however, the necessary basis for the theory of analysis. The identification of a relation of meaning with one of causation becomes thus the second of the fundamental fallacies on which the edifice of psychoanalysis rests.

The third of these fallacies refers to interpretation. It has become clear already that there is no cogent reason—in the mere facts themselves—for connecting a memory arising from the unconscious with a mental fact of consciousness, save only where the revival of the memory causes the disappearance of a symptom. But this criterion is necessarily lacking when the analyst deals with some mental state which by its very nature cannot disappear. In all these cases and also in the analysis of dead persons—Leonardo da Vinci or King Ecknaton of Egypt, to name just two instances—the said criterion cannot be applied. Sometimes—seldom enough—the assent of the analyzed person may replace the criterion of therapy. This assent is not only very often not given, but even after analysis has been pushed back to the deepest layers of the unconscious, and after resistance has been very much reduced, such an assent is utterly without value, when the unconscious material refers, *e.g.*, to the prenatal phase of life.

In all these cases it is left to the analyst to decide whether a satisfactory interpretation has been reached or whether further material is needed to clarify the situation. The analyst concludes that he has unveiled all unconscious facts symbolized in the mental state he analyzes, if and when his reason feels satisfied by the explanation reached. But his reason is satisfied when the interpretation he devises is in accordance with his general ideas about the structure and the functioning of the mind. Or, in other words, the psychoanalyst gathers the empirical material by which he pretends to prove such fundamental statements as those about the meaning of dreams by a method of selection which depends absolutely on the very principle allegedly deduced from the empirical results.

A conscientious critic will always take account of the possible replies his adversaries might have ready. We do well in following the practice of the masters of old. No scholastic ever refuted an opponent's view without having carefully listed all the arguments favorable to this view. And he repeatedly, in his discussion, took account of an answer the other party might eventually give to a remark of his. Adopting this procedure we might ask whether the logical fallacies we comment on here are not inevitable in the development of a new science which has to feel its way and to build up, step by step, its theory. It is for the already advanced science, someone might object, to take care of a neat and irreproachable logical purity. A science that is in process of becoming cannot indulge in such refinements. It has first of all to gather facts, to work out some useful hypothesis which will help it along in its further endeavors. It has to move somewhat in a circle, establishing a provisionary proposition first, verifying it by subsequent research then, and thus, moving not just in a circle but in a spiral, proceeding to develop finally a complete and self-consistent theory. Science oftener than not has to proceed in this manner. But we venture to take issue with our supposed antagonist on this point. It is of course true that the first theoretical statements were suggested to Freud by the observations he had made, by the ideas he shared with Breuer, by the views he had become imbued with during his studies in France. But he fell a prey to the logical fallacy of *petitio principii* almost at the very beginning of his research. The notion of resistance arose, it seems, in his mind as soon as he discovered the gaps in the chain of free associations and remembered Bernheim's experiment. The interpretation he gave to the phenomenon was suggested to him by his general ideas on human nature and the functioning of the human mind. These ideas were not his own; they were rather the current ones of his time. The influences which he underwent and which contributed to the formation of his ideas will be examined in a later chapter.

We cannot reproach Freud for having cherished these ideas. One reproach however, we cannot spare him, and even less his many followers. After it had been pointed out by several critics that Freud's conceptions were open to serious objections, and after psychoanalysis had existed for quite a noticeable time, it was evidently the duty of the founder of this theory and of his school to take account of these objections and to defend their views against these criticisms. But the only defense they ever used was either to tell their adversaries to apply the method of analysis themselves or to accuse them of being under the influence of their own unconscious which hindered them from accepting the truth of psychoanalysis. But the psychoanalysts were not—and are not—apparently capable of seeing that this way of arguing rests on the same logical fallacies of which they have been accused.

One more thing might be stated. A still growing science is entitled to a certain lack of precision and to all kinds of provisional hypotheses. But none ever is justified in committing fallacies against the basic laws of common logic. The very moment a theory disregards logic this theory, whatever its merits may be, loses the right to be taken seriously and called by the lofty name of science. Psychoanalysis has become guilty of other infractions of the primary laws of logic and has sinned in more than one way against the basic rules every science has to obey.

Psychoanalysis has become entangled in a truly difficult situation. Since its statements really rest, not on facts, but on previously introduced views—the very same views that the facts allegedly demonstrate—the method itself and the accordance with the theory is no sufficient proof. All these reasonings move in the same fatal circle which they cannot escape except by a radical change of tactics. If the truth of the propositions of psychoanalysis could be made evident by observations based on totally different methods, the viciousness of the circle would disappear. But this is the one thing impossible to do. Psychoanalysis has committed itself to the idea that its assertions can be made by using its peculiar method exclusively, and that no other method ever can penetrate into the depths of the unconscious. But then there is no way at all to penetrate there, because the one way recommended proves not to lead to objective facts, as they are, but presents them disguised and distorted by the peculiar ideas of psychoanalysis, and so thoroughly masked, that one cannot even risk guessing at their true nature.

One attempt, however, psychoanalysis has made at breaking through the magic circle which encloses it and keeps it from providing any objective proof of its statements. This attempt has been made by referring to data supplied by ethnology and the comparative study of customs, religions, rites and such things. To a lesser extent references to art and other cultural phenomena have been made with the same intention of corroborating the statements of psychoanalysis. But these attempts suffer from the very same defects we have had to point out here. They too presuppose what they are believed to prove. (Cf. below, chapter IX.)

This is not tantamount to saying that Freud and his school have never laid hand on any truth. It is impossible to devote so much pains and so much time to the study of any matter without coming across some of the truths referring to it. But the truths are veiled by the terminology in which they couched. They are hidden behind a screen of unjustified and unjustifiable prejudices. They are distorted by the untenable point of view common to all analysts, so much so, that it becomes exceedingly difficult to guess what truth may be hidden amidst the heaps of absolutely unacceptable statements. Untrue propositions do not become true by being repeated. The incessant repetition of the demand to apply psychoanalysis and the prediction that by doing so the skeptic himself will be convinced carries no weight.

If a man were to tell me that the skies are red and the leaves brown and would, in order to convince me, have me look through a red glass he is using, I would try to make him put away his glass, but he could never compel me to accept his statements.

From the logical fallacies I have discussed spring many ideas that are quite contrary to facts and to reason. With these ideas I shall not deal in this chapter. My intention is merely to expose the basic errors implied in the reasonings of the psychoanalysts. Their factual errors will be pointed out in the following parts of this book.

The logical fallacies belong to the formal structure of the theory. In its material content and in its methodological aspect, the theory rests on certain suppositions, which we call the axioms of psychoanalysis. They have to be studied first, before the statements on facts can be examined.

CHAPTER III

The Axioms of Psychoanalysis

NOTHING is more important for a thorough understanding of a theory and accordingly for a competent
criticism than the discovery of the suppositions that
precede the theory and enter, because they are its very foundations, into every one of its assertions. Nothing also reveals more
of the true nature and the place a theory holds in the history of
human thought than the careful study of those suppositions.
They stand in regard to a special science as the axioms stand in
regard to mathematics. These axioms are first principles, not to
be derived from any statement of mathematics. The statements
of mathematics derive indeed their authority from their accord
with the first principles.

Every material science starts from principles not its own,
principles which are supplied either by another science (in
which case they are taken for granted, because this science possesses the means of demonstrating their truth), or from the
general principles no science dares to ignore, because they are
the very laws of correct thinking. Every science rests on the
principles of logic—which are indeed not only those one finds
in the current textbooks of formal logic, but of a much richer
and deeper character—and on certain material assertions it gets
from some other science. This other science, however, is not
always one of experiment, or a factual science. It is oftener
than not the science we call philosophy. The unveiling of the
philosophy at the back of a theory is therefore as important as
the discovery of the axioms. But it is by the analysis of the so-
called axioms that we learn what kind of philosophy forms
their background. We shall therefore try to state as precisely as
possible the basic axioms, and to inquire in the next chapter

into the particular nature of the philosophy from which they spring or which they express.

So far as we can make out, there are six main axioms of psychoanalysis. They do not follow from the empirical statements—which, as we know already, are indeed not purely empirical, not the result of experience, but very much dependent on theoretical preconceived ideas. On the contrary they precede them and they determine the way these statements are used for building up the theory. I have described these axioms already elsewhere; the following remarks are partly a reproduction of earlier discussions.* But in that earlier work I distinguished but five of these axioms and included the sixth under one of the five headings. It seems better, for reasons of clearness, to list six. Each of these implies certain corollaries and consequences which will be mentioned under the same heading. The six axioms may be stated as follows:

1. All mental processes develop according to the pattern of the reflex mechanism.
2. All mental processes are of an energetic nature.
3. All mental processes are strictly determined by the law of causality.
4. Every mental phenomenon derives ultimately from an instinct. Instincts are the primary material of mental states.
5. The principle of evolution, as stated in the phyletic evolution of organisms, applies to the development of the human mind in history.
6. The chain of free associations leads back to the real cause of mental phenomena.

It is evident that the first five of these axioms are of a strictly theoretical nature. They state something about the explanation and the nature of phenomena—something which cannot be gathered from simple observation. They accordingly truly deserve to be called by the name of axioms. The axiomatic nature

* Cf. Charakter als Ausdruck, Jahrb. f. Charakterologie, 1924, I, 1.; *The New Psychologies*, London, New York, 1932.

of the sixth proposition may seem doubtful. This proposition apparently states a matter of fact; it is, it seems, a conclusion drawn from innumerable observations, an empirical law and not a presupposed proposition. This objection, however, is not really as strong as it seems at first sight and as the psychoanalysts—whenever they condescend to discuss such questions—would have us believe.

Things in truth stand differently. Even if we leave aside, for the moment, the undue identification of relations of meaning and relations of causality—of which something has been said in the preceding chapter—there is a very general idea implied in this sixth proposition; namely the idea of symbolization. It will become clear presently that this notion too is not a necessary consequence of experience, but a theoretical interpretation, resting on pre-theoretical assumptions.

All Mental Processes Develop According to the Pattern of the Reflex-mechanism

This axiom implies the notion that there is no essential difference, either in nature or in the mode of development, between nervous and mental processes. The same laws which physiology discovers as valid in regard to bodily, in particular nervous, functions, are taken to be the laws of mental processes. Physiology considers the "reflex" to be the functional unit of nervous processes. Psychoanalysis assumes that there must be a similar functional unit also in mental life. The idea, however, is not only one of similarity, but one of identity. The more complex functions of the mind are not only built up from functional units resembling reflexes, but reflexes are these units. And the way these units combine to build complex phenomena is the same in both fields.

In considering mental processes as being of the nature of a reflex, psychoanalysis did but follow a current of ideas rather common at the time when Freud was a student of medicine and in the years when he began to build up his system.* The idea of "explaining" mental facts by those known, or postulated, in the physiology of the nervous system was common with most of the physicians and biologists of those days. Though not all had such crude and primitive views as Vogt and Buechner had propagated—the brain secretes thought as the kidney secretes urine—the basic conception was nevertheless of the same kind. Mental facts were considered as but a particular manifestation of brain processes, as identical with them: according to this view, brain processes presented themselves to the observer "outside" as changes in anatomical structure, as chemical alterations, as the conditions of movements and other visible reactions; and from the "inside" as mental states. This monistic conception existed in many shades, but it was the same, fundamentally, with nearly every physician of the nineteenth century. No wonder that Freud, the pupil of Bruecke and of Meynert, trained in physiology and neurology—in his pre-analytic era he published several valuable articles and monographs in this field— and educated in this general mentality, accepted the general conception.

This way of looking at mental things was all the more taken for granted and considered the only "scientific" one by Freud, since he had, before he turned to analysis and the study of neurosis, devoted a very penetrating and inquiring little book to the theory of aphasia. In those years the experimental and clinical researches on "localization" of mental operations in the brain were in full progress. These researches started with the analysis of those disturbances of speech which afterwards were commonly called "aphasia." This state consists, roughly speaking, in an incapacity either of forming words, though the patient

* Since this book hopes to attract the attention of readers not schooled in medicine or neurology, it is necessary to give a somewhat detailed explanation of the notions on physiology and psychology implied in the psychoanalytic system. Such an explanation may be tedious to many; we deem it, however, not out of place, because the clearness of the discussion will profit and the peculiarities of psychoanalytic mentality will become more visible.

understands speech and knows what he wants to say, or in an incapacity of understanding, though spontaneous expression is more or less unimpaired. The articulatory function of the muscles in the vocal chords, the tongue, the lips, etc., is intact in the first case, as the pure faculty of sound perception is in the second case.

Broca had in 1861 demonstrated the first brain dissections of cases with aphasic troubles and shown that to a certain disturbance of speech corresponded a localized lesion of the brain. Nine years later, two German physicians, Hitzig and Fritsch, were able to prove that localized stimulation of the brain-surface caused contraction of single muscles and that each muscle was represented by a definite spot of the cortex. From this time onward publications on cases of brain trouble and on experiments on all kinds of animals became abundant. A new era in the study of the relations between brain and mind seemed to have dawned.

Wernicke, one of the leading psychiatrists of Germany, developed, on the basis of a wide personal experience and a survey of all facts known, a theory first of disturbances of speech and, proceeding from these to wider generalizations, of mental operations. The main idea of Wernicke was that the process of speech might be described in terms of reflex. A reflex is a constant response of the organism to the excitation of some sensory field without the intervention either of will or of consciousness. (This notion assumed the reflexes to be absolute rigid mechanisms; we know today that this is not the case.) The reflex-mechanism has as its anatomical basis a sensory or receptive field; a nerve-path leading from there to the nerve-centers; a nervous connection within these centers from the one where the irritation coming from the sense-organ reaches the brain, to the other from which the impulse starting toward the body has its origin; a nerve-pathway leading from the center to the organ of response and this organ itself. Wernicke conceived of mental reactions or of responses due to mental operations as being identical with reflexes. A man hears a question: the nervous excitation caused by the sound waves in his ear runs through the auditory nerve to the corresponding center in the brain cortex, passes from there, by more or less complicated ways, to another center which sends out an impulse. This impulse reaches the muscles of the throat, of the tongue, of the mouth, and so on, and causes them to contract so that from their co-operation with respiration the voice and the utterance of the answer result.

The reflex, as studied in animals and analyzed in many pathological cases in human patients, becomes thus the schema according to which all human action, even the most complicated, has to be explained. This conception gives rise to a rather curious consideration on the history of scientific ideas. If one searches for the first mention of reflexes, or rather of the notion of them, one comes across a remarkable passage in the *Tracta-tus de Homine* of Descartes. Here the author describes—and also illustrates by a drawing—how the nervous impulse caused in the eye by seeing an object runs along the optic nerve and reaches *la petite glande*, the pineal gland, which Descartes believed to be the seat of the soul. This gland is imagined as a kind of reflecting mirror; it turns according to the needs of the organism and projects the force which causes movement—called in the old terminology the *spiritus animales*—in the appropriate direction. This mechanism causes an object to be grasped by the hand or some other movement to ensue, because of some sensory impression.

If the idea is dropped that the soul wheels around, as it were, the pineal gland and directs its reflecting power, a formula results which is very like the idea expressed by modern physiology in its notion of reflex. Descartes had not, of course, made any experiment in nerve physiology. He had derived his idea about the mechanism of action from introspective analysis. His is in truth merely a translation of introspective data—accessible even to the untrained mind—into terms of physiology. Now we see that the very same idea is used again for explaining action in terms of brain physiology. The new explanation indeed starts from experimental facts. But it could not have applied to action if it did not fit into the introspective data. Introspection gave rise to the conception of reflex, and reflex is used to explain the data of introspection.

This digression into the history of scientific concepts teaches us one thing. Science is sometimes only too inclined to assume a discovery where it has only made use of an analogy. The way Wernicke conceived of action and its disturbances was in truth hardly more than such an analogy, and one which was open to many grave objections. Among the most noticeable criticisms of Wernicke's conception was Freud's little treatise on aphasia. But his criticism referred more to details and the special development of the basic idea; it left untouched the conception of action as a complicated reflex or, at least, as resting on a mechanism of the same kind.

The newer development of the physiology and the pathology of the brain has wrought havoc with the classical theory of localization. The idea of distinct mental operations or faculties residing in circumscribed areas of the brain cannot be maintained any longer in the old way. There is no doubt of some relation existing between brain regions on one hand and mental functions on the other. But the conception, e.g. that visual memory images are stored in a particular part of the brain, had to be given up. Not even the elementary and simple reflexes proved to be rigid and invariable mechanisms as the older physiologists had imagined.

We hear today much of the "plasticity of the nervous system," of even an impaired brain being capable of adjusting its achievements to altered conditions, of reflexes becoming changed when the total situation of the organism is changed, and so on. Neither the old notion of reflex nor that of cerebral localization fits in any longer with the facts and with the newer ideas on the essentials of nervous physiology. They fit in even less with the psychology of today. There is indeed one school which upholds stubbornly the idea of an "explanation" of mental facts by the physiology of the brain. But this school is moved toward preserving these absolute ideas not by cogent facts, but by the philosophy it has adopted. It is the school of the so-called objective psychologists, or psycho-reflexologists, founded in post-War Russia.

There remains, however, enough of the old conception to afford a basis for the construction of a theory based on the analogy of reflexes or, generally speaking, nervous functions, and mental operations. Such a theory would be no nearer to a real understanding of things psychological than the old ideas were or than those of the Russians are. No physiologist, and practically no psychologist for that matter, has today a clear notion of the significance of analogy. They all glide, oftener than not without being aware of it, into hasty identifications. The truth is, as was stated some years ago by the late Professor Arnold Pick of Prague, that we are able to localize disturbances of function psychologically but not anatomically. This means that we are able to indicate, by a psychological analysis of the factors converging in the formation of a complex mental function, which of these factors has suffered by a pathological process, but that it is impossible to allot to such a disturbance a definite spot in the brain.

If it was almost inevitable to conceive of mental functions according to the pattern of reflexes when psychoanalysis was born, today it is urgent to revise this idea. But if psychoanalysis were to do so, the whole system would collapse. The conception of reflexes as being the very exemplar and, even more, the very essence of mental functions, is an indispensable element in Freudian psychology. It is indeed the means by which the conception of energetic dynamism and the other basic notions are linked together. Only by considering mental processes as being basically identical with reflex action of the nervous system can the instincts be credited with the rôle they actually play in psychoanalytic theory.

The reflex organization, as Freud conceives it, has some particular features. The single "reflexes," that is, mental operations and reactions on environmental influences, are not independent of each other. They form a complicated fabric, which extends so to speak, not only over the totality of the mind—conscious and unconscious—at a given time of life, but also throughout time. The present is molded by the past. Every experience and reaction depends, in its special form and intensity, not only on the actual conditions, but also on the past. The "same" experience may receive a very different weight and importance and may condition very different reactions according to past experiences. It has not only an absolute value, determined by what it is, but also a relative value, determined by the moment when it occurs and by what went before. This insight—which indeed is that of popular psychology—had found but little consideration in the "official" psychology of Freud's days, nor can it be said to be very much considered by the average psychology of recent times. Freud did not, so far as we can see, state this principle expressly; but it is implied in his most frequently used formulae, as, for instance, the notion that the instincts undergo changes and have a "fate" (*Triebschicksal*).* Here he takes "fate" not in its original sense—either dictated by predestination or by chance or by some other extra-personal factor—but as signifying the totality of all influences molding a person.

It may well be that in developing this view Freud had been influenced by facts discovered or studies made in the laboratory of Bruecke, the famous Viennese physiologist, of which institute Freud had been a member. It was there that Exner made his experiments on what he called *Bahnung*. He found that a stimulus, too weak for releasing a reflex, might do so if another

* Max Scheler pointed out, as a particular achievement of psychoanalysis, that Freud recognized the *Stellenwert*, the positional value of every mental fact. *Wesen und Formen der Sympathie*, Bonn, 1922.

nervous pathway, connected with the same group of muscles, had been stimulated before but with a stimulus-intensity not strong enough for producing reaction. The weight of the second stimulus depends therefore on the general state of the nervous system as caused by the previous subliminal stimulation. The phenomenon of summation of stimuli, the fact that stimuli too weak in themselves condition a reflex reaction by repetition, may have pointed the same way.

These ideas of Freud deserve to be remembered. They illustrate two sides of his way of thought. He had, on the one hand, a more or less clear notion of the necessity of considering the "whole" of human personality and of human life—hence the use of the term "fate" in regard to instincts—and on the other hand, the tendency to couch his ideas on psychology in the language of physiology which was, of course, characteristic of his time. This physiology was besides very much imbued with the spirit of elementarism—the idea that reality is understood best when it is split up into its ultimate elements.

Another peculiarity of the Freudian conception credits mental—and that means ultimately physiological—processes with a kind of lastingness; they do not, or their traces do not, ever disappear totally. They remain stored up, as it were, somehow; and they may always regain influence on actual processes even if they have been inefficacious for a long time. This notion is, as one sees easily, closely related to the idea Freud had formed of the unconscious. Here too some similarities may be noted with certain conceptions of brain-physiology as it existed then and for a good many years afterwards. The discovery of the pathological state called agnosia—a term first introduced by Freud in the study on aphasia mentioned above—that is, of states in which the sensory function as such is unimpaired but in which the capacity of recognizing things is abolished, had caused some physiologists and neurologists to distinguish two kinds of centers in the brain cortex. It was believed that one center served for rendering conscious perception as such; these centers were called centers of perception. Others were supposed to "contain" the traces left by previous perceptions which would be revived by a new stimulation due to the activity of the perceptual center and, by becoming conscious together with the latter, enable the subject to compare the new impression with the old image and thus to recognize the objects. These centers were called by H. Munk, centers of memory.

The psychological as well as the physiological conception underlying this theory were both rather crude. The authors who devised this interpretation of nervous and mental processes did not bother about a thorough analysis of the operation of recognition; else they might have discovered that things were not as simple as they imagined them. And they were fully convinced that no other explanation of memory was possible save one based on the assumption of material traces left in localized cells. The parallel between this way of looking at mental facts and their relation to brain processes on the one hand, and the Freudian conception of the unconscious on the other hand is very apparent.

Notwithstanding these peculiar modifications of the then current views on brain physiology and on the relations of brain and mind, Freud's ideas remain indebted to the commonly taught theories. It might be recalled here that Exner, Bruecke's pupil and later his successor as the head of the Institute of Physiology at Vienna, had published a monographic study in which he tried to develop a complete theory of the relations obtaining between brain processes and mental phenomena. The book was called: *Entwurf zu einer physiologischen Erklaerung der psychischen Erscheinungen*; it is not without interest to note that only the first volume appeared. The reason is evident; it might be possible, though not without a certain amount of speculation and not without doing some violence to facts, to devise a physiological explanation of very simple mental facts, such as a simple reaction. But the very moment the physiologist tries to apply his principles to an explanation of higher mental processes, he encounters insurmountable obstacles. If he is not willing to indulge in vague speculations to which his actual knowledge indeed does not entitle him, he has to confess that physiology is not—or, as the physiologist of the nineteenth century might have said, not yet—capable of supplying a satisfactory theory of psychology.

Exner was too honest in his scientific work and had too great a reverence for the reliability of scientific statements to attempt such a merely speculative interpretation of psychological data. Exner's book appeared in 1894. Breuer and Freud belonged to the group of physicians centered upon Bruecke and his institute; the former had made there his important studies on the functions of the labyrinth, the non-auditory part of the inner ear, which became—together with the independently undertaken work of Mach—the foundation for the modern views on this sense organ. One will not be mistaken in assuming a mutual influence, if not a dependence.

This conception stating an identity of structure and function of the brain on the one hand and the mind on the other is of a fundamental importance for a true understanding of Freudian psychology. Many of its conceptions, especially the peculiar place allotted to the instincts, rest ultimately on this kind of "physiological psychology." In a way the second of the Freudian "axioms" too is linked closely with this hypothesis.

All Mental Processes Are of an Energetic Nature

This axiom implies the idea that mental processes are governed by the same laws as those assumed by physics. Every physical process may be considered as a change in energy-distribution. Energy manifests itself in various manners, as energy of gravitation, of electricity, of heat, etc. Psychoanalysis supposes that there is a particular kind of energy, particular, that is, in its manifestation but not in its essence, corresponding to mental processes.

This second axiom then states that every mental fact and

process have to be considered as modifications of energy. Originally conceived as defining a particularity of emotional or affective states, this idea has been generalized so as to comprise every mental state whatever. A mental fact, whether an emotion, or an image, or a desire, or an idea, or what you will, is essentially linked to or charged with a certain amount of mental energy. In psychoanalysis, this is called cathexis (cf. above, p. 20).

This idea is closely connected with the reflex-conception on the one hand, and on the other with the theory of instincts being at the bottom of every psychic phenomenon. The reflexes are seen as due to a tension resulting from the stimulus situation, and the reflectory reaction is seen as a discharge by which the tension disappears and the equilibrium is restored. Freud's peculiar idea, however, is that this energy-transformation is not only characteristic of the process and its organic foundations, but that a definite amount or quantum of energy is attached to every mental state or element.

Even if it were not open to serious objections on principle, this idea involves grave difficulties. How is a mental state or phenomenon to be defined? If every one of them carries with itself a definite amount of energy, it becomes important to have a precise definition, not in the sense of logic, but in the sense of setting a division. A definite amount of energy can be attached to a carrier only if this carrier is enclosed within definite boundaries. How can one know where, so to say, one phenomenon ends and another begins? Freud and his followers use the name of emotion, idea, part of a dream, image, etc., rather in the pre-scientific sense of common language and common sense. That which appears to be "one" to the unsophisticated mind is considered as a mental phenomenon *sui generis* and credited with carrying a certain quantity of mental energy. That this is unsatisfactory from the viewpoint of a scientific psychology, cannot well be doubted.

It seems, moreover, that the leading principle which is used, in psychoanalysis, for distinguishing the single mental states is taken from language. What may be called by a name of its own is believed to be a relatively independent element of mental life carrying an energy-charge of its own.

But let us suppose that a greater precision in terminology and a more careful study of the phenomena might be capable of overcoming this difficulty. The energetic conception would not become more acceptable. It leads immediately to consequences psychology cannot acknowledge. Distinct amounts of energy demand distinct carriers. The idea of having the mental phenomena, the mental states, the discernible elements of mental life themselves carrying a definite amount of energy is conceivable only if the mind consists of neatly separated elements, distant from each other, as it were, and if the mind has a structure very much like that which physics attributes to matter.

No division of a total energy-content into discrete parts or amounts can be conceived as existing in a continuous medium. We might refer, for the sake of illustration, to the distribution of electricity on the surface of metallic bodies. As long as there are two such bodies, each has its amount of electric energy with which it has been charged and this energy-quantum is distributed over the surface according to the properties of that surface. The very moment, however, the two bodies are connected with each other by a wire, they form but one body, and become a continuous surface; the electric energy then becomes distributed in a way determined by the shape of this one continuous body. It is quite justifiable to use such an analogy, because the psychoanalysts, and primarily Freud himself, conceive of these quantities of energy as really distinct amounts. They talk of quantities, not in a figurative manner; they even consider—and Freud himself is with them in this—that there will be a time when a measurement of these energy-amounts will become feasible. Even the notion of "entropy" is mentioned in relation to the transformations of mental energy.*

---

* Entropy signifies in physics the amount of energy which cannot be regained after some energy-transformation has been carried through. In every physical process a part of the initial energy is transformed into heat-energy.

This energy, then, is evidently but one manifestation of the energy in general which determines physical processes; it is of the same kind. It is, at least in principle, accessible to measurement. It is divided into definite amounts, and demands therefore that it be, in its parts, attached to equally definite and distinct parts of the mind, or, in other words, this idea implies and necessitates an atomistic conception of the mind.

It is perfectly in accordance with this axiomatic position that psychoanalysis has, from the day of its birth until now, strictly adhered to an associationistic psychology. How far this view is still compatible with the findings of modern experimental and general psychology, is a question which will occupy us later. It is, however, noteworthy that this upholding of a psychological view which is discarded today by nearly all psychologists, becomes explicable by the belief in the axiom of cathexis. This axiom cannot be abandoned, any more than can any of the other five, because giving it up would be tantamount to rejecting the whole theory.

Thus psychoanalysis falls back upon a conception—or, rather, never cared to revise it—which William James made fun of, even before psychoanalysis came to exist, as the "Mind-Dust theory." Instead of taking account of the fact of continuity which characterizes mental life, of what James called the "stream of consciousness," psychoanalysis conceives of mental life as a succession and a co-existence of separate mental atoms.*

The second principle of Thermodynamics states that it is impossible to transport heat from a colder to a warmer body without the help of mechanical work. The energy transformed into heat which is taken in by colder bodies is accordingly lost. Since all processes produce some heat, the total amount of available energy becomes gradually less. This is the reason why one speaks of the "universe dying from cold." It deserves to be mentioned that modern physics has become somewhat skeptical in regard to this idea.

* By referring to the views of James, we do not want to give the impression that we believe the mind or the soul to be nothing but a stream of consciousness, as James would have it. We hold, of course, that there is a substantial soul, really distinct from consciousness which is of this soul or belongs to it, and has not to be confused with it. But as a description of the connection of mental states, or of what is observable by introspection, James' term indeed seems to cover the facts.

A discussion of this kind cannot well omit saying a few words on the notion of mental energy in general. This notion is not the property of psychoanalysis alone. Other psychologists have spoken of it, before and after Freud. But it is rather a peculiarity of the psychoanalytic conception that mental energy and the energy that becomes visible in bodily changes are posited as being the same thing. This view of the problem was evident as early as the *Studies on Hysteria* and in the notion of "conversion" which was introduced by Breuer and Freud.

Conversion, in this view, means precisely the transformation of mental energy into bodily energy or into phenomena believed to be due to a peculiar distribution of energy. An emotion needs its discharge, as we have explained, and it needs it because an emotion is comparable, even identical with a tension, an accumulation of potential energy which has to be transformed into kinetic energy. This transformation takes place in the natural expression of the emotion. If this outlet is denied to the affective state, the tension remains and eventually produces lasting symptoms. This view raises obvious difficulties. If the energy of the emotion does not find its normal outlet, and instead of being relieved by expression is forced into some other channel, causing pathological symptoms, it is not easy to understand why this emotional energy does not become used up and why the pathological symptom does not, after a time, disappear of itself. This is only a minor difficulty, but it exists for the later forms of psychoanalytic theory in the same degree as for the initial stage.

It seems more important to inquire into the correctness of the notion of mental energy in general. This notion has probably several roots. It stems partly from popular psychology, from the common idea of one man possessing more strength or energy in regard to mental operations, just as there are such differences in regard to bodily strength. Another of its sources is the impression we have of making greater or lesser efforts, of being in need sometimes of more mental power or energy—

for instance to resist temptation or to behave with moderation when we feel urged toward excessive reactions—and less of this energy on other occasions. The notion of effort and of energy to overcome resistance and inhibition existing within ourselves has played a great rôle in popular literature, in fiction, in common beliefs, and also in ascetic and moral theology or philosophy. No harm is done as long as these expressions are taken as more or less accurate descriptions, as analogies or illustrations, as a generally intelligible and convenient mode of stating well-known things. But some moderns have given to these time-honored expressions a more definite meaning by establishing a relation with the concept of energy in physics.

Every science coins new terms and introduces new notions. Some of these novel terms become quickly popularized and astonishingly soon are assimilated into popular speech. Many terms, quite usual today in common language, originally belonged to scientific terminology. We speak of "short-circuiting," of a *"potentiel de guerre,"* of "plugging in" and of many other things whose names originally were the property of science or of engineering or of some other branch of special knowledge. The idea and the term "mental energy" was used before physics developed the idea of conservation of energy and began to discuss transformations of energy, the relation of kinetic and potential energy, or to speak of energy being lost, and the "entropy of the universe moving toward a maximum."

The nineteenth century cherished a truly fanatical admiration for science. It became the fashion to know something of the latest progresses and discoveries. The names of Helmholtz and Lord Kelvin, of Clerk Maxwell and of Faraday took the place which those of poets and *bels esprits* had held but a few decades previously. No wonder the terms and the notions of science found their way into common non-scientific language. The term "energy" was assimilated the more easily because it already existed. But this assimilation did not take place without a certain modification of the sense of this term. It ceased to be a mere illustration or to be based on analogy. It was taken as a reality, because the energy of which the physicists talked was believed to be such a reality. Whether it is, even in physics, a reality or merely a convenient formula, an auxiliary idea, is not for us to discuss. We might, however, refer to the remarks of H. Poincaré on this matter.*

The change in the meaning of the term "energy" when applied to mental things was furthered by, and, on its side, did further a definite way of looking at causal relations. The third axiom refers to causality.

All Mental Processes Are Strictly Determined by the Law of Causality

Psychoanalysis considers mental "events" as determined by a strict and inexorable law of causality. This causality is conceived according to the pattern of causality in physics. (Or as physics used to conceive of causality, before the idea had been born that the notion of causality had to be given up and that it was "dissolved" by the latest discoveries of the physicists.)†

For the psychoanalyst, every mental fact, be it a dream or an action, an inspiration or a sentiment, an idea about chemistry or the plan of a book, is strictly determined by causal factors. These causal factors are of two kinds; they are rooted either in the bodily constitution of the individual or in his past history. Every experience, whether conscious or not, leaves lasting traces. Nothing is "forgotten," nothing ever disappears from the mind. What is not actually remembered and what is not at hand on the shelves of memory is still in the mind but repressed into the vaults of the unconscious, only to be better and more carefully preserved there. Thus every experience in fact changes the human individual. Freud, like Heraclitus of Ephesus, might have stated that we do not step twice into the same stream, and

---

* *Science et hypothèse,* Paris, 1900.
† On the true significance of this statement cf. the paper I read at the Convention of the American Catholic Philosophical Association 1938, on *Cause in Psychology,* Proc. of the said Assoc., Vol. XIV, p. 70.

he might have added that we never are the same person in two successive instants.

This is either a trite statement, without any further consequence, or it is a definite view on human nature which cannot but influence all our ideas regarding life, behavior, decision, responsibility, in fact, every side of our being. As understood by Freud it takes on the nature of an important axiom. We are interested here in the fact that such a statement abolishes all freedom of will and allows only for a very strict determinism. This fact and the consequences resulting from it will be discussed when we examine the Freudian philosophy. The question to be raised here is rather about the notion of physical causality itself when applied to mental facts.

Many psychologists and philosophers admit the existence of psychic causality, but very few, if any, care to inquire into the precise meaning of such a statement. The reason for this lack of clarification is that ideas on causality have become in more recent times, and especially in the nineteenth century, rather poor and at the same time rather confused. The classical, that is the Aristotelian, conception of causality came to be regarded as a mere curiosity in the history of philosophy. To talk of a final cause was considered a sure sign of a prejudiced uncritical and unphilosophical mind. Efficient causality since it seemed to rule the facts of the physical world was the only one known and accepted. Terms like *causa materialis, causa formalis, causa finalis* had no meaning; they were empty formulae, remnants of an obsolete and petrified type of mentality.

For a full explanation of the four kinds of causality we have to refer the reader to the textbooks of Aristotelo-Thomistic philosophy. Only some few indications can be given here. The following definitions are taken from C. N. Bittle's *The Domain of Being* (Bruce Publishing Co., Milwaukee, 1939). The efficient cause is "that by which something is produced." The material cause is "that out of which something is made or becomes." The formal cause is "that through which a thing is made to be what it is." The final cause is "that for the sake of which an efficient cause works." Thus, in the case of a man carving a figure out of wood, the man himself or his activity is the efficient cause; the wood is the material cause; his idea of what he is going to make, the image of the statue he has in his mind, is the formal cause; the end for which he makes it, *e.g.* earning his living, adorning a church, etc., is the final cause.

Things have changed somewhat in recent times. Finality is no longer despised as it was when science was at the height of its dominating rule. Biology dares to talk of finality or purposiveness, though these terms have, with many, not the same signification as they had with Aristotle or the Scholastics. Freud himself is a representative of a finalistic conception. This becomes evident when one considers statements like the one crediting dreams with a definite function; they are "guardians of sleep," they are for the sake of ensuring sleep, they have a prospective tendency, they look forward into the future, and are wish-fulfillments of an hallucinatory or fantastical character but are nevertheless directed toward a future end. The notion of instincts, of which we shall have to speak at some length immediately, also implies something of finality. Instincts serve the "ends" of the organism, they exist for the sake of preserving individual life or safeguarding the existence of the race; all their influence on behavior and on mental life is dictated by their longing for a future satisfaction.

Freudian finalism does not, however, contradict in any way the essentially causalistic nature of psychoanalysis.* The "purposiveness" of instincts—to use MacDougall's expression—is in itself strictly determined by efficient causality. It is the nature of the instinct to aim at the realization of future situations by which satisfaction might be gained. Thus the instinct does not "will" its ends. It must strive for their realization. Nor is there

* On finalism in psychoanalysis cf. Sante de Sanctis, *Psychologie des Traumes,* in Handb. d. vergleichenden Psychol., ed. G. Kafka, Muenchen, 1922, Vol. III, p. 306.

any spontaneity in the operations of the instinct. Its essence is determined by the organization of man, which organization is, on its side, determined by phylogenesis and individual history. The manifestations of the instinct, naked or veiled, depend on the nexus of causes for both the time of their onset and for their peculiar kind. There are various ways of conceiving of psychical causality. First of all, various problems must be considered which cannot be solved according to one pattern. Not one problem, but at least six different problems, arise in regard to causality in psychology.* It is not necessary to enter into a special discussion of these problems in detail, but the simple fact of the causality-problem in psychology being very complicated prevents us taking for granted that there is only one definite kind of causality in the mind. Freud himself could not have been expected to take account of these things. Neither by inclination nor by training was he anything of a philosopher. But we miss all consideration of this point in the writings even of those of his followers who aspire at developing something like a philosophy of psychoanalysis. And we miss such a discussion also in the writings of authors who have dealt more or less critically with the Freudian conceptions. A fruitful criticism of this theory, however, has to go back to its very foundations. One of these foundations is the idea that causality of absolutely the same kind as is supposed to rule the material world exists also in the mind.

In the case of most authors and especially the psychoanalysts this view is closely related to the notion of quantity in things mental. Here again is a question which we cannot treat fully at this point. But we might point out that this question too is not easily answered and necessitates careful and subtle inquiries. It has been taken for granted that the notion of quantity applies to everything in exactly the same sense. This view is characteristic of an age which believed in science as the key to all riddles of reality, and as the only reliable approach to all problems.

* The article mentioned above in note on page 64.

Measurement indeed is the basis of science. So far as it regards science, the program of Galileo was quite right; to measure all things and to make measurable what is not yet so. The fatal mistake was, not in making such a statement at all, but in neglecting to inquire into its essential limitations. Galileo's program seemed to presuppose that there is nothing at all which could not, in some way or another, be subjected to measurement. The first thing to ask would have been whether there do not exist things which by their very nature escape measurement. The next step would have been to inquire into the nature of measurement and to find out whether its essence and the signification of the figures obtained are everywhere the same.

It has become clear to many that measurement in psychology, however "exact" its methods may be, has another meaning than it has in physics. Measurement presupposes some kind of quantity. But there are mental phenomena in which no analysis can ever detect anything like quantity. We read sometimes that every mental phenomenon has an intensity and that intensity in mind corresponds to extension in matter. But there are mental facts which are always of the same intensity or rather of no intensity at all. We may speak of the intensity of feelings, or of sensations, or of acts of volition, or of instinctive strivings. But it is impossible to credit judgment with intensity. A judgment is true or false, it is never more or less. Nor can we admit that differences in intensity of evidence or conviction, be they of a kind to permit some quantification, have anything to do with the judgment itself. The act of judging as such, or the mental phenomenon of judgment, remains always the same whether our belief or conviction be more or less developed. Now, if there is even one kind of mental fact which does not allow of quantification, then the general statement that intensity is a feature common to all mental facts loses its sense. Intensity is really not a general feature of mental facts.

Causality, as it is considered in physics or in all prescientific statements on the material world, is closely linked to and dependent on the possibility of a truly quantitative determination of the phenomena. Where there is no true quantity, causality, even efficient causality, must receive a meaning somewhat different from the one it has in the realm of true quantity.* Causality in psychology, referring to the sequence and interdependence of mental states, cannot be of the same kind as in physics. The reason why this truth is so seldom, if ever, recognized is that the notion of analogy has been practically lost. Mind and matter stand to each other in a relation of analogy, as do all the various strata of reality one might distinguish. The categories describing or determining the relations obtaining between the single phenomena of the different strata are also analogical to each other. The conception of a science of the mind, as developed by Freud, is, however, precisely a conception of a kind of physics of mental facts. He prides himself on having devised a true "science" of psychology; and science means to him, of course, a branch of knowledge formed according to the pattern of physics. He was the more able and the more induced to consider the causality reigning in the mind to be of the very same kind as that governing material processes, the nearer his whole conception was to a monistic materialism. The axioms which have been already mentioned point in this direction. But even to the materialist it cannot remain hidden that there exist definite differences between the material and the mental phenomena. Nor did Freud ignore this. But he felt that he had found the bridge by which to cross the gap between these two realms of reality.

The impossibility of identifying simply material and mental processes and states had been the *crux* of all honest philosophers and psychologists of the materialistic school. Only some few, and the least prominent indeed, denied the existence of such a gap which they could not bridge. Many found consolation in the idea that this gap was unbridgeable only "as yet" and that

* A more detailed explanation may be found in the article mentioned above, p. 64.

science would, before long, discover new facts which would allow it to prove the identity of both fields of reality. They felt in regard to psychology and biology the same way as they did in regard to biology and physics or chemistry; as yet life was unexplained, but tomorrow or next year we shall know all about it. Some few of them, earnestly though they might hope for a consistent and satisfactory explanation in terms of matter, still doubted whether this would ever be achieved. They rather shocked their over-optimistic contemporaries by pronouncing a resigned, but very convincing *"ignorabimus."**

Every Mental Phenomenon Derives Ultimately from an Instinct

General psychology talks of many mental phenomena, as sensations, feelings, volitions, thoughts. There was a time when the psychologists believed that all mental phenomena could be considered as complexes of "sensations." This idea was not based on empirical evidence, but belonged to a certain set of philosophical conceptions. The philosophy underlying this kind of psychology was mostly the one of the English empiricists. Sensistic psychology proved to be unsatisfactory; no way could be discovered for deriving in an intelligible and demonstrable manner mental facts like judgments or purposive actions from sensations. Most of the later psychologists were satisfied with stating a number of ultimate mental facts which resisted all further reduction to more primitive elements. It was not recognized immediately that this conception had become incompatible with a monistic interpretation of human mind; that this is the case, has, however, been emphasized, in a convincing manner, especially by Hans Driesch. Materialistic monism needs, in order to be a consistent system, the assumption that mental and material phenomena are essentially of the same kind. One

---

* This was the conclusion at which the famous physiologist and physicist, Emile du Bois Reymond, arrived in a speech he delivered at the Academy of Science in Berlin in 1872.

of the basic features of material phenomena is their being reducible to elementary facts which by combination give rise to the complex phenomena we observe. An interpretation of human nature resting on materialistic and monistic principles needed, therefore, a new "material" or "element" out of which all mental phenomena could be supposed to be built.

The conception by which Freud meant to overcome all the difficulties of a monistic interpretation of human nature was that of instinct. This means that instinct is the original material of which every mental phenomenon is formed. All mental activity is originally—what this word means will become clear afterwards—instinctual. Every mental state, be it a desire or an idea, or whatever else, has its origin in some other state, intimately related to instincts. To understand this fundamental part of psychoanalytic theory it is necessary to inquire first into the meaning of instinct as conceived by Freud.

One further remark is required. The term "instinct" exists, of course, in German. It is, however, not used by Freud who always speaks of *Trieb*. This term is sometimes translated as "urge"; but a psychology making the *Trieb* the fundamental fact in life and mind calls itself "hormic" from the Greek word "ὁρμή" which might be translated as well by *Trieb* as instinct; therefore, as a translation of *Trieb*, "urge" has a special meaning. Though some difficulties may arise from using the word "instinct" we still prefer it to "urge" because the latter word too has some variable connotations. We may feel urged to do our duty, and in such a case no *Trieb* is immediately at work. We are urged by love, but we are under the influence of instincts when craving for food, or flying from danger. There are, moreover, several instances of the terms instinct and *Trieb* being used interchangeably even in German. It is equally possible to speak of sexual instinct as of *Sexualtrieb*. The term "instinct" moreover was used by Freud himself, in his article on psychoanalysis in the Encyclopædia Britannica.

It is not necessary to analyze here the special ideas of Freud on the kinds of instincts or on their number. Something will be said about this in the chapter dealing with the Freudian conception of sexuality. The problem to be studied here is the general idea of instinct and of its place within the whole of human personality.

An instinct is, in psychoanalysis, first of all a function belonging to the biological organization. The instincts as such, are not mental, but of the body. They are peculiar arrangements of bodily functions, serving certain ends, as for instance the preservation of the individual and of the race. It is, however, their nature to be "represented" in the mind. This distinguishes them from mere reflexes which are not represented in consciousness and to whose nature it belongs that they *may* become noticeable to the mind, but do not necessarily become so. We know nothing of the reflectory movements of the iris in the eye, though we may become aware of the reflectory contraction of some muscle of the body. But instincts in man somehow penetrate into the mind, indeed their becoming mental is necessary for their achieving their ends. The instinct, nevertheless, is forever outside the mind; it is a part of the bodily organization and as such inaccessible to direct mental influence. It cannot disappear; it can only, at best, manifest itself in various ways. The instincts are "represented" in the mind by the images of those situations which promise immediate and full satisfaction to the instinctual cravings. There are other sides of these representations or representatives of instincts too. They are not merely images, but images gifted with a strong power of attraction (or repulsion, since there are also instincts referring to escape, flight, defense, and so forth). The instinctual craving itself becomes manifest in a way, as we see in hunger and in sexual appetite. But all these features are, so to say, centered upon the nucleus of the image.

It seems that psychoanalysis holds these representatives of instincts to be the only original content of the mind. It is not easy to understand how they come to be there. The instincts can only supply the necessary conditions on the side of subjectivity; but the contents have to come from without. The principle that every mental object has its origin in sense-impression cannot be denied, even by the analysts. One can, however, imagine that the mind reacts only to those objects presented to it by the tangible world which are in accordance with the primitive and innate instinctual desires. Only what is capable of satisfying these instincts is selected from the manifold possible objects. The more primitive an organization is, the more exclusively is it aware only of those objects which are "of interest" to it. The notion, however, that the images corresponding to instinctual longings are the only primary content of the mind is not without grave difficulties.

Because of this selective power of the instinctual organization, all mental contents, of whatever nature, which in more developed stages fill the mind, have a necessary relation to instincts. An object, which is not ultimately correlated to an instinct and capable of somehow satisfying its cravings, simply cannot exist at all for the mind. Because of this, psychoanalysis feels entitled to state that every mental state or every object of such a state is, basically, destined to satisfy an instinct; it becomes thus a "symbol" of the object, situation or action which originally and nakedly was intended.

Now there are very few original instincts, and all the instincts discoverable by a description of behavior are but manifestations of those basic instincts. We have seen that Freud distinguished only two main groups; one group of instincts refers to the ego, the other to objects. The latter instinct presents itself in two manners, or it has two sides; there is only one instinct urging for closer union with the object, and this instinct is called libido, and another tending toward destruction of the object. Libido, however, is not a *denominatio a potiori*, is not a name given properly to sexual urges and only by analogy or enlargement of signification to other tendencies referring to objects of a non-sexual nature. According to psychoanalysis all instincts directed toward objects are essentially sexual in their very nature. The idea of C. G. Jung, that libido might be the name of a general and undifferentiated attitude in regard to objects, of which attitude sexuality is a specialization or differentiation, has not met with the approval of "orthodox" psychoanalysis.

From this view a difficulty arises. We have evidently to assume that a strict correlation exists between an instinct and the object or the objects capable of satisfying these instinctual longings. To a sexual instinct corresponds and can correspond only a group of objects which are in themselves sexual. If, by sublimation, the libido is directed toward objects which are definitely not sexual in appearance and which nevertheless, satisfy the instinctual, libidinous desires, we cannot but conclude that appearance is deceitful and that these objects are, in truth, fundamentally related to sexuality. From this, however, it follows that the actual manifoldness of reality is to be abolished or to be taken as "mere appearance." Art is appearance; all reality is something related to sexuality. The same statement has to be made of every other possible aim of action and striving. We do not see how psychoanalysis can escape this consequence which contradicts not only common sense, but some of the fundamental principles of philosophy (and, as we want to emphasize here, not only principles of Scholastic philosophy; the phenomenology of Husserl and his followers, for instance, could not agree with this way of looking at the relation of aims and appetitive forces).

The conception of instincts as belonging to bodily organization and having a natural representation in the mind has, in the Freudian system, a twofold function. It allows first to go back to the very roots of every mental phenomenon and thus becomes the basis of the genetic explanation so characteristic of psychoanalysis; and it has to bridge the gulf between body and mind. The instinct is a function or an apparatus primarily of the body; but also, since by the essential laws of human nature it is necessarily represented in the mind, it is a mental phenomenon. It is, one feels tempted to say, one and the same thing viewed from two sides. In a way this recalls Spinoza's famous expression: *una eademque res, sed duobus modis expressa.* The same thing or entity is physical in so far as it is considered in its bodily aspect, and mental in so far as its representations in the mind are envisioned.

Monistic interpretations of human nature have always encountered the difficulty that they could not give any idea of the relations obtaining between, *e.g.*, brain processes and mental states. They simply had to declare these two to be identical and but "two sides" of the same reality, emphasis being laid on the bodily side as the true reality by all authors adhering to a materialistic philosophy. Freud's conception is of another kind. The instincts seem to present a real link between mind and body; to belong, as it were, to a psychophysically "neutral" region—to use an expression of William Stern's—intercalated between mind and body, common to both, though rooted in the latter. A spiritualistic monism, was, of course, something Freud never could have considered.

I am not suggesting that Freud developed this idea for the sake of safeguarding his monistic conception. That it did so, he was probably fully aware; but also, we may suppose, he took it for granted as the only view a serious scientist could adopt, and he did not feel any need to devise notions to strengthen this position. He was sure that history would, before long, enthrone science and overthrow the reign of religion and of metaphysical speculation—which to Freud was nearly as bad as religion—and so make an end of all these "illusions." There remained alive in Freud's mind not a little of the implicit trust in science the nineteenth century had cherished and of Auguste Comte's vision of mankind's future. The age of science was, with the Viennese psychologist, a beloved and never abandoned dream. Accordingly he cannot have felt any need to find arguments in favor of monism; nor was such an idea in his line, since he always professed a definite disregard for philosophy.

But it is probable that in conceiving of instincts and their place within human nature, he was "unconsciously" prompted by his general philosophical ideas.

The instincts themselves are indestructible; they belong to the organism and can no more disappear than the function of the heart. It is, therefore, not the instinct as such which can become the object of repression. If it is occasionally said that sexual impulses or the sexual instinct have been repressed, this has to be understood as a somewhat lax form of expression, used for the sake of simplification. What is repressed is always the mental representation of the instinct; because these representations are the only manifestation of which the mind becomes aware and on which it can exercise its influence and which may, eventually, cause a conflict within the mind. The unconscious does not contain the instincts which as such are non-mental—whereas the unconscious is declared to be part of the mind—but it does contain the representations of instincts.

The instincts continue to function also after their representatives in the mind have been banished, by repression, into the unconscious. In such a case they have to find an outlet somehow. A new representation has to be made available and, corresponding to it, a new object, the possession or realization of which ensures to the instinct its satisfaction. This is done by the process of sublimation in normal cases; by slipping through the barrier of the censor in dreams or in some few other instances; in neurosis it is done by producing a symptom. The relation of the symptom to the instinctual cause cannot be quite the same as the relation between instinct and behavior, because the symptom cannot be said to be action in the same sense as an activity can; but only action procures satisfaction to the instinct and guarantees an "abreaction." Even the psychoanalyst will probably not deny that several points of the instinct theory are in need of clarification.

The notion of conflict deserves special mention. In psychoanalysis conflict has a twofold meaning; at least it is used in reference to two facts which are not simply identical. Conflict means, first, the same situation which common language calls by this name. There are divergent tendencies alive in the mind —they may be conscious or not—and none of them is so definitely superior as to overcome the others. Such a conflict can exist even in the field of pure reason in regard to truth. Two conceptions which seem to be equally probable may "wrestle" with each other. It is, however, probable that the incapacity for decision on truth depends not so much on intellectual reasons but on emotional factors; one statement might appear as more convincing, whereas the other is more to the liking of the subject. The common case is the conflict between duties, or—even more common—between duty and inclination. These conflicts take place between mental contents; they may even exist between contents related to the same instinct, as one sees in the case of a man attracted by two women. The same has to be assumed of every conflict of interest referring to objects, because according to psychoanalysis all interest in an object derives from libido.

But there is also a conflict between instincts. The instinct of death is antagonistic to the other instincts. The ego instincts may be opposed to those of libido, within libido opposite tendencies may arise.

The name of conflict ought to be reserved for those mental situations in which the mind feels drawn hither and thither by two opposed ends. There is a conflict of duties. There is a conflict between our longing for pleasure and our conscience. But the name "conflict" is out of place when we refer to instincts. Instincts conflict as little as physical forces do. There is no conflict between two magnets, each of them attracting a piece of iron. The iron moves toward the stronger magnet. The animal organism will obey the impulse of the stronger instinct. Physical forces or instincts are antagonistic; they never constitute a true situation of conflict. Instincts are conceived by psychoanalysis according to the pattern of physical forces. What applies to these applies equally to instincts. To speak of a "conflict between instincts" is the more inadvisable, since it gives rise but too easily to the idea that true conflicts too are only due to instinctual antagonisms. There is no doubt that this is just the opinion of Freud. But it is not the truth.

To be more explicit: In the discussions on free will mention is often made of "Buridan's donkey." Buridan seems to have been credited with the invention of the story without reason, since the story does not occur in his writings. But the name has come to be generally adopted. A donkey will, it is said, starve when placed between two bundles of hay which to his mind do not present any difference. Being attracted by both bundles with an equal intensity, he will not move at all, and will finally starve, immobilized between the two bundles. Experimental biology affords a rather similar observation. A starfish whose arms are immersed in solutions of salt of equal concentration, while the body is placed on a dry spot, will not move because the stimuli are all of the same intensity. This animal really behaves like the fabulous donkey. It dries up. Psychoanalysis does not see any essential difference between instincts and such simple forms of attraction or stimulation as illustrated by the examples mentioned. The result of an instinctual antagonism is not brought about by choice or decision but it follows from the difference of intensity. The true analogy is, accordingly, not decision or choice, but the parallelogram of forces as drawn in treatises on mechanics.

Free will is indeed a notion which cannot find a place within the system of psychoanalysis. On this point more will be said in the next chapter. Instincts are, as has been shown, the only material of mental life. Since all mental phenomena, whether unconscious or conscious, are of an instinctual nature they have to obey the laws governing the activities and relations of instincts. The identification of a conflict of duties and an antagonism or clash of instincts, an identification manifested by the use of the same term, is a necessary consequence of the psychoanalytic conception of mental life. Consciousness and the "ego" differ from the "id" only in so far as the instincts are undisguised in the latter and masked in the former. But the nature of the phenomena is the same on both levels.

The indiscriminate use of the term "conflict" is one of the means which enable the psychoanalyst to shift imperceptibly, in fact without his becoming aware of his doings, his argumentations from psychology to physiology and back again. The trick is done by using an analogical expression as if it were univocal. Thus an impression is created, as if psychoanalysis had devised a theory of man's nature as a unit. But this is an achievement of which this system is just as incapable as all modern philosophies are. There is only one consistent and intelligible conception which allows us to understand man as a unit and which, at the same time, safeguards the essential diversity of the material and the spiritual. This conception has been proposed by Aristotle and perfected by Aquinas.

If mental phenomena developed gradually out of instinctual ones the right to use the same name for the initial and the final phenomenon could not be contested. The next axiom is, therefore, closely related to the one dealing with the instincts.

The Principle of Evolution Applies to the Development of the Human Mind in History

At the time Freud conceived the basic notions of his system it was a matter of course for every serious biologist and physician to believe in Darwinian evolution. This view had been propagated and popularized in Germany by Haeckel who enjoyed a great fame in spite of certain affairs in which he had been accused of tampering with his evidence. Psychology too would have felt very much behind the times if it had not adopted the evolutionist ideas.

Haeckel had formulated what is known as the fundamental law of ontogenesis: that individual development recapitulates in an abridged manner the phyletic history of the species. Early developmental stages of man were said to be so like the organisms of lesser animals that they could be considered as reproducing these. The fertilized cells from which the organism develops was likened to a unicellular organism, the first stages of the embryo were considered as corresponding to the lowest animals, a later phase of embryonic development reproduced allegedly the organization of a turtle, and so on. Whether this description and analysis of embryonic stages fits the facts or not, is of little concern to us here. There are some biologists who do not accept these statements; but even if they were generally received as giving an exact idea of the facts, they still would not prove the "law" of Haeckel, because this law rests on premises other than the mere empirical discovery of likenesses in bodily shape and organization. The existences of these similarities could, in fact, be admitted without concluding that there is a "repetition of phyletic history." Even if this theory were immune to criticism, it is still doubtful whether a similar idea may be proposed in regard to mental evolution.

Freud's conception is that individual mental development recapitulates the mental history of mankind. The human embryo has but an animal life or is on the level of the animal; the newborn child is still not very far from this state. In the first months the child progresses farther to become like, in his mentality, the most primitive peoples we know; the mind of the child passes, so to say, from a stage of mere animality through one corresponding to the mentality of our prehistoric ancestors, until it reaches, with maturity, the full state of a man of modern times and modern culture.

One sees immediately that this conception implies an equation of two terms which are not to be put on the same level. The phyletic history of the species *homo sapiens* is likened to the cultural history of mankind. Nobody can deny that these two "histories" are basically different. The phyletic history stretches over some hundred thousands of years, perhaps even over a longer time; mankind exists, though we may be unable to say how long, assuredly a much shorter time. The changes in organization from the amoeba to man involve the total plan of the organism. They add quite new features; they produce quite new forms, new species, new genera. The evolution of culture goes on within one species, without bringing about more than accidental alterations.

Great though the differences be between the skeleton of primeval man and of an American of today, they are still much less marked than those between the highest ape and the lowest man. Development of culture, moreover, refers to modes of behavior, to sets of ideas, to forms of living, but not to the material aspects which are believed to change in phylogenesis. The "phyletic axiom" of psychoanalysis rests, therefore, not on facts, but on a quite peculiar interpretation of them. It is simply assumed, without any proof other than the applicability of psychoanalytic categories, that this identity of phyletic and cultural history is a legitimate conception.

The use made by psychoanalysis of its notions in dealing with facts of ethnology and of cultural history will be examined in a chapter especially devoted to this question. It is indispensable, however, for a full understanding of the background of psychoanalysis to see clearly on this point, viz., that the very basis of the so-called confirmation of psychoanalysis by the comparative study of culture is an arbitrary statement which would be exceedingly difficult to prove.

Psychoanalysis contends that by its method of free association and of interpretation it brings forth unconscious material which cannot be considered any longer as belonging to the individual as such; it belongs to or stems from factors which had been at work in generations dead so many thousands of years. The unconscious operates, at least partly, according to the laws not of the modern mind, but of a mind which is called "archaic" and which is believed to be of the kind that was active in prehistoric man. This is in truth a mere fiction, or rather the result of another mistaking of preconceived ideas for facts. What truly exists is but a certain similarity of mentality in children and in primitive man. The assertion of "recapitulation" and of an identity of these two is founded more on theoretical prejudices than on empirical findings. More will be said on this point in the sixth chapter.

The Chain of Free Associations Leads Back to the Real Cause of Mental Phenomena

The last of the axioms states that the associations produced by the subject during the "psychoanalytic situation" are more than mere connections of ideas, memories, or images; they are said to be susceptible of an interpretation aiming at the discovery of causes. Associative connections and causal connections are, according to Freudian psychology, interchangeable terms; perhaps it would be more correct to say that the associations symbolize the real causes which are detected by interpretation. This axiom implies two different though related propositions. The first refers to the factual possibility of discovering causes by following up the chain of free associations; the other identifies relations of content or meaning with those of causation. The meaning of these two propositions will become clear immediately; the topic of the second proposition has already been touched upon (see page 39).

The first proposition is not, as would seem at first sight, one of experience. The only facts which may be alleged as an empirical proof thereof are those cases in which a symptom disappears after a certain memory has been made conscious by this method. But even if this is observed, the causal relation is not self-evident, but assumed. To explain such a fact, viz., the disappearance of a symptom, by a causal interpretation is, of course, the easiest and most obvious hypothesis. But it is not the only possible one. The analyst might refer also to the analyzed person's conviction that the long-forgotten and repressed facts were indeed the causes of the symptom. But the conviction of the subject has, at its best, only a confirmative and not a demonstrative character. If a man is, according to what we are taught by psychoanalysis, so liable to be deceived about his own motives and mental states in general, we can hardly trust him when he makes statements on his hitherto unconscious mental states and their relation to other facts of his mental life. Thus, the only real demonstration available is the curative effect.

We have pointed out repeatedly that this criterion is absolutely missing in all cases of analysis not dealing with a symptom capable of disappearance. It is especially missing in dream-analysis which, we are told by Freud, is the *via regia* into the unconscious. In many cases the relation between the material brought forth by analysis and the phenomenon to be analyzed is patent only to the mind of the psychoanalyst who knows already all about these relations. He needs no confirmation by the analyzed person, because the "unconscious has no No." By whatever reaction the analyzed individual responds to an explanation proffered by the analyst, the response, we read, is always in the affirmative: assent and denial, tears and laughter, indifference and protest, answer or silence—they all have but one meaning, and this meaning is: yes.

The notion implied in this proposition is, therefore, truly axiomatic in character, and not empirical.

This is true still more of the second proposition. It is, of course, permissible to assert that a symbol is "caused" by what is symbolized thereby; but in using this expression, one has to be aware that he is referring to a notion of causality altogether different from efficient causality. The word is indeed "caused" by the meaning it expresses, but it is not caused in the manner of efficient causation, the efficient cause being the will or desire of the mind to give utterance to its ideas. If there is a symbolization such as the one assumed by psychoanalysis, the cause of a symbol has to be sought in an urge or desire for symbolization or in the general nature of the human mind which seeks to express the impressions it has received.

We might remark here, incidentally, that the idea of Breuer

and Freud, of every emotional state being in need of "abreaction," that is of becoming manifest and, as it were, exteriorized by an adequate expression, is in truth but a special and particularly noticeable instance of a general law of the human mind. Every impression is, as Hoenigswald justly remarks, preordained toward expression.* The impression somehow starts a process which ends with expression. But the expression is not to be considered as a "symbol" in every case; there are many expressions which are quite devoid of any symbolic character whatsoever.

The reason why something is clad in a symbol is not the cause of symbolization in general. There obtains, between symbol and thing symbolized, a relation of meaning, the one being the sign of the other. But no sign is caused, in the manner of efficient causality, by the thing signified, and the relation is of quite another nature. (Cf. above, p. 36.) Of this Freud and his school are of course fully aware; it is only in regard to the repressed material of the unconscious in its relation to the phenomena of consciousness that they identify meaning and causation. But this identification too is an axiom and not a fact which could be ascertained empirically. The facts which might be alluded to as proving this assertion are those we referred to above.

For the great majority of cases not even the so-called empirical demonstration which psychoanalysis may achieve is available. We have seen, moreover, that the facts psychoanalysis refers to are doubtful, since the method by which they are discovered is open to so serious objections.

A scientific statement has to be demonstrable in all the cases it pretends to cover. A generalization which rests on a minority of instances can hardly be considered as legitimate.

Since the method itself rests on these axiomatic propositions, the method of psychoanalysis and its general idea or philosophy are essentially one and inseparable. There are some who believe in the possibility of using the method without accepting the phi-

* *Prinzipien der Denkpsychologie,* 2d ed. Leipzig, 1924.

losophy. We hold this to be impossible; such a conception rests, we believe, on a misunderstanding of the principles implied in the method and on an underrating of the importance the philosophy has for the formation of the whole system of Freudian psychology. With this idea we shall deal in a separate chapter because we hold that it is as erroneous as dangerous. But we have first to inquire into the nature of the philosophy of psychoanalysis.

The axioms which have been discussed in this chapter form the basis of the Freudian system. They are included in this system. Whether explicitly stated or implicitly presupposed, they belong as essential parts to the system itself. But axioms of every science whatsoever are not first principles which are evident as such. Such first principles are at the bottom only of pure logic and of pure mathematics. The axioms of all other sciences are derived from somewhere.

Psychoanalysis has become much more than a method of mental treatment or a theory of neurosis. It has developed into a theory of human nature. Its axioms can therefore have their origin only in a field of still larger generality. They are indeed the expression of a definite philosophical conception. We turn now to the analysis of Freud's philosophy.

CHAPTER IV

The Philosophy of Psychoanalysis

EVERY man has a philosophy, though many people do not know they have one and are incapable of telling what they think or feel about the ultimate problems of life. If you ask this man or that, a workman or an official, a student or a man of business, what kind of philosophy is his, he will probably answer that he has none at all and that he would never bother to have one. Nevertheless, there is a philosophical background to everybody's way of life, of his social, political, economic views, of the way he arranges his relations with his fellows, chooses his interests, holds this important and that negligible. Philosophical problems or problems which pertain to philosophy, 'and to inquire into which is the task of philosophy, are more common than we might think at first. Children discover such problems, and they may sometimes worry about them. Education, the difficulties and the pleasures of everyday-life, gradually overlay these interests; they begin to be felt as unimportant, as not of any real help in "real" life, and occupation with them is deemed a useless hobby. But these problems are nevertheless very real, they play a much greater rôle in human life than is generally acknowledged.

This philosophy, whether conscious or not, whether it is the result of some effort at clarification or remains in an embryonic state, cannot but influence whatever a man does. This influence may remain quite unsuspected if the things the man does are far from metaphysics and morals; it becomes very visible, even though the man himself may remain unaware of this fact, whenever his work turns on facts and problems which are close to metaphysical principles.*

* What we mean to convey, has been expressed perfectly by Etienne Gilson,

Some sciences are farther away from philosophy than others. A physicist may do without philosophy as long as he studies only pure physics; he gets dangerously near to philosophy the very moment he begins to reflect on the foundations of his science or attempts to derive therefrom generalizations of a wider scope. The same may be said of most sciences, of nature and of history or society, of facts and of notions. Among the sciences which cannot but encounter philosophical problems within their own field, psychology is the most prominent. The psychologist cannot help being something of a philosopher, because there arise within psychology so many questions which are definitely philosophical. It would take too long to explain here why this is so and why it cannot be otherwise, in spite of attempts to free psychology of all philosophical encumbrances. One cannot escape philosophy, not even by denying it, because a denial of philosophy is in itself philosophical and often implies a metaphysics more hazardous than the one invented by the much despised philosophers.

Anyhow, even today there are many psychologists who are also philosophers and many philosophers who are particularly interested in psychology. This fact is not due to a kind of historical inertia which causes a state to persist though it has become obsolete. Nor is the fact due to mere personal inclinations of some psychologists and philosophers. There are real reasons in the nature of the two disciplines for the persistence of these close relations between psychology and philosophy.*

A comparative study of the many psychologies existing today reveals that the divergences of these schools are mainly caused

---

the philosopher: "It may perhaps be doubted whether . . . there was ever any great historian who had no philosophy of history of his own; even if no efforts were made to make it explicit, it would be none the less real and possibly the more effective as less conscious of itself." *The Spirit of Medieval Philosophy*, New York, 1936, p. 390. What is said here of the historian is true, perhaps even truer, also of the psychologist.

* Dr. Th. V. Moore has, in his recently published work, *Cognitive Psychology*, Philadelphia, 1939, stressed the point that psychology without a philosophical approach would be but a rudiment of what it has to be.

by the differences in the philosophy the heads of the schools prefer. It is the *Weltanschauung* which makes the greatest difference. The behaviorist does not discard consciousness as an object of scientific study because he is not aware that conscious phenomena exist, but because his philosophy does not allow for considering these phenomena as facts of importance to science. The mechanistic psychology of the reflexological school is not forced upon them by facts, but by their pre-scientific or, at least, pre-psychological conception of human nature; and so on.

It is not otherwise with psychoanalysis. This school too has philosophical convictions of its own. Freud indeed had no liking for philosophy, nor did he ever attempt to state his own philosophy. That he adhered to some philosophy is very patent; he never could have professed such a faith in the future of mankind when finally enlightened and guided by science, if he had not held some very definite views which cannot be called by any name but philosophy. It is not science which tells us what place it holds or has to hold in the totality of human life; nor is it science which states anything about a happier state of man in years to come, or defines religion as an illusion. Such statements are the offspring of philosophical convictions.

The philosophy at the back of psychoanalysis is obvious. Nobody who ever became acquainted with the principles of this Freudian psychology can doubt that its foundations are utterly materialistic. It will not be difficult, therefore, to prove that psychoanalysis belongs to a group of systems born from the spirit of naturalism and materialism. Nor is it difficult to see that the moral outlook of psychoanalysis is a pure hedonism. These attitudes have some definite and far-reaching influence on the way one conceives of human nature, of the dignity of the human person, of the basic ends of life.

It has been urged that the philosophical outlook of Freud and of his followers has but little importance for the question whether psychoanalysis be true or not, and whether it gives a true idea of man and his mental life or not.* In science, it is said, the philosophy of the scientist is of but little importance; facts may be observed and stated independently of all philosophy; and psychoanalysis is science. Here is where the great mistake is made. Psychoanalysis is not and cannot be science in the same sense as physics is. Nor can any psychology ever develop into a science of this kind, notwithstanding all the measurements, figures, tracings and statistics. Psychology is, by its very nature, for ever dependent on philosophy; it is indeed a science dealing with facts, but it is on the other hand so close to metaphysics that without clear ideas on the problems of philosophical anthropology it becomes the victim of the worst confusion and gets lost in the most amazing errors. Psychoanalysis, being an attempt at building up a science of the human mind and of human life, is not exempt from this general law. If, therefore, psychoanalysis is proved to rest on an unacceptable philosophy, it becomes unacceptable itself.

The following objection is frequently urged against this position in regard to psychoanalysis. Maybe, it is said, psychoanalysis as a theory and as a philosophy of human nature is mistaken. But this does not touch its usefulness as a method for curing mental ailments, for preventing neurosis, for regulating education, and for exploring the laws governing human behavior. This objection will be dealt with in a later chapter. Here we remark only that we believe it to rest on mistaken conceptions. Those who urge it often refer to the fact that the discoveries of physics are, in many cases, absolutely independent of the particular theory. The equations expressing, *e.g.*, the laws of the reflection of light are true, whether the physicist holds the emanationistic conception, or the undulatory hypothesis, or the electromagnetic theory. But the case is very different with psychology. The said objection is partly based on a lack of discern-

* Cf. for instance Hartmann, *Ueber genetische Charakterologie, insbesondere ueber psychoanalytische,* Jahrb. f. Charakterologie, 1929.6.73.

ment; the essential differences between psychology and science are overlooked.

The "facts" psychoanalysis envisions are, moreover, even more philosophical or subject to philosophical criteria than those of psychology generally are. A study of color-vision, or of the laws of association, or on the development of decision may, up to a certain point, stay far enough away from philosophical implications; but statements on man's very nature, his moral attitudes, on the factors determining his total personality are not of such a kind.

It has, furthermore, become clear already, and it will become still more evident in the following chapters, that psychoanalysis —and not this school alone, of course—is rather liberal in the use of the term "fact." What is put before the reader as a simple fact is, in truth, usually an empirical finding clad in the terminology of a theory. Thus the theory is implied already in the elementary statements on which the theory allegedly rests.

The philosophy of any system whatsoever can be discovered only by a consideration of its principles or of what we term the axioms. It is not to be discerned with any reliability by a study of certain applications to, or assertions on, special subjects. It is always possible that even the most "orthodox" followers of some doctrine misunderstand it or introduce ideas which in truth do not belong there. One can never be sure of the capacity of logical consequentiality; too often, in history, an idea has been used as a basis for procedures and views which were in flat contradiction to it.

Many people have felt shocked by certain statements made by the analysts in regard to the rôle played by sexuality in human life. Many have recoiled from other statements on morals or religion. Wrong and even dangerous though many of these assertions are, they are not the important point which a serious criticism has primarily to consider. Moral disapproval, the revolt of feeling, the protest of offended faith and such like, are no arguments in a dispute on psychology and its foundations. Only the careful analysis of the principles can demonstrate the true nature of psychoanalysis or, for that matter, of any other system.

Nor is the reference to successes obtained in the treatment of neurotic patients an argument which could be opposed to a criticism of principles. Besides the fact that, as we shall see in a later chapter, therapeutic success is no proof for the truth of a theory in medical psychology, there is always the possibility of extrinsic influences to be considered. So many factors enter into the therapeutic situation between the medical psychologist and his patient, and success may depend on motives very different from those of which the theory talks, that an evaluation of the results becomes practically impossible. The only way to arrive at a clear and definitive judgment on the nature of a theory in psychology is the careful analysis of the principles.

The principles on which psychoanalysis rests have been detailed in the foregoing chapter. They need not be listed here a second time. But they have to be examined to find the general conceptions underlying them. It is, however, necessary to proceed to some further generalization by inquiring into the whole attitude from which these axioms or the conviction of their truth spring.

The following propositions may be safely called, so far as we can see, the very characteristics of Freud's mentality and, since nearly all his followers are "orthodox" and willing to accept *ad verbum* the statements of their master, also of the whole school of psychoanalysis.

(1) The only scientific approach to questions of psychology, of human character and behavior, and indeed to all the phenomena which depend somehow on mental factors—like art, religion, culture in general—is by putting the genetic point of view in the foreground.

(2) Every apparently complex and, at first sight, uniform phenomenon has to be considered as consisting of simpler elements. The genetic study accordingly means the discovery of these elements which are supposed to exist in a simpler man-

ner, eventually in isolation and as independent of each other, in more primitive stages.

(3) The methodological principles by which to study mental phenomena and those of social and cultural life are essentially and necessarily the same as the methodological principles underlying the study of biology. They are essentially the same, because there is no difference of nature between mind and body or between facts of matter and those of the spirit; and they are necessarily the same, because they are the principles of science, and science is the only legitimate approach to reality.

We do not mean to say that these principles were consciously alive in Freud's mind when he set out to discover the nature of neurosis and later to develop a comprehensive theory of the human mind. But they are the·very principles which determined his outlook on the whole complex of problems he had to face. Nor do we imply that these principles were peculiar to Freud alone or to psychoanalysis; they are indeed the very ones which governed research and theory in nearly all fields during the nineteenth century and which dominated the minds of scholars as well as laymen. It will be shown in the twelfth chapter how and by what channels these ideas came to influence Freud and to mold his views.

We have called Freud's philosophy materialistic; it is indeed an unmitigated materialism. None of his axioms, and none of the leading methodological principles, can in fact be maintained unless it be against a background of an absolutely materialistic philosophy. It has become evident, by the study of the axioms, how psychoanalysis holds that the same categories have to be used in the study of the mind as in the study of matter. Psychoanalysis is proud of being a "science," that is, of looking at the problems of psychology as if these were of exactly the same nature as those of physics. The concept of energy is supposed to be the same in both fields. The method of analysis, used with such a tremendous success in physics and allied sciences, has to be applied to the study of the mind. The only law governing the connections and successions of events is, in both cases, the law of efficient causality. Everything, both in the world of matter and in the realm of the mind, is predetermined by the past because everything is linked to some precedent cause by the despotic rule of causality.

There can be no doubt about the materialistic nature of psychoanalytic philosophy. It cannot by its own principles ever arrive at the acknowledgment of an essential difference between mind and matter. It has no place for the notion of freedom, because determination and causality are the only laws linking the single events to each other.

Materialism cannot but adhere to determinism in the field of ethics. An undeterministic materialism is a contradiction in terms. Psychoanalysis as a theory of human nature is, accordingly, open to the same objections which have to be raised in regard to materialistic metaphysics and deterministic ethics. It is not our task to criticize these conceptions, since this has been done repeatedly by better men than we. It is, however, worth while to remark that the psychoanalysts, by accepting blindfold, as it were, these philosophical ideas, fall a prey to an attitude which is characteristic of them and which is partly a consequence of their considering exclusively the genetic point of view. They disregard almost completely all description or phenomenology; they are not in the least interested in the particular features a mental fact presents, they ask only wherefrom it stems. Thus some obvious aspects of mental facts apparently escape them. Nobody, not even the most enthusiastic deterministic philosopher, can overlook the fact that man feels that he experiences free will. Every person is fully convinced that, at least in average situations, he may freely choose his ends and employ the means he believes to be the best; he is equally convinced afterwards that he could have decided otherwise, had he been willing.

This fact of free will exists; the deterministic philosopher, however, gets rid of it simply by calling it an "illusion." It might be one, though the existence of such a general illusion, its persistence and impressiveness, would be rather astonishing. But the mere assertion that it is an illusion is not enough. To make this statement acceptable the deterministic philosopher would have to explain to the unsophisticated mind why and how such an illusion came to exist at all. Facts are not dealt with by decrees. Proclaiming free decision to be an illusion is quite unsatisfactory; definite proof is needed. There is no such proof, nor has any of these philosophers ever been able to point to such a proof. All they did was to appeal to the necessity of the chain of efficient causes remaining unbroken. This is no necessity but a mere postulate, and an unjustified one too, because the existence of other ways of causation is disregarded. Until determinism can prove—not merely declare—free will to be an illusion, the immediate evidence of common experience remains unshaken by all speculation. Every phenomenon has to be taken as what it is or appears to be, unless it can be satisfactorily explained as consisting in truth of other elements than those obvious to direct inspection, and unless it can be shown why these other elements or factors appear as this phenomenon. The reverence science professes generally for facts deserts many scientists when they turn to facts not of matter but of mind.

Materialism, comprising all facts under the heading of material processes, cannot know of any other causality save that of *causa efficiens*. It can therefore not know anything of freedom. The statements made by some modern physicists on freedom existing in the world of matter need not be discussed here. Freedom is indeed very different from indetermination or chance; and even more different from indetermination resulting from the inadequacy of method and, perhaps, the limitations of human reason in general.

The axioms listed in the preceding chapter are compatible only with a materialistic philosophy. Few words are necessary on this point. The first axiom, of the reflex-nature of mental reactions, rests on the materialistic identification of bodily and mental processes. The indiscriminate use of the energy-concept applied to mental facts presupposes the same basic idea. So does the notion of the mind consisting of an aggregate of discrete "atoms," which notion follows necessarily, as we have seen, from the energy-concept. The inevitable dependence of the causality-principle as applied by Freud to the explanation of mental facts has revealed itself as compatible only with materialism. It may seem questionable, however, whether the fifth and the sixth axiom, referring to the principle of evolution and to the identification of meaning and causality, are equally linked to a materialistic philosophy. It is with them, however, not otherwise than with the four first axioms.

A criticism of evolutionistic theories would exceed by far the limits set to this book. To carry through such a task one would have, besides examining a great many factual statements, to investigate carefully the general mentality behind the various conceptions of evolution. This cannot be done here. One point might be mentioned which has a definite importance as well in general as especially in regard to the opinion one forms of psychoanalysis. It has been too often overlooked that evolution, like so many other terms, has many significations which indeed have something in common and at the same time differ in very essential points; or, to use the classical expression, that evolution is an analogical term.

Evolution is originally a name for the growing-out of a mature organism from a germ or an embryo. The mature individual "evolves" from the seed, the primitive form, the egg, as if it had been included therein, and had but unfolded, as a flower unfolds itself and frees itself from the leaves which enclosed it. Evolution in this original sense presupposes material continuity; there is an uninterrupted series of gradually changing stages from the germ to the mature organism. Every other signification of the term evolution is by metaphor and comparison. The term takes on different significations according to the matter which is compared with evolution in the original and strict sense. All these significations have this in common that they rest on some similarity between the matter they refer to and organic evolution.

But it does not follow from this that they have more in common to them than this one feature. Whether this is the case or not can be found out only by a careful analysis of the kind of similarity obtaining between original evolution and the other processes called by the same name. We might of course use this name for every sequence proceeding from apparently simpler and more primitive stages to more complicated and more "developed" ones. (What has to be said of evolution applies, of course, equally to development.) Thus we are fully entitled to speak of evolution in regard to economic, social, cultural history. We may speak of the ideas of Aristotle developing from Platonism to his own philosophy; we may say that some technique developed gradually, for instance the construction of automobiles. But one cannot but be aware that all these "evolutions" have in common only the single feature of being a succession of stages which differ in certain features so that they impress us as some kind of "progress." There is no real likeness between the evolution in engineering and in the art of painting, or between the evolution of housing and of Aristotelian philosophy.

Even if we would take it for granted that the idea of evolution as applied to the world of living organisms is a correct statement of facts, we should not thereby be entitled to consider every other evolution as being of the same type. This is the logical mistake of which so many evolutionists, and among them Freud, have become guilty. This mistake is caused partly by simple prejudice and by the seduction exercised by words; the *idola fori* of Francis Bacon are today as powerful as they ever were, and there is a market-place of science and one of general business which do not differ very much in their habits.

There is another reason for the acceptance of this fallacy. Evolution in its original sense is founded on material change; in the development of an organism there is a material substratum which gradually changes, passes from one intermediary form to another and thus moves from the germ as *terminus a quo* to the mature organism as *terminus ad quem*. If matter comes to be considered as the only true reality and if the inquiring mind feels that it gets near to the ultimate secrets of reality only insofar as it is capable of applying the notions, categories and methods which have been successful when dealing with matter, it will easily, not to say necessarily, arrive at considering material evolution as the only true evolution and as the very archetype of every particular evolution. If reality is material, and if true evolution is material too, then all truths which can possibly be stated about any kind of evolution have to be couched in terms of materiality.

This seems to be the reason why evolutionists are as a rule materialists, though one might also conceive a non-materialistic theory of evolutionary character. Hegel's philosophy is an example of this. So, centuries before Hegel, was the emanationistic conception of Plotinus. The particular meaning the term evolution has with Freud—and we repeat not with him alone but with the majority of scientists believing in evolution—is possible only on the basis of a thoroughly materialistic philosophy and in connection with it.

Lengthy explanation is not needed to show that the way instincts are regarded by psychoanalysis is in perfect accordance with materialistic evolutionarism and that only this philosophy allows for the Freudian conception of the genesis of mental phenomena.

The close and necessary relation between materialism and the axiom of association, or of the identification of meaning and causal connection, becomes visible also in the fact that mechanical causality or causality of material change is interpreted exclusively as efficient causality. It does not matter here that, according to the classic philosophy, other types of causality play a definite rôle even on the level of material and mechanical changes. Since these types of causal relation are disregarded by science we need not refer to them. A theory which, though

dealing with forms of reality different from matter, acknowledges only efficient causality and states this causality to be exactly of the same kind in matter and in mind, is necessarily
materialistic. And this is the position taken by psychoanalysis.

Evolutionarism in this sense has another characteristic; it believes in progress not as a mere succession of phases but as a
gradual ascent to higher forms. The notion of progress itself
cannot be analyzed here. We refer to the very enlightening
statements, historical and analytical, by Christopher Dawson.*
This notion is implied in the conceptions of most evolutiona-
rists, certainly in those of Freud. It supposes that the stages which
appear later are more perfect than the earlier ones, and furthermore that they do not, in spite of their greater perfection, contain
any element or factor which had not been already present in the
lower states in a rudimentary or latent form. Thus evolutionarism assumes that life originated out of lifeless matter without
any new element being added to those already contained in dead
matter. Animals grew out of plants or out of an undifferentiated
mediate form and developed more and more highly; nothing
new appears in animal life which had not been present as *Anlage*
even in the most simple animalcule. The defenders of such theories would probably feel definitely shocked if they were told
that they are still applying notions belonging to the Scholasticism they so utterly despise. *Anlage* is only a name for *potentia*
and a name which in fact does not indicate any real "progress"
beyond the statements of Aristotelian philosophy.

This manner of looking at things—which we felt entitled to
call the "way from below"†—is the inevitable corollary of materialism. That philosophy is forced to credit matter with all
capacities or potentialities which are ever observed, because
nothing besides matter is believed to exist. But is it true that
the view from below is as necessarily materialistic as materialism
is necessarily "from below"? We believe that this admits of no

---

* *Progress and Religion*, New York, 1938 (Catholic Masterpiece series).
† *The New Psychologies*, London, New York, 1932.

denial. Every attempt at explaining the higher by the lower, ignoring thereby the essential differences of the various levels of reality, cannot but be materialistic. This manner of looking at things cannot but push its attempts at explanation farther and farther "down," until it arrives at the lowest level of reality we know. The view from below ends with materialism and cannot end otherwise.

The instinct-axiom is, therefore, not less a sign of a thorough materialistic philosophy than are the axioms which have already been examined. This axiom is in fact merely a specialization of the general evolutionary conception and its immanent materialism.

The sixth axiom, which identifies causation and meaning, remains to be studied. We have spoken hitherto of identification; yet there might be one objection. It seems possible to interpret the psychoanalytical viewpoint by saying that the instinct and the dynamic power of the repressed material act as efficient causes in determining their manifestations in the conscious phenomenon, but that a different relation obtains between the content of this material and the particular symbol. This seems, however, not to be the idea of the psychoanalysts, nor is such an interpretation compatible with the principles of psychoanalysis. The statement, namely, that by following the chain of free associations the causing element is revealed, leads necessarily to the conclusion that the meaning and the causation depend on the same factor. One could not otherwise understand how association, which is determined by meaning, could ever lead back to the cause of the symbols from which the chain started. Thus the interpretation of this axiom as asserting an identity between relations of causation and of signification stands. Such an identification is again only possible within a materialistic conception of the mind, and, accordingly, of being in general. Since meaning determines certain events in the same manner of determination which exists in the world of matter, meaning itself has to be conceived as a function of material factors.

The general metaphysics which underlie psychoanalysis are, therefore, thoroughly materialistic. Giving up the materialistic philosophy results in a destruction of the very principles of the Freudian system. Nobody can, without getting involved in self-contradictions, adopt this psychology and still believe himself capable of choosing another philosophy. There is no other compatible with psychoanalysis.

Materialism is, perhaps, not necessarily linked to a hedonistic conception in ethics though these two are generally found closely associated to each other. But psychoanalysis is frankly hedonistic. No other goal of human behavior is recognized but pleasure. We have seen that by passing from the pleasure-principle to the so-called reality-principle, man merely adopted new ways of ensuring the greatest possible amount of pleasure and of avoiding unpleasantness, but that his goals remain unaltered throughout. This hedonistic conception is an inevitable consequence of the instinct axiom. If indeed all strivings, all desires, all actions are, basically, modifications of instinctual cravings and if, accordingly, the essential structure of mental operations remains the same in spite of the original manifestations becoming modified until they are not recognizable any more, then the nature of the ends at which these strivings etc. aim, cannot be of a completely different nature. This conception of the aims man pursues is, however, mistaken. It is not true, as we shall state in a more detailed manner, when discussing the relations of psychoanalysis and general psychology (v.i., p. 138, chapter VI), that pleasure is all of one kind, the one which psychology calls the pleasure of satisfaction and which corresponds to the attainment of instinctual ends. Nor is it true that man's attitudes and actions aim exclusively at pleasure.

It has been said often, by philosophers, by moralists, and by common people, that human nature is so base that it pursues only egoistical aims and that it desires only its own pleasure even if the actions are apparently altruistic, even if they imply sacrifice, even if they, at first sight, seem to have only unpleasant and painful effects. If we do a good action by overcoming some desire of the "lower parts of the soul," and thus impose restrictions on our sensual longings, for instance, we are willing to put up with a momentary unpleasantness, because we foresee that the pleasure we are going to feel because of our goodness will be more than a simple compensation; also because both the displeasure caused by our sentiments not being as lofty as we want them to be, and that caused by the disapproval of our fellows are shunned more than that which will result from resisting some impulses of our nature. This view, though older by innumerable centuries, is definitely the same as that expressed by Freud in his reality-principle. It has not become more true by being restated in a new terminology.

Unprejudiced observation teaches us that man does many things without envisioning any pleasure in the future. If he acts in a moral manner it is not, provided the idea of moral goodness be the really efficacious motive, because he foresees the pleasure caused by having a good conscience or because he wants to avoid the discomfort resulting from having a bad one. We know by experience that our foreseeing the unpleasantness of remorse is often enough incapable of holding us back from actions we feel sure are wrong. We know too that sometimes, even if only in exceptional cases, we do things of which we foresee only unpleasant consequences simply because it is right to do them. A sacrifice is not made because of some secret pleasure to be derived from it—not for the sake of gratifying some deeply hidden masochistic instinct, but because the value realized by sacrifice is conceived as so much higher than the other value which we have to renounce.

No doubt the attitude assumed by the view we are criticizing exists oftener than not. No doubt, too, there are many people whose moral actions are not dictated by an insight into the height of the values realized thereby and that in a very great number of cases the motives prompting such actions are of a rather inferior kind. But the essence of things is not determined by what is observable in a majority of cases; essence becomes visible best in the most highly developed instances. We would never think of discovering the truth about human nature by studying only cripples, idiots and insane people, even if these, by some misfortune, should come to be the majority. Thus, the nature of moral action cannot be discovered by a study of a kind of behavior which is determined, at least to a large extent, by immoral motives.

In nearly every human life there are, we suppose, moments in which the person feels that he has to do this or that, however painful the action may be. But there are also many instances of actions which are not felt as painful, and which are nevertheless not performed because of some pleasure resulting therefrom. A mother nursing her sick child does not think, in the first instance, of the pain she would suffer if the child were to die, nor of the pleasure she will experience by seeing him gamboling around again. She thinks only of the child, of his needs, of his sufferings. True love does not seek its own satisfaction; *non quaerit quae sua sunt.* And this is true of all kinds of love, be it the love of a child, of a mate, of a friend, of one's neighbor, of goodness, of one's country, of God.

Freud is blind to these facts, because he conceives of love only as a particular way of attaining instinctual satisfaction. Moreover, he has never shown any interest in descriptive psychology. He has never cared to find out whether the things which he, adopting mostly a terminology of common language, calls by the same name, are really the same by nature.

Hedonism, as implied in psychoanalysis, is of a primitive and simple kind. It lacks the refinement of Epicureanism, which at least recognized essential differences of values and of the pleasures they procure. The morals of psychoanalysis do not know of degrees or levels of value; that man has to behave according to certain rules is not dictated by the nature of the values these rules refer to, but merely by the necessities of reality, the avoidance of unpleasantness, and by the desire to gather in, as it were, a harvest of pleasure as rich as possible with a minimum of pain. Psychoanalysts will declare that they are not concerned with morals or with values. Theirs is only the task of scientific investigation, of preventing and curing certain troubles and malformations of character. But this cannot be true. Psychoanalysis speaks much of education and pretends to tell educators how to deal with normal children and with those we call "problems." Education presupposes patently certain aims; an aimless education is no education at all. Psychoanalysis can no more help being faced by moral problems than any other endeavor aiming at helping man, at making him more capable of coping with the difficulties of life, at enabling him to adjust himself more perfectly to the actually existing conditions. There must be, therefore, a definite morality implied in the psychoanalytic world of ideas. These morals are, however, necessarily hedonistic and, by consequence, extremely subjectivistic.

Subjectivism is another basic feature in the philosophy of psychoanalysis. It would not be an exaggeration to call the psychoanalytical conception a solipsistic one. Apparently neither Freud nor any of his pupils has given much thought to these consequences. If they had, it would probably not have mattered much to them, because they would refuse to consider any philosophical reflection and would deny it all importance. They would declare, we suppose, that they are interested exclusively in empirical facts and the immediate conclusions to be drawn from them.

Reference has already been made more than once to the expressly unphilosophical attitude of Freud himself and of many of his followers. There are, however, some who seriously wish to bring psychoanalysis into accord with the principles of some philosophy. We have pointed out that in truth only one philosophy is wholly compatible with psychoanalysis—and, accordingly, that psychoanalysis is compatible with but one philosophy —namely, a thoroughgoing materialism in metaphysics and an equally thoroughgoing hedonism in ethics. But it can be shown that the psychoanalytical mentality is, when its last consequences are drawn from the implied ideas, of such a kind as to end in an extreme subjectivism which abolishes in fact every possibility of objective existence, objective truth and, of course, objective value.

Psychoanalysis can know nothing about reality or about objectivity. There is a stronger trend of Schopenhauer's ideas in Freud's system than has been generally recognized. It is very probable that Freud was subjected to the influence of this philosophy though he hardly studied Schopenhauer. On this point chapter XI will have to report. For the present we are not occupied with the historical antecedents of psychoanalysis, but with criticism of the theory itself.

For the sake of placing ourselves on the terrain of psychoanalysis itself, we shall neglect the difficulties concomitant with the notion of "cathexis," of a certain amount of "libido" becoming attached, as it were, not to a mental state but to its object. We shall treat this notion as if it were a legitimate one.

Objects, then, are valuable only in proportion to the amount of cathexis and because of it. Their value results from their becoming loaded with a definite amount of libido. They are not desirable because they have a certain value by their own nature, independently of the human mind, but they become valuable because they are desired. Thus far the idea is not different from the well-known notions of axiological relativism.

Cathexis is but another name for this notion or the attempt to penetrate somewhat deeper into the reasons why certain things are credited with values. If a prominent follower of Freud once stated that he believed in the existence of objective values, this statement contradicted flatly the very principles of the theory.

The relativistic conception of values is unavoidable. The very moment things are conceived of as endowed with some value or goodness of their own inherent in them because of their proper nature, the whole theory has to be abandoned. Values are aims of action. Action, according to psychoanalysis, is always due to a transformation of instinctive forces. Instincts have no knowledge of values and do not need any; they are pre-ordained towards the good of the individual or the race. Things or situations satisfying the instinctive needs become good or appear good as soon as the instinctive organization reaches the developmental height of rationality, or as soon, to speak the language of psychoanalysis, as the super-ego is established. The super-ego is a peculiarity of man. However small the psychoanalysts may think the distance between the higher apes and man to be, they have not overlooked the essential differences. Even Hermann, whose biologism induces him to apply the principles of psychoanalysis to the study of the behavior in apes,* does not go so far as to identify the "psychology" of apes with that of man.

This basis of the psychoanalytical views on values—or rather, the view implied by the psychoanalytical conception of human nature—is overlooked by H. Hartmann in his plea for maintaining the notion of the objectivity of values and combining it with psychoanalytical ideas. He† points out that psychoanalysis in its practical endeavors has to start from some definite value-ideas, *e.g.* that of health. The analyst in attempting to restore health to his patient has acknowledged health as a value. He does not create or posit this value, but accepts it. Hartmann denies also to psychoanalysis the right of stating anything about the goals of education, morals, and so on. He is right in both his statements. But his conclusion does not follow. Nobody, of course, accuses the individual psychoanalyst of positing a system of values. But this is not the problem. One has carefully to distinguish between a theory of the nature and the origin of values and that of the recognition and acceptance of them.

Psychoanalysis is wrong in letting values develop out of the needs of human nature. It believes that real things are gifted

* *Neue Beitraege zur vergleichenden Psychologie der Primaten,* Imago, Lpz. 1936.
† *Psychoanalyse und Wertproblem,* Imago, Lpz. 1929, *14.*

with values because they happen to satisfy some instinctive needs. The criticisms do not refer to the relativistic attitude of the psychoanalyst but to the relativism of psychoanalysis. Such a theoretical relativism does not hinder a certain group of values from being recognized by a great number of individuals; the question of individual attitude in regard to values and the other questions of individual predilection for this or that kind of value have nothing to do with the question of the genesis of values.

The basic error in psychoanalysis will become perhaps still clearer by considering some other fields in which the extreme subjectivism of psychoanalysis becomes in fact disastrous. We take at random three publications, contained in the "orthodox" psychoanalytical periodicals of the last three or four years. These articles illustrate in a striking manner the subjectivistic attitude and its evil consequences. But they illustrate also the fact that the psychoanalysts gradually become so much blinded by this subjectivism that they are no longer capable of seeing truth and facts as they are. Here too the "creed-character" of this system, its "pseudo-religious" nature makes itself felt.

In an article by Hermann on the Ego and Thinking* the author states that formal logic stands in the service of defense; this statement may have an intelligible meaning if it is intended to convey the idea—not a new one by any means—of logic being a tool given to the human mind for finding its way in and through reality. Logic, however, is said by Hermann to look at things objectively through the eyes of an idealized rigid super-ego. One would rather suppose that looking through these eyes endangers objectivity very much. Logic is furthermore called an imposed morality of thinking, which statement is evidently the reversal of the idea that morality is the totality of the laws of behavior just as logic comprises the laws of thinking.

Incidentally, it is characteristic of the mentality of the author of the article that he evidently believes logic to be a complex of

* *Internat. Zeitschr. f. Psychoanal. 1929, 15.*

laws regulating "thinking" and that he is unable to see it as a system of statements on the formal relations of truths. It is amazing that there are still so many for whom the critical analysis and refutation of psychologistic ideas, as for instance the one by E. Husserl in 1900, does not exist. Hermann indeed seems not to know what the formal logic of which he speaks really is. He describes the fundamental attitude of formal logic as a turning away from immediately perceived sense-data to collective representations, by which badly chosen term he means universals, species, genera, and so on, which are held to be more essential than individuals. Everyone knows that formal logic has to do only with formal notions and their systematic order, but that contents—of which alone, "essentiality" could be asserted—have no place at all in formal logic. All this is but the talk of an uninformed mind, though the author of the article under consideration is probably less uninformed than prejudiced.

But there is something more. Hermann proceeds to draw a parallel between the logical attitude and what he supposes to be the corresponding attitude of the primitive mind. The prototype and, as one is given to understand, the ancestor, as it were, of the universal is—the totem animal. Logic does not care for the individual, but for the family or the class; the character of the totem is attached not to a single animal, but is common to every representative of the species. (The author seems to disregard the obvious fact that the same might be said of so simple a thing as a name.) Logic seeks the essence of things in order to get into contact with reality; the primitive is brought by the totem into contact with reality or nature. He becomes nature through his totem.

Even if one sets aside the mistaken ideas on the nature and the rôle of the totem, and the arbitrary statement that totemism is a general state of early civilization, Hermann's ideas still contain enough to make one wonder. Formal logic as a means of getting into touch with reality? Formal logic dealing with essences? The primitive needing an animal, his totem, to get into contact with nature? An astonishing conception, indeed, and one utterly lacking proof.

How could a mind ever conceive such an idea? The answer is that according to the general principles of psychoanalysis everything observable in the human mind has to be traced back to and to be derived from some original instinct-situation. That logic might be a system of propositions dealing with the formal side of truths is a thought which cannot enter a mind completely obscured by the fog of subjectivism.

Freud, himself, made the impossible attempt to derive negation from the instinct of destruction. In doing this he obeyed the tendency, inherent in his whole system, toward an exaggerated and self-contradictory subjectivism. If negation has to be related to some purposiveness of human nature at all, one might as well have it derived from what might be called an instinct for construction or rather for perfection and completion. Negation is indeed not only a statement on "not any more" but also on "not yet." The corpse is the negation of the living man who is no longer there; but the child is the negation of the adult because he is not yet grown up. And it is quite possible that expectation is more basically related to negation than one would suspect at first sight.

Subjective attitudes like expectation, however, are related to negation, although not as the soil from which the logical category springs; they are merely the subjective counterpart of logical reality, or of a side of trans-subjective reality which can be expressed and has to be expressed by this category of logic. Things are not here; the fact of absence is evidently prior to the experience of destruction. Even in the realm of animals the fact of absence plays a rôle; though, as has been pointed out by some critics of an unduly exaggerated notion of animal "intelligence," animals are incapable of conceiving anything like negation; but the animal expects to find its food and does not find it because it is not there.

The experience of development is prior to that of destruction; that the child grows to be an adult, that the seed grows to be a plant, that unformed matter grows by being formed to be some useful object—all these are very primitive experiences. But first of all, there is the experience of achievement and the attitude of purpose the former presupposes. Purpose means "not yet." Even the instinct of destruction—provided that it exists at all outside the mind of some psychologists who probably are led astray by an unconscious anthropomorphism or "horaiomorphism" (ὡραῖος meaning adult)—cannot become active, at least in man, without some purpose or some envisioning of the future result. In other words: Freud's idea is self-contradictory, because the very notion of instinct in a rational being at once implies the relation to the not-yet-achieved.

What Hermann attempts to do in regard to logic another author tries to do for mathematics. P. Schilder* writes on the "Psychoanalysis of Geometry, Arithmetic and Physics." We shall deal with this astonishing piece of psychology very briefly. The argument rests on the following equations: counting means divisibility. Divisibility is experienced by partition; partition means tearing to pieces. Ergo: counting, which is at the bottom of all mathematical reasoning, goes ultimately back to the instinct of aggression and destruction. Here again we cannot but notice that the passion for psychoanalytical interpretation and for "reducing" any activity of the mind to primitive instinctive behavior, blinds the author to very obvious facts. The original experience which becomes the starting-point of counting is evidently not division as resulting from tearing to pieces, but distinction as following from the diversity of observable objects. Not destruction, but the wondering at the manifoldness of reality and the necessity of taking account of things, of possessions, of facts and of distinguishing by names or by numbers, is the basic fact. It is highly improbable that man started counting

---

* *Zur Psychoanalyse der Geometrie, Arithmetik und Physik.* Imago, Lpz. 1936, 22, 389.

by making out the number of fragments after he had broken, torn or destroyed a thing.

We take our third example from an article of E. Bergler dealing with the psychology of gambling.* "All gambling is at bottom a desire to compel love through an unconscious masochistic attitude. Hence the gambler always loses in the long run." Hence? We always thought that the gambler's losing was due to the laws of probability. And to the limitations of his purse. If Bergler's conception were true one might become a successful gambler and a danger to all gambling houses by having a psychoanalyst changing the masochistic into a sadistic attitude. It does not matter whether, according to the ideas of psychoanalysis, such a change is feasible or not; the mere fictitious assumption is sufficient to demonstrate the absolute ignoring of reality implied in such a statement.

These examples are enough to prove the thesis proposed above. Psychoanalytic mentality has become the slave of subjectivism to such a degree as to become utterly incapable of seeing objective reality. There are no laws but those of psychology. The laws of probability are disregarded; simple facts of psychology do not exist, if they do not fit in with the preconceived ideas. The nature of logic is misunderstood because of an extreme psychologism which is but one form of a thoroughly mistaken and erroneous subjectivism.

This subjectivistic attitude may be described, without exaggeration, by stating that reality to the psychoanalyst is nothing but an opportunity for satisfying instinctive desires. Reality has no importance of its own. It has hardly a being of its own. The psychoanalytic conception of man's position, if the principles of the theory are followed up, has to be solipsistic.

Psychoanalysts will, of course, reject such an imputation and declare that it rests on a total misunderstanding of psychoanalysis. They will refer to the great rôle the attitudes of others play in their system, because the development of instinctive be-

* *Zur Psychologie des Hasardspielens.* Imago. Lpz. 1936, 22, 409.

havior, repression and sublimation, adaptation to reality, and the like are brought about by the influence of other persons; they will point to their notion of identification which too implies the influence of other persons; they will speak of the fundamental importance of sexuality or, as they like to call it, of love. But it is precisely their attitude in regard to love which reveals, better than anything else, the truth of the statement made above.

It is, in fact, not true that the other person appears in Freud's theory as another person to be loved and to love. His name is not person, his name is—object. He is a "sexual object." There was never a name given to the human person which more clearly disregards the essential dignity and the particular position of the human person. The beloved or desired individual becomes an object among objects. His value depends on cathexis, on the amount of libido attached to him, just as every object receives its meaning, its importance, its value for the subject by the very same process. What is there to distinguish, basically, essentially, a human person from any other environmental element? There is nothing. The human person as such has been denuded of all distinguishing characteristics. "All things have a price; man alone has dignity." This famous saying of Kant has lost its meaning in psychoanalysis. Man has a price as things have a price. Man's price is measured and expressed in units of libido.

Psychoanalysts usually feel offended when they are told that their theory is incompatible with morals. They contend that they do not want anyone to lead an immoral life. Like Hartmann in the article quoted above, they point to their acknowledgment of moral values. They do so, but only because they cannot help being human besides being psychoanalysts. But they are right in objecting to the reproach of immorality. Their theory is in fact neither moral nor immoral. It is inframoral; it moves on a level where such a thing as morals does not exist at all.

Morality starts with the recognition of the particular dignity of the human person. It is perfectly nonsensical on the infrahuman level to talk of categories belonging to ethics. The ideas proposed by some physicists, who talk of freedom in nature, because of certain results of modern physics, are absolutely meaningless. One cannot prove freedom by referring to statistical physics and to the law of probability. This is but another kind of shallow monism. It may be another type, no longer the materialism of 1880, but it is no whit better. Man, as he is envisioned by psychoanalysis, is not a moral being. He is not more moral than the infra-atomic particles which are said to move without any efficient causality forcing them to move. The laws of probability are not more moral than the laws of mechanical causality. But a conception of man which does away with morals, not by replacing it by "immoral" ideas but by rendering the use of ethical categories quite impossible, is no longer a theory of man. The capacity of moral behavior is as fundamental to human nature as rationality is; the former is indeed but a particular manifestation of the latter.

Thus, the philosophy of psychoanalysis reveals another fundamental trait: it is essentially impersonalistic. The axiomatic principles of psychoanalysis and its general attitude do not allow the true concept of person to have any place in the system. We need not refer to the classical definition of person as an individual rational substance and to the fact that rationality as a distinguishing factor cannot be recognized by psychoanalysis; rationality becomes indeed, because of the general evolutionarism, merely a higher degree of development of instinctual functions. It is impossible for psychoanalysis to permit any absolutely new factor to be introduced. We shall see later that this is the reason for the serious neglect of which psychoanalysis has become guilty. But even if we do not take account of this definition and consider only what common sense and the naive convictions of every man imply when the word "person" is mentioned, we perceive immediately that this notion cannot be brought into accordance with the notions characteristic of Freudism.

Person evidently means a whole which comprises many sides

and functions. These functions are necessarily conceived as being "of" the person, as "belonging to" the person but not as elements, not as something of which person consists. However independently we may imagine these functions to operate, however great eventually their opposition against certain central tendencies of the person may become, they are invariably subordinated to a whole which is, to use the famous words of Aristotle, prior to them. Even if we consider the instincts or anything else as relatively independent elements which are bound together into the unity of person, there has to be something or some power which unites them and gives them the peculiar character of function of and within a whole. But in psychoanalysis there is no place for such a uniting power. It is hardly possible to credit some instinct with the capacity of uniting the other instincts and itself into such a whole. There must be something outside and above the instincts, which creates the whole and guarantees its existence. A philosophy which envisions man as a "bundle of instincts" has no means of considering such a uniting and unifying bond.

The true idea of person is incompatible with psychoanalysis. This psychology is therefore rightly called an impersonalistic one. That this amounts to a total disregard of obvious and important facts, even to a disregard of what man's true nature is, ought to be clear. The psychoanalysts cannot help, of course, speaking of human person, because one cannot speak of man and overlook this basic property of his being a person. But in using this term the psychoanalysts commit a real sin against the spirit of their own philosophy.

CHAPTER V

The Theory of Sexuality

THOUGH it is not true that psychoanalysis may be simply identified with "pansexualism," it is nevertheless evident that sexuality holds a very prominent place in the Freudian system, and that in psychoanalysis there is more talk of things sexual than in any other psychology. For this reason alone it would be justified to dedicate some consideration to the Freudian notion of sexuality. Such a consideration is the more desirable as this notion offers some peculiarities which distinguish it rather markedly from pre-scientific ideas and from those held by many other psychologies.

Sexual instinct, or rather the group of sexual instincts, is designated in psychoanalysis by the common name of libido. Psychoanalysis does not mean the choice of this name to imply that sexuality is one instinct among others, which for some reason are grouped together with it. The idea is precisely that all the instincts are essentially of a sexual nature and that they remain so whatever modifications they undergo. Of this we have already spoken when sketching the fundamentals of psychoanalytic theory. Libido takes indeed the wide sense of all instinctual tendencies tending toward any object whatsoever outside the organism itself. This is not intended to weaken the sexual implication of the term libido, but rather to underscore the sexual nature of all tendencies, striving, interests, concerning objects. To sexual libido man owes all his capacity of aiming at objects. The cathexis, the amount of mental energy or the affective charge connected with an object, has its origin in the activity of the sexual instinct.

It would be a misunderstanding of psychoanalysis to believe that, according to this theory, the satisfaction realized by attaining some object, not immediately related to sexuality as such, is like sexual satisfaction. The pleasure conditioned by friendship, by scientific endeavor, by the pursuit of economic success, all these remain what they appear to be to the consciousness. It is stated only that they are derivatives of sexuality and that their capacity to give satisfaction is based on the amount of discharge being ultimately booked, if we might use this comparison, to the account of the sexual instinct. Therefore, one wrongs the psychoanalysts by accusing them of identifying all pleasure with sexual satisfaction. Indulging in a given interest, aiming at given objects does not mean looking for sensuous pleasure; but that man can have such interests at all is due to sexuality and to the function it fulfills in the organization of human nature.

It has become clear already and will become still more clear that the only viewpoint psychoanalysis recognizes is that of genetic analysis. Science, as Freud conceives it, has to discover origins. The Freudian theory of sexuality is accordingly mainly genetic. As in the other parts of his theory on the nature and the origin of features in human personality, Freud goes back to childhood in regard to sexuality. In 1910 he published a little work, *Three Articles on Sexuality,* in which he first made known in a systematic and detailed way his conception of infantile sexuality. This conception rests on two sets of observations. One group comprises, of course, statements obtained by psychoanalysis of adult persons (psychoanalysis of children was, so far as we know, not yet practiced in these years); the second group refers to observations on the behavior of children.

If all tendencies toward objects are ultimately libidinous and if such tendencies are observed in children, then we have evidently to assume that the sexual instinct is active long before sexuality in the commonly accepted sense manifests itself. The notion of infantile sexuality is a necessary consequence of the way "libido" is conceived. This conception had been elaborated by Freud even before the publication of the volume mentioned, though the full development of the theory belongs to later years; but C. G. Jung published his treatise on *Changes and Forms of Libido* in 1911, and this work implies the existence of the complete theory, even so early.

Freud did not refer in his statement to this systematic necessity. He probably was not aware of it. It is indeed easy, in retrospect, to perceive the framework of a theory, but it is often very difficult to be conscious of the various mutual connections between the different conceptual elements while a theory is still developing. Instead of deducing the notion of infantile sexuality as a consequence implied in the conception of libido, Freud pointed to the results of analysis and to extra-analytical observations. Arguments of the first kind have no power to convince us, since we know that they rest on logical fallacies and are therefore in need of confirmation by non-analytical methods. The second group of evidences deserves some attention.

In examining these alleged proofs the reader immediately discovers a curious attitude on the part of the author. Freud declares—and he is careful to note that he is not the first to conceive this idea—that the habit of infants of sucking their fingers or whatever part of the body they may get hold of is a way of attaining sexual satisfaction. He writes: "This pleasurable sucking is linked to a full consumption of attention and leads either to falling asleep or even to a motor reaction of the body. . . . No observer ever doubted the sexual nature of this activity." And immediately follow these words: "Whoever sees a child sinking back from the breast, saturated, with red cheeks, and blissfully smiling, will have to confess that this image remains also in later life determining the expression of sexual satisfaction." And Freud concludes that sexual satisfaction is also the experience of this infant.

Such a statement cannot but amaze the unprejudiced reader. First, it is always doubtful whether a similarity of expression justifies the conclusion that the emotions or experiences are in fact the same. Our eyes are not trained sufficiently to remark slight differences of expression which when noticed would show that apparently like expressions do in truth depend on different emotions. Secondly, there is no reason for denying the possibility of one expression being linked to the experience of satisfaction by whatever factor this satisfaction may be caused. Freud simply assumes that identity of expression means identity of experience. He may or may not have been acquainted with the famous theory of James-Lange-Sergi which became quite widely known soon after it had been proposed in the last decade of the nineteenth century. The essence of this theory was stated by William James in a rather paradoxical form—but this eminent psychologist and philosopher had a definite liking for paradoxes—by saying: we do not weep because we are sad, but we are sad because we weep. The idea is that emotions are nothing but the conscious reflex of bodily changes. Among these changes there are those we call expressions. If an emotion is but the sum-total of the bodily changes, then indeed an identity—provided one can make sure of its existence—of expression proves an identity of experience.

Freud's ideas moved very much in the same direction. The bodily side of mental phenomena could not but appear to him as the most important factor, since he defined the instincts as apparatus belonging to the bodily organization and only "represented" in the mind. His conclusion regarding the sexual nature of the satisfaction experienced by the suckling infant is, however, hardly convincing. Examined from the viewpoint of logic this conclusion is about as valid as saying: if a man takes amytal, he will sleep profoundly; here we have a man sleeping profoundly; therefore we may safely conclude that he has taken amytal.*

Freud indeed says that the behavior of the suckling child "remains determining" and he avoids calling it directly sexual satisfaction; but obviously this determination of behavior in

---

* These remarks and some of the criticisms of Freudian theory of sexuality were made by us many years ago; cf. *Psychologie des Geschlechtslebens*, in Handb. d. vergl. Psychologie, ed. G. Kafka, Munich, 1922, vol. III.

later years is possible only if this infantile behavior is itself
sexual. The further remarks of the author leave no doubt on
this matter. He declares also that the habit of children in the
first months of their life of playing with parts of their body,
with their fingers, their toes, their ears, and eventually with the
genital organs, indicates the existence and efficaciousness of
sexual instinct. This statement too implies a previously accepted interpretation. If this interpretation were not previously
accepted it would be as permissible to liken the play with the
genital organs to the play with the ears or with the fingers as to
make the first the pattern of the second. The Freudian statement
becomes plausible, only if the primacy of sexuality is already
made the foremost principle, or to say the same thing in other
words: the so-called empirical proofs for the existence of infantile sexuality as psychoanalysis teaches it become proofs only
after the theory they supposedly prove has been assumed as
valid. The objective observer notices nothing but a tendency for
moving whatever part of the body may be reached and moved;
the Freudian interpretation is an offspring of the theory. We
are again faced with a *petitio principii*, this time not in regard
to the theory but in regard to the "fact."

Perhaps someone would feel like arguing that these activities
of the newborn child cannot be considered as sexual because
according to the definition of psychoanalysis libido refers to
objects outside the organism. This objection is, however, not to
be upheld, because the libido turns only in later years definitely
toward objects, a modification resulting from developmental
factors. Moreover there is a reflection of libido toward the
person himself, called by Freud "narcissism." We are also told
that every other pleasure the child derives from bodily activity
in the years before adolescence and the onset of sexual maturation is essentially of a sexual nature. As one easily sees, this
statement rests on the very same kind of reasoning we have had
to expose above.

The invalidity of alleged proofs does not disprove the existence of a thing. A person to prove that he has been promised something may produce a forged letter. The proof is worthless, but he might have received the promise just the same. Thus the invalidity of the Freudian "facts" does not dispense us from inquiring into the factual problem. We are, however, occupied here not with a study of facts and with opposing a true interpretation to a wrong one, but only with criticism. It is therefore not for us to make any detailed use of the observations made by modern child-psychologists using methods of direct study of infantile behavior, which throw some light on the question of the development of sexuality and its eventual manifestations before the years of adolescence. But it is worth mentioning that what there is of pre-adolescent sexuality is found to present an aspect other than the one psychoanalysis believes it has discovered.* The Freudian school has overlooked many important details and has misconstrued others. It was bound to do so, because it approached the whole problem with a biased mind. This becomes obvious also in other parts of the Freudian conception of sexuality.

Freud believes that every interest in objects, *a fortiori* every interest implying anything like love for persons, is necessarily libidinous, that is, sexual. He cannot understand a loving inclination other than by the influence of sexual desire, be it already fully developed or still latent, unmistakable in its manifestations or so much veiled that it becomes recognizable only to the initiate and by particular methods. Hence he cannot conceive of the relations of a child and parent except in terms of sexuality. If the situation between parent and children which psychoanalysis describes as the "Oedipus Complex" exists at all, it must be interpreted differently from the psychoanalytic theory.† One is fully justified in doubting that the statement which psychoanalysis makes concerning this relationship is true; it rests

* Cf. R. Allers, *Sex-Psychology in Education,* transl. by Raemers, St. Louis, 1937, p. 122.

† Cf. the valuable statements by Dr. K. Horney (who still believes herself a psychoanalyst) in her book: *New Ways in Psychoanalysis,* New York, 1938.

on the results of psychoanalytic exploration and, therefore, on all the logical and methodological fallacies characteristic of the system. Unless other proofs are found the whole conception remains doubtful indeed. Psychoanalysis has tried to strengthen its position by referring to mythology and ethnology; but on this point Freud has become guilty of a very serious neglect of the prudence and the critical attitude a scientist is required to apply. We shall see that the ideas he and his school cherish in regard to ethnology, prehistory, and culture are quite wrong and based on a rash acceptance of absolutely unfounded speculations.

The Oedipus-situation which psychoanalysis believes to be a necessary and common one in individual life as well as in the life of mankind and which is accordingly supposed to have existed everywhere and to have crystallized, as it were, into the legend is, as specialists assure us, found only among the Greeks and in one single tribe in Asia. It seems to us that it would be much more probable to assume the Greek legend to be a dim and far-off reflex of some historical fact than to give it a psychological explanation. There are, after all, many legends which have been shown to preserve the memory of historical events. We have heard of many instances in which archeological discovery has demonstrated the historical background of some legend, for example, of the Homeric Saga. Such an explanation of the tale of Oedipus is at least as probable as the constructions of the psychoanalysts.

Freud tells us that in childhood sexuality is diffused over the whole body; there are many "erogenous zones" the stimulation of which gives rise to sexual sensations. The restriction of sexual pleasure to the sexual organs and some few other parts of the body is brought about by the process of maturation. Parallel to this bodily rearrangement of sexuality goes a psychological development described by psychoanalysis as the synthesis of "partial instincts" into the kind of sexuality we observe in adult persons. Crediting these other regions of the body with the capacity of conditioning sexual sensations rests on the assumption, of course, that bodily pleasure is essentially sexual in its nature. Thus the psychoanalysts speak of muscular, of oral, urethral, and anal eroticism. No need to discuss these things here. The psychological notion of partial instincts, however, has to be examined somewhat more closely.

First of all, it must be pointed out that psychoanalysis in general, and not this school alone, overrates the importance of sexual development in the so-called crisis of adolescence. Nobody indeed will or can deny that sexuality, the arising of sexual problems, the new experience of sexual desire contributes much to the general picture of adolescent mentality and adolescent behavior. More recent studies of these things, however, have drawn attention to the fact that sexual development is only one side, if an impressive one, of the adolescent period. The main thing can be described as the consolidation of the definite and lasting personality, and the main psychological feature is not so much linked to the sexual phenomena as to the uncertainty caused by the rebuilding of personality and the entering into a new world.* By considering only sexual development one gets therefore an incomplete and distorted picture of adolescence. Psychoanalysis, because of its general tendencies, has neglected to inquire into the non-sexual aspects of adolescent mentality. Its attention has been riveted on sexuality. Yet the views proposed on this point are no more acceptable and no better founded than those on other matters.

The notion of "partial instincts" encounters serious objections. The basic idea is that before adolescence or sexual maturity there exist several instincts which, in the mechanism of satisfaction, are not linked to the sexual organs and which are not integrated into one sexual instinct, but which nevertheless are definitely of a sexual nature. These partial instincts owe their

* More detailed remarks on this point may be found in our *Sex Psychology in Education* translated by S. A. Raemers, St. Louis, 1937, in *Psychology of Character*, New York, ed. 1939, and in *Character Education in Adolescence*, New York, 1940.

relative independence partly to the lack of differentiation of sexuality in the body, that is, they are related to the various erogenous zones of the body; some of them correspond to certain tendencies which are observable as aspects or features in mature sexuality and which are supposed to have an independent existence in childhood. The first group is exemplified by the sexual qualities attributed to the stimulation of various mucous membranes, of the urethra, for instance. The second group comprises instincts which condition allegedly sexual satisfaction by looking, by cruel actions, by suffering bodily pain and so on. The notion of the partial instincts has been derived from data gained by the psychoanalysis of adult persons. Even without any "depth-psychology" one knows that there is a sexual curiosity, a definite pleasure in looking at things sexual, and that pain and sexuality sometimes enter into a close combination. Nor is it unknown that cruelty is often observed in children, that they display a sometimes disconcerting curiosity, and that they evidently obtain somatic pleasure in various ways. The question is whether the existence of such features of sexuality justifies the interpretation devised by Freud.

There is no cogent reason for considering the pleasure connected *e.g.* with the infliction of pain, as being sexual merely because it may be found in connection with sexuality in certain abnormal cases and, to some extent, in normal individuals also. (It is exceedingly difficult, for that matter, to say where in regard to sexual behavior normality ends and abnormality begins. If one limits one's considerations to sexuality alone without taking account of the total personality, this question is in fact unanswerable in many cases. Abnormal sexuality is a feature in an abnormal personality, and the former is abnormal because the latter is.)

The only reason for calling tendencies sexual, which taken at their face value have nothing in common with sexuality, is the preconceived idea of the generality of libido. Psychoanalysis is incapable of even conceiving the idea of sexuality as being on the same level with anything else; it has to be the very foundation of all tendencies or activities referring to an object.

Psychoanalysis, in assuming that several partial drives are integrated into the one instinct of mature sexuality, became perhaps the victim of a principle which is one of the secret powers which sponsored psychoanalysis at its beginning and contributed not a little to its success. We allude to the idea of a "whole" as opposed to that of a mere aggregate. This motive doubtless played an important rôle in 1894 in starting the fathers of psychoanalysis on their way. It had then not the strength nor had its time yet come to break through certain barriers. But it had been there and is still active, as we shall see when examining the historical conditions of the origin and the development of Freudism. (Cf. below p. 242, chapter XI.)

Because of this perspective the idea of considering mature sexual behavior as due to the co-operation of several, relatively independent, forces was felt to be contrary to reality. Sexual instinct had to cover all the various aspects and manifestations observed in behavior centered upon sexual desire. But a right principle may be easily misused; its field may become unduly enlarged in the mind of one who has once grasped its importance. Though there are wholes, and though this category is basic to all science dealing with life and mind, it cannot be applied everywhere and without previous inquiry as to its applicability. If we are moved, in some situation, by the sentiments of love and of pity, pitying a beloved person, no real whole is formed out of these two sentiments; they are both alive and both active in our mind. It is no contradiction to the principle of "wholeness" if we concede that there are mere associations or aggregations too.

The definition or even the recognition of instincts presents certain peculiar difficulties. Man is only too inclined to fall back upon a certain anthropomorphistic attitude and to see in animal, or, for that matter, in infantile behavior the very forces at work which he would expect to condition the same behavior in himself. To make this clearer we might refer to the so-called instinct of destruction, which is supposedly active in animals and especially in little children. The statements of animal psychology being unreliable since we have no means of checking it and cannot really picture to ourselves what it means to be a cat or a finch, let us consider only the child. No doubt that children destroy things and that they find this a pleasurable occupation. We have to bear in mind, however, that the term destruction is one which has a meaning only in our, the adult person's, mind but not in that of a little child.

Destruction can be spoken of only if there is a construction which we want to be preserved. An individual incapable of appreciating a thing in its wholeness is also incapable of destroying it. The child who tears a book to pieces or who smashes some other thing is not really indulging in a pleasure of destruction; he is probably moved by quite another desire. If we free our mind from the categories which we habitually use and try to look at the situation without prejudice and by realizing as far as possible the attitude of the child himself, we might get another impression of the child's doings. The result of these doings is evidently that something new is "created," instead of the book there are a number of scraps, instead of a closed form which perhaps has become boring there are many things, each of them presenting a new and interesting shape. It would be as probable, or perhaps more probable, to attribute this way of behavior in childhood to an instinct of creation as to one of destruction.

The desire for creation, which is doubtless an essential feature in human nature, is still very much handicapped in the child who does not know anything of material, of technique, and who has no experience and no skill. There is indeed a very close relation between knowledge of material and the transition from mere playing or toying with things to the first attempts at "work."* Work is impossible without a certain knowledge of

---

* Cf. Ch. Buehler, *Kindheit und Jugend,* 3d ed., Leipzig, 1931.

the properties of the material. Construction, furthermore, demands a higher state of intellectual faculties than does mere "destruction." We do not pretend to have given, with these few allusions, a satisfactory explanation of the acts of so-called destruction in children; but we think that we have shown at least an explanation other than the usual one to be possible. That such an explanation may be found warns us against accepting the *prima facie* aspect of instinctual behavior as a sufficient basis for its theory.

Psychoanalysis, if we understand its statements right, considers the instinct of destruction as a special manifestation of a general instinct of aggression. It is doubtful whether this notion is as assured as the analysts want us to believe. We might talk of an instinct of aggression if we take the term aggression in its most literal sense, as signifying nothing more than approach; *aggredior* means in fact originally only walking toward a thing, getting close to it. But aggression has, even in Latin, the definite connotation of hostility. It is questionable whether in crediting children with such an instinct we are not again falling back upon an undue anthropomorphism, or rather, "horaiomorphism." * Incidentally be it said, that the endeavors of comparative psychology to free itself of anthropomorphism are not too successful; it is often forgotten that a term like aggression implies from the outset an interpretation presupposing our personal experience.

The various instincts which, according to psychoanalysis, are alive in the child and of which a large group belongs together as all being libidinous, are because of the difficulties alluded to above, not indubitable facts but mere constructions or interpretations, probable ones, if you like to think so, but not ascertained beyond 'all doubt. Even if the difficulties we have mentioned were overcome, or were regarded as not of too great importance, it would still be questionable whether anything is really gained by introducing this notion of partial instincts. It is stated that

* Cf. above p. 109.

the partial instincts have become integrated to the full sexuality and that they modify the latter's manifestation by their relative intensity. Fully developed sexuality is said to contain, as it were, the instincts of sexual curiosity, of exhibitionism, of aggression and its opposite, and perhaps other instincts too. The gratification these instincts receive by corresponding behavior contributes to the total of sexual satisfaction.

Now this sexual satisfaction can be obtained only by establishing a relation to another individual. There are no other ways of establishing such a relation except by "getting into touch" with the second person, by looking for and at him, by making oneself noticed by him, by displaying a certain amount of "aggressivity" and by letting the other behave in the same manner in regard to oneself. Does the statement of the psychoanalysts do more than translate these obvious facts into the language of their theory? And does calling these features of behavior partial instincts of sexuality, say more than that man has, in order to "get hold" of another person, to use the same faculties or powers he needs to get hold of some object? It seems as permissible to define these partial instincts, or sides of mature sexual behavior, as the manifestations of certain abilities, habits, instincts, if one insists on the term, in connection with sexuality. They can be called sexual themselves, only if one previously accepts the theory that every striving for an object is essentially "libidinous."

We have remarked above that Freud's conception might depend somehow on his having felt, though vaguely, the need of overcoming a too "analytical" way of looking at things of life and mind. There is no doubt that analysis might go too far, and Freudian psychology is a striking example of this being the case. But there is another basic tendency in the psychoanalytical mentality which might have influenced the particular form the theory of sexuality was given. This tendency is related to the first named, though not identical with it. We might call it the monistic attitude. Monism is, after all, an attempt at simplifying reality far beyond the limits set by objective facts. Complexity is thus reduced to simplicity; all is one and the same, however various the aspects may be. The theory of sexuality too becomes simpler if it is assumed that phenomena, which are experienced as related directly or indirectly, are throughout nothing but manifestations of instincts which are purely sexual in nature. If the "partial instincts" were not what they are supposed to be, *i.e.*, parts or rudiments of sexuality, one would have to acknowledge that there are other powers in the human mind besides sexuality. But the very moment this is granted— the ego- and death-instincts have nothing to do with an individual's relation to the objective world—the whole edifice of psychoanalysis crashes. This collapse is inevitable, because psychoanalysis rests on the assumption of the uniqueness of libido. If there are other tendencies, also related to the objective world, and not of sexual nature, the conception of libido cannot be maintained any longer.

Freud's theory on infantile sexuality, one of the points which particularly aroused the wrath of his adversaries, is not forced on him by facts, but by the immanent necessities of his general conception. He had to adopt this view if he wanted to avoid self-contradiction.

Sometimes a critic of psychoanalysis is asked by its admirers: if you reject our theory, what theory have you to propose for replacing ours? Is it not better if you feel that our views are not quite in accordance with facts to accept it for the time being, since it offers at least a working hypothesis? (The second sentence is one a true psychoanalyst would probably never utter, because he is sure that he possesses the full truth and that unwillingness to accept it is due to unconscious factors in the critic's mind. But perhaps once in a while even a psychoanalyst would condescend to talk more or less like this.) To this we would have to reply that having no theory at all is better than having a wrong one. As long as we are without a theory there is still hope that we might discover one which could enable us to cope with the facts. But a wrong theory bars the way to truth. Ignorance is a lesser evil than pseudo-truth.

In all discussion on the Freudian theory of sexuality there is one pivotal point: the question of the place and rôle allotted to sexuality within the totality of human nature. By this is meant not the space taken by sexuality in conscious life, not whether it be right to accord to sexual feelings and experiences so great an importance but the much more weighty problem of the function of sexuality in the structure or the set-up of the human person as such. Freud does not say that we ought to seek more sexual pleasure, though he holds "repression" of sexuality to have, in certain instances, evil effects; indeed he lays great stress on "sublimation" by which libido is turned away from its immediate and, so to say, its crude goals and directed toward other aims, toward science, for instance, or toward art. But all these questions pertaining to morals, or practical life, or consciousness are not the point which is important in regard to an evaluation of psychoanalysis as a system, as a theory of human nature and as a philosophical anthropology; because that is what psychoanalysis in fact amounts to. The real problem is the position which sexuality occupies within the totality of the human person, according to Freudian anthropology.

Libido is, as we are told, the great motor force which urges man to transcend himself and to become attached to or interested in objects of the non-ego, whether these objects be real things or persons or ideas or values. And we have seen also that, according to psychoanalysis, interest and truth and value do not reside in an object because of this object's being this or that, its belonging to this or that class of beings, but because of its relation to libido. The value of an object depends on the amount of satisfaction its realization may give to the libidinous instinct. This view alone shows that sexuality or libido becomes, in psychoanalysis, one of the most important and decisive factors of human nature. All relation to the non-ego is determined by libido and by the mutual relations between this instinct and the objects.

We have been told also that the libidinous behavior of earliest childhood determines all later reactions of the same kind. But all reactions in regard to objects depend on libido. Therefore we have to conclude that libidinous behavior in childhood, and since this behavior depends on them, all influences molding sexuality, supply the pattern according to which all behavior of later years is formed. This is stated, to refer to just one work, expressly in C. G. Jung's lengthy book on *Changes and Forms of Libido*. This book was published in a periodical edited by Freud himself and belongs accordingly to a period when Jung was still acknowledged by Freud as his pupil. It is known that Jung later developed ideas of which Freud disapproved and that a secession was the result of this conflict. Jung says that sexuality supplies the pattern or exemplar for the development of personality; sexuality and its successive phases are called *vorbildlich* for the form personality will acquire in later years.

This remark of Jung's belongs to a still earlier phase of psychoanalysis, but it anticipates clearly what was stated later more explicitly and what was especially expressed by the concept of the "id," to which sexuality, as an instinctual structure, essentially belongs. The "id," however hidden its operations may be and however influential its reflexes may become in the other levels of personality, is once and for all the great reservoir of forces which determine the nature and the special modifications of human personality. It is the sexual instinct which determines personality; it is not personality which influences the instinct, except, of course, by inhibitions emanating from the super-ego. But these inhibitions are, so to speak, artificial: they are so because they are ultimately due to identification and therefore to the taking-over of attitudes which originally were alien to the personality, even in a certain sense antagonistic to the true personality. Personality, in the eyes of the psychoanalyst, does not possess sexuality, but is obsessed by it.

Sexuality is credited with a curious kind of independence from what a naive psychology would call the personality. We get the impression that, strong though sexual impulses and temptation may be, there is still a chance of reacting against them or, better, of making them obey our conscious will and conform to its ends. This idea is considered by the psychoanalyst as an illusion or a deception; when we believe we resist sexuality, we are in truth serving its ends though these ends may be perfectly camouflaged.

There is one side of this whole question which has never been felt to be worthy of consideration by the psychoanalysts. Sexuality might well be an "expression" of certain attitudes or tendencies of a non-sexual nature as any other side of human behavior might be.* There can be no doubt of this if one cares to look at facts without prejudice.

It is quite instructive to consider the reasons why such an idea could never arise in Freud's mind and why it is utterly unacceptable to his school. The notion of expression, which is a basic one for every other psychology, scarcely figures among the terms used by psychoanalysis. It is partly replaced by the notion of symbol. But though an expression is in a way a symbol, not every symbol need be an expression. We speak indeed of words expressing thoughts, and some other sign, a flag for instance, expressing that the admiral is aboard. But in such cases the use of this term is not quite the same as if we say that blushing expresses shame or that a gesture expresses contempt. The general term under which all these forms—there are several of them— may be comprised is that of signification. The fundamental notion of sign is no more considered by psychoanalysis than that of expression; all these things are merged into the one idea of

---

* We cannot here discuss the facts pointing to this interpretation, nor can we discuss the interpretation itself. We have done this elsewhere in the treatise on the psychology of sex mentioned above, p. 117, and also in *Psychology of Character* and in *Sex Psychology in Education*. Dr. Horney, to whose book we referred above, makes statements which point in the same direction.

symbolization.* A symbol in psychoanalysis is caused by the element symbolized therein, that is by the instinctual force, and it receives its particular character by being charged with a definite amount of mental energy. The mere logical relation of sign and thing signified is something which psychoanalysis could not take into consideration, because logical relations are considered themselves symbols of dynamic constellations. But expression is primarily related logically to what it expresses; only because of this relation it becomes expression. The causal relation is, so to say, superposed on the logical relation. Both are not simply one and the same thing, though they co-exist in one and the same phenomenon. Being caused by something and being expressive of it ought not to be confused.

Thus every phenomenon of behavior—taking this word in the widest sense—whatever else it is, is also expressive of something. This becomes particularly visible in language. A word or a proposition signifies a thing or a fact; they are meant to release some reaction, by what Buehler calls appeal, and they express the person's mood, personality, attitude, intention, or the like.†

There is no doubt that sexuality and its manifestations depend on instinctual factors. They do not depend exclusively on them, because other "parts" of personality sometimes play an important rôle. But even if instinct were the only cause of these phenomena, this would not invalidate the statement that they are expressions too. Now, expression is never solely of one single idea or sentiment or mood; expression is always of the total personality. Personality expresses itself in sexuality, as it

---

* Because of this lack of clearness and of terminal analysis it is not possible simply to replace the term "symbol," which is indeed rather an unhappy choice, by the term *"expression psychique"* as Dalbiez, of whose work more shall be said later, desires. First, there are so-called symbols which are not mental, as for instance, neurotic disturbances of bodily functions; secondly one would have previously to analyze very carefully the various significations of all these terms. In doing so it would be indispensable to take account of the study on signification—*Anzeige*—made by E. Husserl, *Logische Untersuchungen,* 2nd, ed. Halle, a. 1913, vol. 1, p. 23ff.

† K. Buehler, *Sprachtheorie,* Jena, 1934.

expresses itself in other kinds of behavior. Thus sexual behavior depends not on the nature, intensity, kind of sexuality alone, but on the total personality to which sexuality belongs. It is perhaps only a quarrel on words if one wants to distinguish between sexuality and its manifestations, letting the latter be subjected to total personality whereas the former results only from the bodily constitution and conditions personality as a pre-existent factor. At least the manifestations of sexuality have to be regarded as expressions, or one has to take account of their being also expressions.

The position of psychoanalysis might be described by stating that personality depends on and is formed by sexuality. What kind of person one is depends upon what kind of sexuality one has and upon the influences to which this sexuality has been subjected. But it seems truer to say that the kind of sexuality a person possesses and has developed depends very much on what kind of a personality he is.

Account has to be taken of the existence of mutual inter-relations. It is a mistake to see in sexuality nothing but a peculiar mode by which personality expresses itself. But it is even more wrong to hold rigidly the opposite view. The latter is the way in which psychoanalysis looks at these things. Psycho-analysis misses therefore essential sides of human life and thoroughly misunderstands many things.

CHAPTER VI

Psychoanalysis and Psychology

PSYCHOANALYSIS is acclaimed as a new way in psychology. It is believed to be the most important progress the science of the human mind ever made. Not only the Freudian school in the narrower sense of the term, but many psychologists, sociologists, and psychiatrists hail Freud's ideas as the royal road to a real understanding of mental processes, of total personality, of its behavior and its social relations. Though they do not directly assert that all other psychology is practically meaningless and contributes nothing truly useful to the knowledge of man, their general conviction is that psychology did not exist before the Freudian notions had been introduced.

We have to inquire into their right to make such sweeping assertions. But we have first to point out that, however great the progress achieved by psychoanalysis may be, this kind of psychology cannot claim to cover the whole field. Psychoanalysis is essentially the study of genesis and of dynamics, and does not aspire at being anything else. It is not in any sense descriptive psychology. Psychoanalysis is, of course, entitled to choose its field of work; specialization is a general feature in the development of modern science. But no specialist is entitled to ignore and disparage the work of other specialists. He has to pay careful attention to facts ascertained by methods other than his own.

Psychoanalysis feels little respect for descriptive psychology, holding it incapable of discovering what the Freudian deems to be the real nature of mental phenomena. This real nature is interpreted, as we have seen, in terms of a biologistic dynamism. Even if psychoanalysis were right in every one of its statements, it would still have to consider the descriptions supplied by common psychology. A theory of science endeavors to explain the phenomena observed. To be equipped for such an explanation it has first to make sure of these very phenomena. The operations of human reason consist, as we were told long ago by Aristotle, in combining and dividing. A theory is the more useful the greater the fields of phenomenal reality it covers and the greater the number of apparently different phenomena which it can comprise under one heading. But no theory can ever do away with the diversity of the phenomena. If a theory which gives one uniform explanation of a great diversity of phenomena is to be taken seriously it has to demonstrate how and why the varieties of phenomena arose from the general principle which the theory formulates. In psychology as elsewhere the theory of genesis is legitimate only when it fulfills this condition.

Many phenomena of mental life do not come under the observation of the psychoanalyst. Several authors belonging to the Freudian school are accordingly willing to concede that analysis is not the whole of psychology. But there are others who honestly believe psychoanalysis to be not only the last word in psychology but also able to cope with every problem that may possibly arise in regard to mental life. This is obviously a gross exaggeration. Mental life depends on more factors than merely those of dynamics, topology, and economics, to use Freud's own terms. The question of causation does not exhaust the range of psychological problems.

Certain rather serious objections have to be urged against psychoanalysis in the name of descriptive psychology. It is hardly necessary and surely not fitting to justify the method of description in psychology here at any length. We are quite aware of the opinion held by many authors that description is "unscientific," because it does not state its findings in terms of quantity and because its results are not controllable by experimental methods. We remark, rather casually indeed, that these criticisms are quite beside the point. They forget that even an "objective" psychology—like behaviorism or the reflexology of the Russian psychologists or, rather, physiologists—had to start originally from introspection. If we could not rely on the knowledge of our own mind, which is due to introspection, behavior and suchlike words would be quite meaningless. We know what behavior is, because we know that we behave. However "objective" psychology may become, it will never be able to disengage itself absolutely from introspection.

Even if introspection is rejected because of its lack of objectivity and because of other reasons of the same nature, there are some facts which are universally recognized. That there is a difference between perception and imagination, between both of them and thought; that emotion is a phenomenon different from judgment, and that strivings, conations, all forms of orectic states are *sui generis* cannot be denied. A theory of psychology may try to "reduce" these various classes of mental phenomena to one or to some few elements which, by combination, produce the states we recognize as being essentially different from each other. This impression might be a mistake, just as the idea of the sun moving across the skies is erroneous. But if such a mistake exists and is common to all men, it becomes the task of science to demonstrate why this mistake exists and what conditions it.

There was a time when psychology believed in sensistic philosophy and tried to appraise every mental phenomenon as nothing else than a peculiar combination of sensations. This theory proved to be contrary to fact and incapable of giving a satisfactory idea of mental states. Sensistic psychology was never able to explain the peculiarities of those "higher" mental states which, so it asserted, consist in combinations of sensations. Nor did it ever explain how and why these complexes of sensations exist at all. A psychological theory of this kind is apt to fall a prey to easy simplifications. Simple theories appeal to the mind. They offer certain advantages and there is a widely accepted idea that reality is essentially simple and that, therefore, the simpler a theory is the nearer it will be to reality and truth.

This belief has proved a very efficient motive in the advance of science. But it is, at the same time, a dangerous because a double-edged weapon. One can never say beforehand whether reality, in a particular aspect, is simple or complicated.

The tendency toward simplification has wrought much havoc. It has given birth to the nonsensicalities of monism. For a long time it has blinded the eyes of the scientists to the essential differences of matter and mind. It is at the bottom of the "nothing-else-but" mentality which characterized so largely the attitude of the nineteenth century. Modern science, addicted to this principle of simplification and unification, sometimes refers to the old rule—*principia praeter necessitatem non esse multiplicanda* (the number of principles ought not be needlessly increased)—usually credited to William of Occam, with what right may seem doubtful. But whoever coined the saying, he was careful enough to limit its application by another rule which, however, is but too often neglected: *principia praeter necessitatem non temere esse minuenda* (the number of the principles ought not be rashly diminished). If it is right to look for unity in diversity, it is not less necessary to take diversity at its face value as a fact, and to look for the reason of its existence. If it prove impossible to discover a uniting principle, which allows for the reduction of apparently distinct phenomena to one basis, we have simply to accept the fact of diversity. We are not allowed to disregard facts merely for the sake of satisfying our desire for unity and simplicity.

We discover within ourselves diverse mental states which we feel to be different by nature and not reducible to one common element. No psychology has as yet been able to devise a satisfactory explanation of this diversity. All attempts at such an explanation have been, in truth, mere postulates. They were not based on facts but on wishes, not on science but on a prejudiced metaphysical conception. The facts, however, command respect; they cannot be discarded. A theory which does not take account of the facts whether by simply accepting them or by eventually explaining them is not entitled to the name of science. Psychoanalysis is guilty, at least in one point, of overlooking certain facts. And of certain others it is incapable of supplying an explanation.

According to Freud's theory there is but one aim of human behavior: man strives for the greatest amount of satisfaction or rather of the peculiar pleasure resulting from the satisfaction of instinctive desires. The so-called principle of reality, on which we have reported in a previous chapter, is in fact merely a particular method of attaining the pleasure of satisfaction; it does not imply any essentially different attitude; it merely takes account of the obstacles which reality presents and it provides a better technique of gaining satisfaction. This idea of Freud's presupposes a thoroughgoing uniformity of pleasure. But this is contrary to fact.

It is of course true that man strives for pleasure, or to use the much more accurate formula of the older philosophers, for happiness. This has been stated by every philosopher who ever studied the nature of man. It is in Aristotle and St. Thomas, in St. Anselm and in Duns Scotus, in Kant as well as in Shaftesbury. Happiness is not an univocal term; there are many kinds of happiness which differ from each other not only in degree but also in kind. The happiness a child feels when given candy is not the same kind as that which a scholar experiences when he has found the solution of a baffling problem. Nor is the latter's state of happiness the same when he puts the last stroke of his pen to a manuscript as when he is listening to a symphony of Mozart.

The psychoanalytic conception implies a thorough uniformity of pleasure. All pleasure goes back, ultimately, to instinct satisfaction. It is, therefore, basically the same in all cases and at all times.

Descriptive psychology has pointed out that there are several, at least three, kinds of pleasure which are so different from each other that they cannot be reduced to one common denominator. They differ in quality. They differ also in their development and in the reaction they condition after having passed away. Buehler has distinguished three forms of pleasure: the pleasure of function, as it is observed best in the playing child; the pleasure of satisfaction, as illustrated by satisfying hunger or sexual desire; the pleasure of creation caused by the achievement of some work. Mueller-Hermaden has tried to show that there are even more than these three kinds of pleasure. But it is sufficient, for the aims of our present discussion, to consider the three kinds as distinguished by Buehler.

It is neither necessary nor helpful to consider the relations between these three kinds of pleasure and the instincts or urges or, generally speaking, the orectic tendencies underlying them. We are simply aware that they are different. They differ in the quality of the pleasantness felt. They differ in the way the intensity increases, persists and decreases in time. They differ also in the time-relation and in the intensity-relation to preceding or subsequent phases of unpleasantness. Pleasure of satisfaction, for instance, is characterized by a gradual increase of tension which becomes steadily more steep and which is in itself pleasurable notwithstanding a certain note of unrest associated with it; it reaches a climax and is replaced suddenly by another state of mind which may be either a quiet restfulness, or indifference, or an actual distaste.

The pleasure of function is of quite a different nature. It too may rise gradually, though it often sets in at a higher level which is then maintained throughout the whole situation; but the most characteristic feature is that the activity engendering this pleasure—for instance, playing—does not aim at any particular moment of satisfaction but rather goes on producing this pleasure continuously. Playing does not intend to bring about some final situation of satisfaction. It is verily its own end and has no other goal. Some activities which we also call playing are somewhat different; this is particularly true of games in which the desire to win and the aim of realizing the "attitude of triumph" (Janet) modifies the kind of emotional set-up. But true play has no goal outside of itself. The curve of pleasure shows accordingly no climax. It goes on more or less levelly. A child playing gives the impression that he might go on playing indefinitely apart from interruption or fatigue. If he is forced, by fatigue, to give up playing, it is with regret that he abandons his occupation, manifesting thereby that no final satisfaction has been attained.

Pleasure of creation is different from both the forms we have mentioned. It develops often through phases of definitely unpleasant character, of doubt and of wrestling with difficulties. It rises suddenly, as an *attitude de triomphe*, when the work has been achieved. It lasts for a certain time and may even increase still more. It disappears gradually or suddenly and is replaced by a feeling of emptiness. Perhaps the pleasure of contentment after having done what one ought to do is a fourth form which is unlike either satisfaction or the pleasure of creation. Were we to expatiate more on these points of descriptive psychology, we might allude to certain curious modifications of attitude; a situation originally meant to end in satisfaction may be transformed so as to provide pleasure more like the pleasure of function—stilling one's hunger gives rise to the pleasure of satisfaction, but the pleasure the glutton derives is mostly one of function.

Such modifications and combinations, however, are no arguments against the evident phenomenological differences of the various kinds of pleasure. Psychoanalysis knows only of one kind, because it wants all orexis to be originally instinctual. Also after "sublimation," or the transformation of the primitive instinctual strivings, the nature of the pleasure derived from complying with the instinctual urges must be the same. No transformation can be imagined by which the instincts, however transformed or masked, would become capable of producing a new form of pleasure completely opposite to their true nature. This is the more to be maintained in regard to psycho-analysis because this theory does not acknowledge any instincts except those of "libido," of the ego, and of death; this point has already been discussed sufficiently. Some other psychology of instincts which would recognize a larger number of primitive instinctual strivings—as, for instance, the psychology of Mac-Dougall—might try to cope with the difficulty we have just mentioned. Such a psychology could, eventually, introduce the notion of instincts which condition another type of pleasurable experience; this is indeed the case with MacDougall's psychology which admits, among other instincts, that of playing.* Psychoanalysis, however, does not concede the existence of other instincts; if there are various manifestations, they are due to secondary modifications of the original instincts, the true nature of which can never be lost.

It would be extremely difficult for a psychoanalyst if he were called to give a satisfactory explanation of the existence of these other forms of pleasure. He does not feel called to do it, because description and taking account of phenomenological differences is something for which he does not care. The fact of play did not, of course, escape the attention of Freud. But the only question he felt to be of importance is concerned with the instinctive forces at work in play. He did not trouble to find out what play really is, as a phenomenon. The psychoanalytical theory of play is anything but satisfactory.

The idea that there is only one kind of pleasure and that all the varieties which might be eventually observed are reducible to this one kind, namely pleasure of satisfaction, makes psychoanalysis become guilty of a grave neglect of facts. The problem which the analyst has to face is serious. If a solution according

* It seems, however, that the essential differences in the kinds of pleasure would create a certain difficulty. One might doubt whether instinct whose activity conditions such different emotional states may be rightly placed all on the same level. One cannot but feel that the notion of instinct is much in need of clarification and that by placing the "instinct of play" on the same level with the instinct of self-preservation some violence is done to fact.

to the principles of psychoanalysis cannot be found and cannot be expressed in terms of Freudian psychology, the position of psychoanalysis becomes precarious. The peculiar nature of all pleasure which is not of satisfaction does not allow us to limit the forces which are originally at work in the human mind to the three groups of instincts which psychoanalysis considers. Either there are phenomena which are of another origin than the one stated by psychoanalysis as the general one; in which case the theory can no longer claim to be a complete view of mental processes. Or other instincts have to be assumed as taking part in the original organization of the mind; in which case the same conclusion imposes itself and psychoanalysis is forced to modify its statements and its principles to a degree which in truth amounts to an overthrowing of its basic ideas.

There are other facts to be considered. Psychoanalysis claims to be "the" psychology. In listening to the words of its followers and admirers one gets the impression that to pursue studies in psychology otherwise than along the lines of Freudism is little better than a waste of time: it is only psychoanalysis which tells us things about the mind worth considering. If this claim is to be justified psychoanalysis has to prove itself capable of covering the whole field of mental facts.

The psychoanalyst has a complete explanation at hand why, in the history of an individual as well as in the history of mankind, a feeling *e.g.* of guilt, arises. He will explain to us that the influences to which the individual was exposed during early childhood; that the "Oedipus-situation" and the insufficient elaboration it went through, that this or that conflict between the forces of the id, the ego and the super-ego contributed to cause such a feeling of guilt. Let us, for one moment, pretend to be satisfied by this explanation. What is explained by such a statement? The only thing which is explained—and, in truth, the only one the psychoanalyst cares to explain—is the fact that a feeling of guilt developed in this individual person at this particular time. The psychologist, hearing that psychoanalysis explains all and that it is the only complete and trustworthy science of the human mind, wants to know a little more. He wants to be told why such a peculiar phenomenon as a feeling of guilt exists at all, why there are so many different mental states. Supposing even that the origin of these states is due to the working of the factors envisioned by the Freudian school and granted that these states have to be interpreted as transformations of contents which originally "represented" the instincts in consciousness,* the question remains unanswered why such states exist at all. Why did an instinct, by being repressed and by undergoing all the influences described by Freud, develop into a feeling of guilt? No reference to the position of authorities, to the experiences of the child in regard to prohibiting and punishing sanctions, or such like, can ever supply a satisfactory explanation. The theory leaves this question unanswered, however far back into the early history of individuals and of the race it might push its inquiries; it also remains utterly incapable of explaining the qualitative properties of the various mental states, allegedly due to the transformation of instinctual phenomena. There is the feeling of guilt; there is the other feeling of reverence; there is the sense of beauty; there are so many other kinds and shades of mental experience whose particular natures remain forever a mystery. The psychoanalyst is not permitted to accept these facts as ultimate data of experience; he is obliged, by the very nature of his theory and its being proclaimed as the only true and the only complete theory of the mind, to give an answer. He cannot admit that

---

* Since instincts are the only material out of which all mental phenomena are formed, the instincts supply also the whole content of consciousness. An instinct is part of the physiological organization, and as such not mental. It is "represented" in consciousness originally by the images, anticipations, strivings, etc., referring to those situations which provide immediate satisfaction. Repression, actuated by environmental forces, eliminates these original contents from consciousness and relegates these outcasts into the depths of the unconscious. Their place is taken by other contents approved by the ego. The original contents of the mind yet undisturbed by cultural, social, or educational influences, are called *Triebrepraesentanzen*; they represent the instincts as the ambassador represents his country.

anything exists whose nature and presence cannot be fully explained by the principles of his theory. But his theory offers not the least opportunity for a satisfactory answer to a question that the psychologist cannot help asking.

We do not think—though we may of course be wrong—that this question has been asked so insistently as to force the psychoanalyst to give a clear and unequivocal answer. But we doubt whether he would have found such an answer if he had been asked. Psychoanalysis has in truth no answer and it cannot have any. It cannot explain how and why such phenomena as the sentiment of guilt came to exist in the human mind, because the theory does not contain any element suitable for supplying such an explanation. But if no explanation can be found, then the existence of mental states independently of instincts has to be acknowledged. This, however, amounts to confessing that a good many facts of psychology are utterly beyond the power of psychoanalysis to explain. The very moment the independent existence of phenomena not stemming from the instincts is conceded, the whole fabric of psychoanalysis collapses. It ceases to be a complete theory of mental facts and processes; so far as it is true—there is indeed but little truth in it, as I think—it shrinks to a partial theory of conditioning certain mental events, but it loses all claim to be considered an all-comprising theory of mental life. Much less can it be considered as "the" psychology, the one which has to be exclusively recognized, the one which has to replace all other attempts at building up a science of the mind, the one which the students of mental facts have hoped and wished for so many years.

Let us state the dilemma once more so that the necessity of an answer may be seen inescapably: either the qualitative nature of the many mental states we feel to be *sui generis* and different from each other can be explained by psychoanalytic principles, or the independent existence and peculiar properties of these states have to be recognized; that is, we have to acknowledge that there exists a great number of elements or factors in mental life which elude all psychoanalytic interpretation. The first answer cannot be given, because the principles of psychoanalysis do not offer any means of explaining qualitative particularities. If the second position is asserted, psychoanalysis is no longer what it pretends to be and what it is believed to be by so many who have been blinded by its apparent "scientificality."

Psychoanalysis has become involved in this dilemma because of two of its basic features: the passion for quantity and the passion for the idea of evolution. In evaluating so highly these two ideas, psychoanalysis proves to be a true child of the nineteenth century. This theory, far from looking forward to the future, is in truth loaded with the burden of a past which is either dead already or on the point of death. The hope of psychology is not psychoanalysis but the unprejudiced study of facts. The disregard which the psychoanalysts have always professed for experimental psychology and the use of apparatus, and even more for introspective psychology, bears its fruits. These are not healthy—for the psychoanalysts.

The "metapsychology" of Freud introduces, as we saw in the first chapter, three points of view which are called respectively that of dynamics, of economics, and of topology. Economic and dynamic considerations refer to two sides of the same thing. Dynamic consideration deals with the kind of instincts involved, economic with the amount of instinctual energy displayed and the manner of its distribution. Thus the impression is created that psychoanalysis has a psychological conception of its own, different from the one held by general psychology. But on the other hand, Freud's psychology is mainly what is known as associationism. It is true that the famous laws of association as they have been stated by Hume* appear to play hardly any rôle

---

* We might record here that Hume is credited with the discovery of these laws though he became acquainted with them by the study of Aquinas. They are indeed named and fully described in the commentaries of the great Scholastic on the *Parva Naturalia* of Aristotle. Cf. J. K. Ryan, *Aquinas and Hume on the Laws of Association,* The New Scholasticism, 1938, *12*, 366.

in psychoanalysis; they determine of course the succession of the single ideas, images, words in the free associations, but this determination is, partly at least, but the effect of deeper forces, of instinctual constellations which are the real factors behind the display of conscious elements. Thus one could be led to conclude that psychoanalysis has given up associationist principles and replaced them with a purely "dynamic" conception.

The essence of associationism is, however, not that there are associations, but that there is nothing else. This means that there are no mental phenomena which are not due to the working of the associating forces and that every complex or higher mental state is in truth a combination of elements held together by certain forces. On the nature of these forces the older associationist psychology made no conclusive statements. Psychoanalysis supplies such a theory of these forces: they derive from the instincts. But the essential idea remains unchanged; the complex phenomena are still aggregates of elements. This is a necessary consequence of the instinct-axiom. Since there is no other material out of which mental states could be built except the instincts and their representations in mind, no other explanation is possible.

Another instance might be mentioned which illustrates strikingly the habits of psychoanalytic thinking. It had been observed by many authors, even before psychoanalysis gave an explanation of its own, that there are some similarities between the mentality of children on the one hand and of primitive people on the other. Much has been written in recent times on the "magic thinking of children" and the close resemblance to magic customs and ideas observed among primitive tribes. Freud himself contributed a very valuable remark, one of the few which refer to immediate observation in psychology; he pointed out that one of the characteristic features in the way children look at the world is what he called the belief in the "omnipotence of thought." Children indeed believe that it is sufficient to think of something to make it become real. And there are doubtless close analogies to this habit in the magical rites and formulas of primitive culture.

We cannot discuss here the psychoanalytic conceptions of magic and of primitive mentality. They have been influenced rather by ideas belonging to the sociological school of E. Durkheim of Paris, especially by the ideas which Lévy-Bruhl developed in his book on the mentality of inferior societies. One has to acknowledge, however, that Freud had stated his ideas at a time when he certainly knew nothing of the teachings of the French sociological school, and before Lévy-Bruhl's book appeared. The notions of the latter were welcomed by the psychoanalysts only as a confirmation of their own conceptions. This confirmation is, however, of a somewhat doubtful value, because the theories of Durkheim and his followers are far from being recognized by all or even by the majority of the scholars working in this field.*

Nor can we inquire into the precise nature of the alleged similarities and into the characteristics of "magic thinking." It deserves only to be noticed that neither children nor primitives indulge at all times in this way of thought. It was the mistake of Lévy-Bruhl to believe that the primitives use a logic quite different from ours because they seem sometimes to neglect the principle of contradiction. But this neglect never goes far enough to make them take one thing for another when the first is useful to some end and the other is not. A man may apparently identify himself and his fellow tribesmen with parrots, but he will not try to pluck feathers from his friend, nor will he expect him to fly away and to perch on a tree; he may call a wooden stick a kangaroo, but he will never feel tempted to cook it. Thus children may believe in magic or cherish thoughts reminiscent of such ideas, but they expect mother to give them candy and are not satisfied with wishing for it, powerful though they may believe their wishes to be.

* For a critical study of these ideas, see S. Deploige, *The Conflict Between Ethics and Sociology,* transl. Ch. C. Miltner, St. Louis, 1938.

The "omnipotence of thinking" is, after all, only one side of the general attitude of children who have to learn how to distinguish between facts and ideas, between reality and images. Their occasional incapacity or unwillingness—both factors play a certain rôle—to make such distinctions does not mean that they are always living in a confused world of both dream and reality.

Yet Freud had noted a remarkable fact. Only, as usual, he proceeded immediately to devise an interpretation which has no sufficient basis in his findings; it rests mainly on certain preconceived ideas. This interpretation is summarized by the term "archaic thinking." The likeness observed between primitive and infantile mentality is translated into the terms of evolutionarism and of the phyletic axiom. The child thinks in this manner because his stage of development "reproduces" the stage of early civilization when such a mentality was common.

We may put aside, for the present, the fact that the ethnological conceptions of Freud and his school are mostly unacceptable and that for the most part they are based mainly on statements by quite unreliable authors. Even if this were not the case, these features in infantile thought and their similarity to primitive mentality could be explained otherwise. It is characteristic of Freud's monoideistic way of looking at things that he never considered the possibility of another and simpler explanation. His pupils are even less inclined to look around for a non-Freudian explanation; they are afflicted in a high degree by what Gilson calls, in a quaint word, the trouble of "ipse-dixitism."

The following remarks are not intended to propose a satisfactory theory of the phenomena under discussion. Whether my explanation be true or not, is of no concern here (though I believe it to be better founded and more in accordance with facts and with the principles of a sound psychology than the psychoanalytic ideas are). The only point which matters is that there is possible at least one other explanation; and, further, that this possible explanation has to be considered by the psychoanalysts and if possible refuted by them. That they have not condescended to look into this matter at all, is due to their incapacity to see things objectively. They are so utterly wrapped up with subjectivity that they deem an explanation right only when it rests on their notion of intrinsic principles of human nature.

If instead of remaining riveted to the viewpoint of subjectivism one takes account of the extrinsic factors too, one becomes aware that there is a striking similarity between the *situation* a primitive is in and the average situation of the child. Both are ignorant, both are at a loss in face of so many occurrences of everyday life, both are surrounded by powers whose operations they cannot understand or foresee—the primitive by the forces of nature, the child by adult persons—both feel impotent and helpless in a strange and powerful world. Why, both being human and obeying the same laws of human nature, should they not develop a similar mental attitude and similar ways of thought? The same explanation would even apply to the mind of the schizophrenic which falls back to an "archaic" level because of "regression." It has been pointed out by several psychiatrists that schizophrenia often sets in with the "experience of a world catastrophe"—*Weltuntergangserlebnis*—and that by this a new and unknown world appears to the bewildered soul of the patient.

We do not feel that psychology has gained anything by the introduction of the notion of "archaism," which in any event is too closely related to mistaken ideas on ethnology and on primitive culture to be acceptable.

CHAPTER VII

Psychoanalysis and Medicine

FREUD started on his way because he wanted to understand and to cure certain troubles which proved refrac-
tory to the ordinary methods of therapy. His work began
as a study in pathology and therapeutics. It remained such with
him and with most of his pupils. A great part of the articles
and treatises dealing with psychoanalysis, however, go beyond
this and are on the theory and the treatment of neurosis or on
the clinical history of neurotic cases. Some psychoanalysts, however, go still farther and indulge in a wide extension of the
scope of their activity. They believe that organic troubles are
caused by mental factors and are, if not able to be cured, at
least explainable, according to Freudian principles.

Some of these applications of psychoanalysis to bodily medicine are definitely fantastic. We are told, for instance, that there
is a possibility of interpreting organic disease as "unconscious
partial suicide," the unconscious mind not going so far as to
kill the whole organism, but being content with destroying, or
attempting to destroy some part of it.*

There have been also attempts at applying psychoanalysis to
physiological phenomena. These attempts are no more appealing than those mentioned already. Menstruation, surely a physiological process, and for that matter one whose conditions have
been pretty thoroughly studied, is envisioned as a "conversion
symptom," according to the pattern worked out by Freud for
a definite kind of neurotic trouble; menstruation is said to be

---

* *Organic Suicide*, Bull. Menninger Clin., 1937, *1.*, 192-198. Grodek, in
Germany, has proposed somewhat similar ideas. They need not be discussed,
because they are not essential to psychoanalysis. But they are characteristic,
not so much of psychoanalysis as of the mentality which gets hold of certain
of its adepts.

due to a union of opposed wishes and contrary instinctual impulses, of genito-sexual excitation on the one hand and of defense against it on the other.* The use of psychoanalytical notions in biology has given rise to the development of a particular "bioanalysis." Its statements apparently have shocked even some of the "orthodox" psychoanalysts.† The most astounding ideas are those proposed by the late Dr. Férénczi of Budapest. We know already that the notion of evolution plays an important rôle in the Freudian system. It is used as a basic conception, allowing one to bring together ethnology, prehistory, and psychoanalysis, and also to offer an explanation of individual mental development. So far as these attempts go, they treat the statements of the evolutionist as true and as useful for strengthening certain positions of psychoanalysis.

Férénczi turned things the other way round. He wanted to "explain" evolution and phyletic descent by means of psychoanalytic conceptions. One example of his mode of reasoning will suffice. Psychoanalysis teaches that the human mind unconsciously longs for the return to earlier developmental stages, for the opportunity to indulge exclusively in an existence ruled by the "pleasure-principle," and therefore for a repristination of childhood down to its very first days, even farther, back to the period of life in the womb. The reasons for introducing this strange idea are bad enough. But now comes the reversal of the argument. Férénczi asks himself whether the same process does not also rule evolution in general. According to paleology there lived originally only organisms adapted to a life in the water. When evolution progressed, the animal organism left this medium and became adjusted to a life outside of water. But the new organisms did not cease longing for the lost water-paradise. Therefore they developed organs which allowed at

---

* M. Balint, *A Contribution to the Psychology of Menstruation*, Psychoana. Quart. 1937, 6., 346.

† Cf. S. Bernfeld, *Zur Revision der Bioanalyse*, Imago, Lpz. 1937, 23., 197.

least the embryo to lead such an existence.* *Difficile satyram non scribere.*

There have been always in every branch of human endeavor some thinkers whose imagination ran wild. Their ideas are no disparagement to science in general; nor can we bring an indictment against psychoanalysis because of the extravagances of some of its followers. But one wonders at these ideas being taken seriously by the Freudian school. It is difficult to understand how articles such as these could ever come to be published in the school's renowned and highly "official" periodicals.

We may touch incidentally on the attempts made by some authors to bring certain notions of physiology into line with those of psychoanalysis. There was a time when Russian physicians and psychologists held psychoanalysis in high esteem. They have since then discovered that its ideas are opposed to true Marxism and are of a nature too "bourgeois" to fit in with Bolshevist ideology. We do not feel competent to judge this particular point. We shall point out that there are reasons for upholding the first, now condemned, view. But this is, for the present, unimportant. Merely for the sake of completeness, let us refer to the parallels which some believe can be discovered between the notion of "conditioned reflexes" as they were developed by the experimental work especially of Pawlow, and the psychoanalytic view on the genesis of symptoms. The notion of reflex has been explained above (v. p. 51). A conditioned reflex becomes established by having an animal perceive, together with some sensation which releases a reflex, another sensation which has originally nothing to do with the reflex. If after a great number of repetitions the original and adequate stimulus is left out and only the inadequate, additional stimulus is applied, one observes that the reflex is nevertheless released. For instance: the smell of food releases in the dog, by way of reflex, the secretion of saliva or of gastric juice. The dog hears,

---

* For instance: S. Férénczi, *Male and Female,* Psychoana. Quart. 1936, 2., 349.

whenever he smells food, a bell. After many repetitions the bell alone is capable of releasing the secretion. Russian neurologists and psychologists have laid great stress on this point. So has Dalbiez; but his remarks are far from being convincing, because his second-hand knowledge of physiology prevents him from having a precise idea of the nature of the phenomena in question. However, Schilder, a psychiatrist and physician, and one of the leading psychoanalysts today, warns against superficial and hasty parallels. It is indeed doubtful whether such a *rapprochement* is permissible and whether it rests on more than superficial analogies.*

It is quite natural that the psychoanalysts should desire to bridge the gulf separating mere vital phenomena from those of the mind, especially the human mind. We have already seen that the basically biologistic attitude of Freud causes him to assume a monistic point of view, though not even his ingenious construction can really do away with the essential differences obtaining between mind and matter. The more impossible the task of establishing a thoroughly monistic theory is, the more fantastic must be the attempts to do so. The instances quoted— and they are not isolated curiosities—may suffice for an illustration.

The relations of psychoanalysis to medicine are, however, of great interest to the critic for several reasons. Medicine is, as was stated before, the very birthplace of psychoanalysis. The psychoanalytic method is primarily one for treating patients. And its successes are often referred to as a decisive proof of the theory's truth. We have to examine particularly the last point.

Before discussing the signification of the good results obtained by psychoanalysis in a remarkable number of cases, one may allude to a fact which is not devoid of importance. Psychoanalysis is far from being generally accepted. There are many famous physicians and psychiatrists who do not feel inclined to

* *Psychoanalysis and Conditioned Reflexes,* Psychoana. Rev. 1937, 24., 1.

make use of Freudian principles in the cases of neurosis which come their way. If they held the idea of psychoanalysis as the only method or the best method of dealing with such cases, assuredly they would have tried to apply it. They would have felt obliged to adopt it; and if they were told that they could not do so without having studied with an approved psychoanalyst and without having been analyzed themselves, they would certainly have taken the trouble to become initiated. The physician has no other goal than to help his patients. He is obliged, by his professional conscience, to apply any licit method which gives hope of success, especially in cases where his usual method of treatment has proved inefficacious. But, strange to say, many psychiatrists continue to treat cases of neurotic disturbance without making use of psychoanalysis. I do not mean only that there are psychiatrists who are unwilling to adopt the *whole* of Freudism, yet who accept the earlier phases of psychoanalysis or use the method merely as one of exploration or who try to combine Freudian ideas with their own general psychiatric technique. I refer to psychiatrists who do not make use of psychoanalysis in any sense. It would be difficult to accuse all these physicians of lack of professional conscience. And it would be quite untrue to pretend that they are unsuccessful.*

There is, in fact, no empirical proof for the statement of the psychoanalysts that their method is the only one allowing a thorough cure of neurosis and the only one giving good results in certain serious and difficult cases. No method of treatment whether mental or physical yields one hundred percent success. There are always cases in which the best methods, the greatest experience, the purest intentions are of no avail. Even the psy-

---

* Perhaps I ought to emphasize that "psychoanalysis" is the name reserved exclusively to Freudian psychology. There are, of course, other theories of neurosis and other methods of dealing with neurotic troubles. My remarks aim only at the idea of Freud and his "orthodox" followers, including some dissenters who, like Jung or Stekel, go on believing the bulk of Freudian ideas. But it is a misuse against which Freud himself has forcibly protested to call by the general name of psychoanalysis all kinds of medical psychology.

choanalysts cannot but fail in some cases. How large the percentage of success and how large that of failure, is difficult to say. The peculiarities of the troubles with which psychotherapists have to deal often forbid a control of the results after the patient has finished the treatment.

In a neurosis the healing is demonstrated by the fact that the patient becomes able to deal with all the difficulties and worries of real life. Now one can never say, with absolute certainty, that a neurosis has been totally uprooted. One cannot predict that the patient, his mental health being restored by treatment, will be capable of facing all difficulties, because we cannot submit him experimentally, as it were, to any such conclusive test. The conviction of the psychoanalysts, that their method is the only one entitled to the name of a thorough and successful treatment, rests partly indeed on the successes achieved, but mostly on their believing in their theory with an unshakable faith. Successes are achieved by non-psychoanalytic methods also. Adlerian psychology, for instance, claims to be a better way of dealing with neurosis than psychoanalysis is. Other psychiatrists, and among them very famous ones, use neither method. Janet's large treatise* is a striking illustration of this.

The psychoanalysts cite cases which have been unsuccessfully treated by other methods and which yield to treatment by analysis. But psychiatrists of other schools of thought can quote experiences in the opposite sense. They too have known many cases of neurosis in which a psychoanalysis even of long duration proved inefficacious and which profited very much by a different method of treatment. The analysts will credit the analysis, even though it had been incomplete, with the success ultimately obtained. But the non-analysts may do the same with the cases which proved recalcitrant to their treatment and which yielded ultimately to psychoanalysis. Thus, statistics of successes and failures do not really prove anything.

* *Les médications psychologiques,* Paris, 1930.

Neurosis is a trouble of a peculiar kind. What can be asserted of bodily diseases does not always apply to neurosis. Neurotic troubles ought to be classed neither with bodily nor with mental diseases. They are not true diseases, in the sense which this term has in general medicine. They are better described as disturbances of behavior due to mental factors, mostly acquired and therefore susceptible of being changed by equally mental influences. The only thing which neurosis has in common with bodily disease is that it usually—but not always—causes suffering. There are, however, definitely neurotic states which do not trouble the subjective well-being; this is true for instance, of certain sexual abnormalities. Neurosis is like true mental disease insofar as its symptoms are mostly of a mental nature or, at least, insofar as mental symptoms are never missing even when bodily manifestations of the neurosis, as in heart-neurosis, stand apparently in the foreground. But the nature of neurosis is quite different from that of true psychosis and from that of bodily disease. Symptoms and clinical pictures must therefore be evaluated otherwise in the pathology of neurosis than in general medicine or in psychiatry.

Such questions, however, cannot be discussed here; they belong in a treatise on psychotherapy or on medical psychology. One fact nevertheless is worth mentioning. In general medicine there is a more or less definite parallelism between the impressiveness of the symptoms and the gravity of the disease. Generally speaking, it is possible to assert that the more developed the symptoms the more serious is the case. This is not true in the pathology of neurosis. Here the symptoms may be but slightly developed, they may be even insignificant, and nevertheless not yield to treatment; or we observe apparently serious symptoms, and have practically no difficulty in restoring health. Because of these reasons, and several others of the same nature, it is difficult to evaluate statistics on successes obtained by any mental treatment. The successes which psychoanalysis achieves do not prove anything. They might have been achieved not by, but in spite of, the method applied. Neither the one nor the other statement can be proved or disproved by appealing to statistics.

Thus the psychoanalysts are in a way right in laying more stress on the validity of the theory than on statistics of therapeutic results. But this procedure has one serious drawback. The statements of the theory were derived originally from observations on cases of neurosis. The proof of their truth was found in their being efficacious and capable of causing neurotic symptoms to disappear. Here again we seem to move in a circle. One might, of course, raise the same objection against any other theory of neurosis. None of them can rely on its successes as a convincing proof of its being true. We are, therefore, thrown back on the immanent criticism of the theories and their compatibility with the totality of facts observed, or on some system of comparative psychology of the normal and of the abnormal mind.

One thing is sure: that one may deal, and successfully too, with neurosis without making any use either of the notions or of the methods of psychoanalysis. A comparison of the reports made by followers of the various schools would probably show that the percentage of successes and failures is everywhere more or less the same. One cannot of course refer to the times when medical psychology did not yet exist. This one merit will remain forever Freud's: he started the movement which led to the development of medical psychology and he pointed out forcibly the necessity of applying mental methods to the cure of mental troubles. (This does not refer to true psychosis which is mostly caused by an organic brain-trouble and which therefore will hardly yield to a purely mental treatment.)

To suppose, as we do, that psychoanalysis is wrong in its theoretical foundations and incompatible with well-ascertained facts of psychology, yet to credit it with undoubted successes, seems to be contradiction. But there is really no contradiction. There would be, to a certain extent, in bodily medicine, where it is improbable that a totally wrong method could achieve any noticeable success. But it is different with neurosis.

Even in the treatment of bodily disease we are often unable to say whether the success is to be credited to our treatment or to other causes. We may be sure of the therapeutic efficacy in surgery. We are much less sure in internal medicine. Physicians have complained, in a half-playful manner, of the ingratitude of their patients. If the sick man gets well, the physician says, it is ascribed to the patient's strong constitution; and if he does not get well, it is the fault of the physician. There is some truth in this saying. Not only is it a true description of the behavior of certain people; but it is also true, in a way, objectively. We can never be sure of the efficacy of our methods because we see them fail in cases which we deemed to be hopeful and because sometimes amazing results are achieved when we despaired of being capable of doing anything. Even in dealing with bodily disorders we have to take account of many factors besides those we consciously use. The same is true, to a far greater extent, in medical psychology or in the treatment of neurosis.

One factor which is of the greatest importance and of whose intensity we can never make sure is the will of the patient; if he is really willing to become normal again, he may amaze us by the rapidity of his recovery. But this will is not a thing of which the patient is conscious. He nearly always believes that he wants to get rid of his symptoms; if he did not feel this way he would hardly come to see a physician. But we discover, in certain cases, that his alleged will-for-health is fictitious, a make-believe, by which the neurotic patient manages to conceal from his own mind what is going on there. We make this discovery sometimes by observing the patient's behavior during and after treatment; sometimes it is just the failure which convinces us of the existence of "another will possessing all the strength which the first [that is the conscious] will is lacking"; these words are St. Augustine's, in the eighth book of the Confessions. We can

never say what rôle the will-for-health or the unwillingness
have played in success or in failure.

Psychotherapy creates a peculiar personal relation between the
physician and the patient. Personal relations may exist, of
course, between every physician and his patient. But this relation is not essential to the cure; an appendix may be taken out
successfully even by a surgeon whom the patient dislikes; and
malaria will respond to its specific treatment whatever idea we
may have formed of the character of our physician. Our liking
or disliking him has but a small influence on the efficacy of the
cure. But in psychotherapy it is different. We have seen that
psychoanalysis takes account of this fact in its term of "transference"; we take this to be a name of a situation which we may
describe and understand perfectly even if we discard all psychoanalytic notions. But who is to say how far the therapeutic success depends on the development of a personal relation between
physician and patient? We cannot, of course, accept the statements of the psychoanalyst of the necessity of transference and
its specific rôle, since their acceptance would depend upon a
prior acceptance of the whole theory.

There are even some among Freud's pupils who acknowledge
that there are in psychoanalysis other influential factors besides
those belonging to the treatment itself. Confidence, faith in the
capacity of the analyst, the fame this method enjoys to-day, the
personality of the therapist, even a certain degree of suggestion
may contribute very much to success. And there is one fact more.
The neurotic is generally an isolated person. He is but little in
touch with reality and especially with his fellows. He behaves
like a person who has to conceal some secret and therefore has
to be careful not to come into close contact with others. He has,
moreover, repeatedly experienced that his sufferings are not
taken at their full value by others, that his personality is not
appreciated. Meeting the psychotherapist, he finds himself in
a situation altogether different from every other of his daily
life in his family, in society and in his office. For the first time

there is someone really interested in his case, who will listen indefinitely, to whom he may talk of his personal affairs, who will not divulge anything. No wonder he becomes attached to this person. No wonder the physician becomes in many cases the bridge by which the once isolated personality may proceed towards reality and social existence. Nobody can truly evaluate the importance this experience may have.

In all theoretical developments of medical psychology, there is one unavoidable circle. It derives its ideas from the very same material and by the very same methods on which and by which they have to be tested. The study of abnormal personalities, especially of neurotic patients, the attempt at bringing such personalities back to normality supplies the empirical data; the success of the treatment based on the conclusions drawn from these experiences provides the test of the truth. As one may easily perceive this test may claim at its best only a greater or less probability; but it has not the weight which we rightly attribute to the tests controlling the statements of physicists and even physicians. The accordance with facts obtained by other methods and with the statements of general logic and methodology become therefore much more important than they are elsewhere.

If we have convincing reasons for believing a theory in medical psychology to be mistaken, no success can force us to accept it. Results may be obtained, and not be less frequent or less satisfactory, by other methods of treatment too. The experience of many non-analytical therapists is sufficient proof. We may add that we know by personal work that a successful treatment of neurosis may be carried through without making appeal to the ideas and methods of Freudian psychology.

CHAPTER VIII

Method and Philosophy

S OME authors who reject absolutely the philosophy of Freudism believe that one might disengage its methodological aspect, thus retaining psychoanalysis as a method of psychological investigation and as one of medical treatment, and discarding at the same time the philosophical principles. This is the opinion of L. Dalbiez* who has devoted two thick volumes to a description of psychoanalysis, a recommendation of its method and a refutation of its philosophy. This is apparently also the idea of Dr. M. J. Adler† who tries to preserve the methodical side of psychoanalysis and to ensure it a sound foundation by basing it on the principles of Aristotelian and of Thomistic philosophy. The same point of view is shared by Maritain‡ whose opinion is based, as it seems, mostly on the discussions of Dalbiez.

A proposition applauded by men like Maritain and Adler obviously deserves serious consideration. We shall have to look carefully into this matter, since we feel obliged to oppose the opinion of these scholars. To state our thesis at the very outset of our discussion: we hold that method and philosophy are indeed inseparable in psychoanalysis and that a disapproval of the philosophy includes implicitly the rejection of the method. For once we feel in full agreement with the psychoanalytical school. In his preface to Dr. Adler's book, Dr. Alexander, one of the leading psychoanalysts of America, attempts to refute the position taken by Adler. Alexander's arguments are not always well chosen. He takes for granted many ideas which in truth are anything but evident. But his main position, so far as we can see, is

* *La Méthode Psychanalytique et la Doctrine Freudienne*, Paris, 1936.
† *What Man Has Made of Man*, New York, 1938.
‡ *Quatre Essais Sur l'Esprit dans sa Condition Charnelle*, Paris, 1939.

impregnable: the basic conceptions of human nature which form the background of Freud's psychology cannot be abandoned without that psychology becoming meaningless. It cannot be given another foundation than the one upon which it was originally built. To attempt to take away the old foundations and to replace them by another philosophy is like trying to stabilize a square building on circular foundations; the equilibrium will be anything but satisfactory and the edifice is liable to crash sooner or later. In previous chapters we have pointed out the essential "axiomatic" suppositions on which the theory of Freud rests. We have tried to show that these propositions are implicitly contained in the very foundations of psychoanalysis and that not one of the more special propositions can retain its meaning if it becomes detached from the whole of the system. Freud's mind was thoroughly and consistently constructive. It would be a poor compliment to this powerful, if erring, mind to think the method he developed separable from the philosophy which formed its background.

The authors who side with Dr. Adler and Maritain have been, it seems, impressed by the success of psychoanalysis as a therapeutic method and by the approval this theory has found with so many psychologists. But the successes, as we have just explained, are not sufficient proof for the truth of such a theory. And the admiration which psychoanalysis enjoyed and still enjoys among many psychologists, psychiatrists, sociologists, and others, is the effect of a quite peculiar historical situation of which we shall speak in chapter XII. With a man like Dr. Dalbiez things stand apparently a little differently. He seems to have become acquainted with psychoanalysis as a method of treating certain cases which were neglected by the average psychiatrist. He was struck with the opportunities the method seemed to offer for helping patients who would not have been helped otherwise. But he omitted to look around for another method which eventually might do the same service without necessitating the acceptance of many unusual ideas. Dr. Dalbiez evidently knows of no other way of dealing with neurosis and therefore believes psychoanalysis to be the only one. This is definitely untrue.

The essential elements of psychoanalysis as a method are said to be free association and interpretation. This statement is, however, not quite true, or at least, not quite complete. Interpretation is not only the translation of symbols and reminiscences into the language of instinctual situations, but also the diagnosis of resistance and the seizure of the right moment for presenting the translation to the patient. The method moreover implies the acknowledgment of such things as instinctual situations of the kind described by psychoanalysis. Psychoanalysis falls to the ground if we refuse to believe in the existence of the Oedipus-situation or in the existence of libidinous bonds between parents and children or in the process of sublimation or in the effects of repression. And we can believe in these things only if we place ourselves exactly at the viewpoint of Freud. This last statement only repeats the thesis already stated. The method implies and contains the whole of the theory. Just as every single proposition of psychoanalysis has a meaning only if all the rest of them are acknowledged, even so the method is meaningful only if the whole system is posited as being true. That this is indeed the case will become visible, we hope, if we proceed to consider some of the steps or elements of psychoanalytic method. We cannot avoid the repetition of some things spoken of in earlier chapters; to restate these things is necessary for the sake of clearness. The chain of associations on which the whole procedure rests is practically and by its very nature endless. It can go on forever. Everything is connected somehow with every other thing in the human mind, and the memories stored up within it and the ideas which may arise, new ones and old ones, can be multiplied infinitely. There is no reason for this process ever stopping. It is interrupted from time to time by the pauses psychoanalysis regards as indicative of "resistance" and as preceding the entrance into consciousness of things contained in the "unconscious." These things were either originally conscious contents and became repressed and inaccessible to consciousness, or they had been never really conscious, as *e.g.*, prenatal impressions. But if resistance is overcome by the analyzed person and by the insistence of the analyst, the chain is taken up again and may run on until the next manifestation of resistance occurs.

This fact has been one of the reasons for pushing the real causes of symptoms or normal attitudes further and further back into the past of the subject. Originally one had but to discover the "traumatic" incident, the repressed emotional experience to which the adequate "abreaction" had been denied. In a later stage, psychoanalysis had to discover the forgotten impressions of early childhood. Finally it had to go back to the very first days of life, to the hour of birth, and—with some—even beyond. This development could never have set in, if analysis had not proved to be indeed endless. If the chain of associations should sometime reach an absolute end, we should have to conclude, according to Freudian principles, that the ultimate cause of the mental fact from which this chain started had at last been revealed.* The notion of multiple determination too could be introduced only because of this condition of things.

It becomes necessary for the psychoanalyst, therefore, to have some method at hand for determining when to break off the chain of associations. He alone can know whether a point sufficiently removed from the actual mental fact has been attained. He can no longer rely on the disappearance of a symptom, because in the overwhelming number of cases he does not start from symptoms and because he does not aim at merely causing a pathological phenomenon to disappear. In analyzing a normal person's dream, for instance, the sign of therapeutic efficacy

---

* But if we have gone back to prenatal life and if the associations are still running on, there is always the explanation at hand that we are digging down to the layer of "racial memories." We read, *e.g.*, in an article of Nunberg, *Psychological interrelations between physician and patient,* Psychoana. Rev. 1938, 15. 297, that the myth which once may have been history is revived in danger; the physician becomes the sacrificing priest and the patient the sacrifice.

is missing. The same is true of many other facts of which analytical explanations are given.

There is no objective criterion of significance. Whether the material dug out of the unconscious is significant or of any relevance can be decided in all those cases only by applying the principles of psychoanalysis. "Significant" like "important" and "primary" and every other similar term means that which deserves to be called so according to the conceptions of analysis.* We can never know whether some matter coming to the surface after resistance has been broken has any importance unless we have previously the knowledge of, *e.g.*, the Oedipus-situation. This is one point in which the necessary and indissoluble connection between theory and method becomes visible. The theory, however, has been shown to exist only as long as its basic philosophical notions are held to be valid. The method can therefore be handled only by a person firmly believing in the truth of the theory, and a person can have this belief only when he adheres, consciously or not, with an equal firmness to the philosophy.

One cannot forget that many of the statements made by psychoanalysis rest, not immediately on empirical evidence, but on interpretations derived from such evidence. The foundations of not a few of these statements are moreover of a non-psychological nature, since they make use of data supplied by ethnology and the history of culture; it will become clear in the next chapter, however, that the alleged facts are of doubtful character and become "facts" only because the psychoanalytic theory is presupposed. When discussing this question, we shall encounter another vicious circle very much like those we have had to point out already. It is also important never to forget

* Freud remarks that false interpretations have no significance to the personality; even if they are accepted they do not find any lasting response. (*Constructions in Analysis,* Internat. Journ. of Psychoana. 1938, *19.* 377.) But how is one to know whether a response will prove to be a lasting one? And how does this principle apply to the analysis of persons dead for ages, of Leonardo da Vinci, Heinrich von Kleist, King Ecknaton of Egypt, etc.?

that every theoretical statement of psychoanalysis is, without any exception, an integral part of the whole system and presupposes it. Here indeed, to quote the famous saying of Aristotle though not quite in its original sense, the whole is prior to the parts.

The whole theory and its basic philosophy are implied as soon as we are willing to consider the material revealed by free associations as having a causal relation to any mental fact whatsoever, be it a symptom, a dream, an emotion, a slip of the tongue, etc. Causal relations of this kind can be stated only if the peculiar idea of dynamism and of mental energy as it has been developed by Freud is recognized as true. If this conception is rejected we are allowed only to state a relation of association or, to use a still more neutral term, a relation of connection, but none of causation. Whatever idea one may form of the relation of the material produced by free association to the fact which had been the starting point of the association, it is certain that by considering this relation as one of causation, one has accepted psychoanalysis as a philosophy. This is not tantamount to a rejection of the method of free association as a means for the study of the human mind, but it amounts to a denial to the non-psychoanalytic psychologist of the right to make use of the particular views of psychoanalysis on the nature of the relations obtaining between the single links of this chain.

It may be that the rôle of instinctual forces is greater than some psychologists care to admit and that psychoanalysis is right in stressing this point. Whether this be the case or not cannot be demonstrated by a mere study of free associations. These associations supply us only with raw material. It is the interpretation of this material from which psychoanalysis derives its views on the place held by instincts in the totality of the human person. The interpretation, however, is not one forced upon us by the nature of the empirical evidence; it is due, as every interpretation necessarily is, to the combination of empirical statements with some general ideas. We have to have some rules of interpretation before we can attempt any discovery of meaning in this material.

Let nobody object that the psychoanalytic interpretation is justified by the success realized in pathological cases. The invalidity of this argument has been demonstrated in the foregoing chapter. But even if we should be willing—we are definitely not—to concede the truth of psychoanalytic interpretation in those cases in which pathological symptoms have been made to disappear by an interpretation according to Freudian principles, it would not follow that such an interpretation is necessarily right when applied to other facts which cannot, by their very nature, disappear. The identity of nature, of the pathological facts on the one hand and of the other phenomena on the other, is not to be observed by immediate comparison; such a statement results only from the interpretation given to both groups. Since the criterion of disappearance does not and cannot exist in the great majority of normal mental facts, the declaration of identity is a statement of theory, based on the preceding conception of such a thoroughgoing identity.

This conception is not itself precisely of a philosophical nature. Nor is the idea of a basic identity of pathological and normal facts the property of psychoanalysis alone. The statements of psychoanalysis, however, go farther than that. It is declared not only that the phenomena as such are of the same nature and that there exist intermediary states between normality and abnormality, but also that the origin of both is exactly of the same kind. This is not to be deduced simply from the phenomenon as it is given to the observer; it is a conclusion based partly on certain theoretical conceptions which are again closely bound up with the axiomatic philosophy of Freud's system.

We may safely retain the method of free associations—though one does not need it for medical ends, and though the knowledge of normal psychology which it provides may be obtained by other methods too—but one cannot apply the inter-

pretation according to Freudian rules without implicitly accepting the theory and with the theory also the philosophy. Whoever feels unable to adopt the materialistic conception of human
nature and the hedonistic conception of morals preconized or,
at least, presupposed by psychoanalysis will hardly be able with
any consistency to make use of interpretation as demanded by
psychoanalysis.

It is not our intention to criticize the position taken by Maritain or by Adler. They are, after all, outsiders, in a sense, since
they look at the method from the viewpoint of the philosopher
who relies on the statements of the specialist and who, having
no first-hand experience of these things, is ready to believe in
the usefulness of the method since he is told of such magnificent
results. But all this is no justification of the theory, even in its
psychological aspect. Not even the personal experience of the
patient has any importance; he least of all is capable of telling
us what really helped him and whether the same success could
not have been obtained by other methods too.

We know of but few psychologists or psychiatrists who, while
rejecting absolutely the theory and its philosophy, nevertheless
apply the method. Some who apparently have adopted such a
procedure have in truth modified the method so far that it is
no longer that of true Freudian psychoanalysis. These so-called
analysts are not recognized as such by the "orthodox" Freudian
school. Some of them have not been aware of the philosophical
implications, and they therefore felt justified in using the
method. Others of them were not capable of discerning the
basic contradiction of the philosophy they themselves professed
and the one they inadvertently adopted when they began to
apply psychoanalysis. It is a misfortune that so few of these
psychologists have a sufficient training in philosophy and that
the philosophers mostly have no experience in practical psychology. Those of the first group feel that they may go on preserving their personal philosophy even if it is at variance with
that of psychoanalysis, and those of the second group believe

that one might retain unaltered the psychology and give to it a different philosophical foundation. The reason why such very odd ideas arose at all is that modern man has forgotten one fact: that there is no psychology without a philosophy and that every psychology among the many existing to-day owes its peculiarities precisely to its philosophical background.*

There are, of course, methods in psychology which may be used independently of the philosophy their proponents cherish. One can study behavior without adopting the peculiar philosophy of the behaviorist. The very moment, however, the student of behavior passes from mere description of reactions in certain conditions to statements on the nature of mind and to other generalizations, for instance, declaring behavior analysis to be the only legitimate method of psychological inquiry, he has left the field of empiricism and taken his stand with a definite philosophy. It is exactly the same with psychoanalysis. As long as we merely adopt the simple method of free associations we take no obligations in regard to any particular philosophy. But if we proceed to interpret the data supplied by the associations according to the notions of psychoanalysis, we are not only close to accepting the whole theory and its philosophy: we have already accepted both; interpretation cannot be done without looking at things from the peculiar viewpoint of psychoanalysis. The notion of psychoanalysis being compatible with any other philosophy besides the crudest materialism arose probably from the fact that the defenders of this thesis believe that the psychoanalytic method meant only free association and that they overlooked the basic importance of interpretation.

---

* Dr. Thomas V. Moore lays great stress on the philosophical approach to empirical psychology and on the definite influence of philosophy on psychological theories; cf. his new work: *Cognitive Psychology*, Philadelphia, 1939. He writes in the preface: "The tendency to avoid philosophical issues is unsatisfactory to a serious student of psychology. And so the present text frankly faces metaphysical problems."

CHAPTER IX

Psychoanalysis and Ethnology

THE statements of psychoanalysis on ethnology, the early history of mankind, comparative sociology, and so on, are rejected by the great majority of scholars possessing any competence in those fields. Freud's ideas on social evolution at first attracted the attention of students of history and ethnology; but they soon ceased to be seriously considered, because they were based on arbitrary assumptions and because they referred to the ideas of certain authors who did not enjoy the respect of their colleagues. It is noteworthy that Freud never thought it necessary to correct his statements if they happened to be disproved by the discoveries of the special sciences he was referring to. He never took account of the fact that the authorities on which he relied were in truth no authorities at all. Criticism from authorities in ethnology, comparative sociology, and early history destroyed much of the evidence he had used but failed to trouble him. For instance, the later editions of his book *Totem and Taboo* mention none of the newer discoveries and retain the references quoted in the first edition, though the alleged facts have been shown to be no facts at all but either mistaken interpretations or mere speculation without any actual background. This way of procedure is surely not the one scholars are accustomed to follow. In his last work, *Moses and Monotheism*, Freud refers, for the first time so far as we know, to those criticisms. He answers them in a very curious manner which throws a rather interesting light on his scientific mentality. He is aware, he states, that the authorities quoted by him are much criticized and that their assertions are held in little esteem by others. He does not feel capable of forming a judgment himself, not having specialized in these fields. But he is going to continue to rely on those authors, because their ideas and the conclusions derived from them fit in with the conceptions of psychoanalysis.

We have pointed out in a previous chapter the various logical circles, the frequency of the logical fallacy of *petitio principii* (begging the question) in Freud's system. We discover now a new and striking instance of this unfortunate habit. The data employed by Freud and his pupils, referring to ethnology and allied sciences, are supposed to strengthen the psychoanalytical thesis by showing that this thesis is in accordance with facts observed by scholars altogether independent of psychoanalysis. But the facts quoted by the psychoanalysts are chosen by a unique process of selection. They are not chosen because they are more conclusively proved than others, nor because they are reported by scholars of universally accepted fame, but because they fit in with the ideas of psychoanalysis. If there ever was a *petitio principii* here is an example of it.

Such a procedure strips psychoanalysis, at least as an explanation of ethnological and sociological facts, of the dignity of an objective science. It reveals itself to be more of a creed than of a science. It is believed to be true *a priori*; therefore it feels entitled to use this peculiar method of selecting evidence. Such a method could not but create very marked contradictions between psychoanalytical statements on the one hand and those of the other sciences mentioned above, on the other. With these contradictions we shall deal presently, though in reporting on them we cannot but confess our incompetence. We too have to rely on the statements made by the leading authorities and are unable to base our remarks on any first-hand knowledge.

Common sense and prudence warn us that in such a case one cannot do better than to rely on the generally recognized authorities and to side with the opinion held by the most renowned scholars of one's day. It is quite true that even the greatest scholar might be mistaken and that his views may become obsolete and may be proved to be wrong even in a very short span of time. This peril of being misled by opinions of only a temporary validity is, however, not to be feared as long as we deal with plain facts. If we are told that Freud's idea of totemism as a necessary and general stage of social development is wrong because there are many peoples in whose history no trace of totemism is to be found, we may rely on this statement, even if we should feel that the explanation given of this custom is insufficient. It is not the explanation with which we are concerned, but the fact.

Before, however, entering into a discussion of the particular views of Freud and his school on ethnology and the early history of mankind, we have to examine the principle which enables these authors to deal with the matters in question. Hardly one of them is an ethnologist or a student *ex professo* of prehistoric data. They are, nearly all of them, physicians and psychologists. What were the reasons why Freud felt entitled to form an opinion on ethnological and sociological and historical processes and to make use of the findings of these sciences for his own ends?

In trying to answer this question we come across a peculiar principle. Psychoanalysis is perhaps not alone in acknowledging this principle; but it has hardly ever been put to such an extensive use and it has never been credited with such a general and practical importance as by the followers of Freud. The principle may be stated best as G. C. Jung once did: having lifted the veil from the individual soul, we are enabled to understand the conditions ruling over the fields of history and sociology. Or in other words: it is held that the very same laws believed to be valid in individual psychology govern the evolution of mankind throughout the ages. This principle has to be examined closely. We have to inquire into the *quaestio iuris* before entering into a discussion of the *quaestio facti*.

As we have remarked above, this principle is not the exclusive property of psychoanalysis. It underlies indeed such notions as psychology of the masses, psychology of races or of nations, psychology of certain social groups. The term "psychology of races or nations" is not without a certain equivocation. It is a quite legitimate notion if it implies only the idea that the psychological make-up of individuals depends, in its particular properties, partly on the individual's belonging to this or that nation or race. There is no doubt that cultural factors, historical conditions, tradition and custom fashion, up to a certain degree, the individual mind. It is asserted—and we have no reason for investigating this assertion here—that the inherited racial type determines individual mentality to a great degree. As long as this term "racial psychology" means nothing but the study of the factors influencing the individual mind, it is a legitimate notion. Its rights become doubtful as soon as the idea of a "racial soul" is introduced.

The same remarks apply to the concepts of mass psychology or of psychology of groups and of classes. As long as these names are intended to signify the peculiarities of an individual belonging to these classes or groups, or being involved in a mass, we deal with a true and legitimate problem of psychology. If, however, the idea is that a mass of people is animated by a mass-soul, or that a group of human beings possesses a group-soul, this idea becomes a pure mythology. One may speak, metaphorically, of a mass-soul, to express the fact that a mass seems to behave as if it were animated by one uniform will or as if it felt in a uniform way; one may use the same metaphor for describing the unity of action and of reaction shown by a social class. But one must never forget that one is using merely a metaphorical expression and not the adequate name of some reality.

The study of the historical development of these notions would not be devoid of interest, though to indulge in such an inquiry would doubtless lead us too far away from our main topic. Some few words, however, may be permissible. It seems that the notion of a group-soul—to use this most general term—goes back to antiquity, at least to Plato and to Aristotle. Those two thinkers conceived of the history of nations or states as being analogous to that of human life, having a period of child-hood and of youth, leading up to maturity and being followed by the decay of old age. To the Greek philosophers, however, this was but an analogy. Aristotle indeed thought of the state somewhat as a living being, of which the single citizens and officers were in a way the organs. He saw the state as the whole of which the individuals are the parts; and he stated, as one knows, the principle that the whole is prior to the parts. But it is doubtful whether the master of Stageira would have con-sented to the idea that this social organism is gifted with a soul, a substantial form of its own.*

The idea of a soul living, as it were, in the body of a nation, a race or a group is incompatible with the principles of any realistic philosophy. It is difficult to imagine what kind of being such a group-soul might be, unless its conception is based on a pure and even an exaggerated Platonism. In that event, the "idea" of the state might indeed be conceived as existing really in a "supercelestial place"; this idea is, however, not the idea of one definite state, not of Athens, or Sparta, or England, or France, but of the state in general, and every concrete state would owe its existence and its being to "participation" in this general idea. Individual state-souls, or for that matter, group-souls are not to be thought of in a truly Platonic philosophy.

The notion of a group-soul has evidently another origin. It is the child of a mentality which has been tremendously impressed by the fact of life and the fact of order in reality. Both appear, to this kind of mentality, as equally mysterious and, perhaps because of this, as closely related. The Romantic mind easily conceives of reality as the manifestation of an all-comprising vitality. Romanticism has always shown a very definite prefer-ence for pantheistic notions. One might detect in this attitude

* Such a notion seems incompatible with the principle of matter and form the union of which conditions, for Aristotle and his followers, the real, exist-ing being. It is impossible to imagine the matter which was to be informed by the form of a group-soul.

again some remnant of certain Platonic ideas which have appealed strongly to Romantic minds of all centuries.* It is a mistake to restrict Romanticism to a short period of the nineteenth century; there have been spells of this mentality in earlier times. One is not very far from truth, we think, in speaking of a definitely Romantic trend in the twelfth century. It is not because, under the influence of the pictures drawn by the Romantic artists, or of our own Romantic interpretation of Malory's tale, of the lays and *chansons* of the *troubadours*, of the many stories we have heard of knights and knighthood we interject, as it were, into these times of long ago a color of Romance they in fact did not possess. There is a good deal of what we have become accustomed to call Romantic in the mentality of the twelfth century. The ideas those times had of love as mirrored by the poets and by the quaint treatise on love the Chaplain Andreas left to posterity, the idea of honor and of duty laid on the true knight, the spirit of the crusades and the pilgrims—all these various manifestation of the "spirit of the age" have something which reminds the student decidedly of Romanticism. It fits in with this impression that there lived in the twelfth century several eminent scholars who fell in love with the idea of a world-soul, *anima mundi.*

It matters little that some of these scholars, probably less to safeguard their orthodoxy, but out of this orthodoxy's naiveté, identified the *anima mundi* with the Holy Ghost. The important thing is that this notion could be conceived of at all, that the school of Chartres—where, for that matter, an equally Romantic Pythagoreanism was the philosophical fashion—propagated this idea and that the clear-sighted, oversharp intellect that was Abelard's fell prey to it. But Abelard, logician though he was, had a definitely Romantic strain in his personality; by

* Some similarities of Romantic and psychoanalytic mentality have been pointed out by two authors whose articles we unhappily could not study in the original. T. A. Passmore, *Psychoanalysis and Esthetics,* Austral. J. of Psychol. a. Philos., 1936, *14,* 127, and T. Anderson, *Psychoanalysis and Romanticism,* ibid., 210.

this we do not mean to allude to the famous tragedy of his love and his marriage with Heloise and their separation, but to the philosophy of the famous teacher. His blind trust in logic as a key to reality led him into what cannot be better described than as intellectual adventures, not less adventurous than the achievements of Tristan or Launcelot of which his contemporaries told such moving tales.

The idea of a world-soul came to these medieval scholars from Plato. The little they knew of Plato's writings by personal study they obtained from a translation and a commentary of the *Timaeus* by Chalcidius. This side of Platonism had, however, survived in the Neo-Platonic tradition, handed down to the scholars of the twelfth century by many writers, by Dionysius the Pseudo-Areopagite, whom they read in the translation of Scotus Eriugena, in passages taken from Maximus the Confessor which the same author had included in his work and which itself was thoroughly imbued by the spirit of Neo-Platonism, and by certain other intermediaries. Thus we come back to Plato as the father of this curious notion of a world-soul. From a world-soul there is but one step to the conception of souls animating smaller "wholes." Whatever appeared to be an organic whole, something ruled by intrinsic laws and showing a kind of spontaneity, easily came to be thought of as being animated in some way.

State and society have always made such an impression on the inquisitive mind. In confirmation of this, one has only to recall the many expressions used in politics and in sociology which in truth are metaphors taken from life. A state has, in its state-departments, its "organs"; a complicated "organization" is necessary to run the state and to assure stability to economic life; the capital is the "heart" of the state; the supreme power is its "head"; and so on. True, these are all metaphorical expressions, based on certain, often superficial, similarities; but they have to correspond to some general conviction, to a generally received impression, to become elements of common language.

A metaphor becomes intelligible and, therefore, acceptable to the average mind only if it refers to some notion this mind understands. Similarities, as such, do not justify more than a mere metaphorical use of certain names. But the human mind is easily led to take for reality what in fact is but a name for some slight similarity. The general acceptance which these expressions received is no justification for their being taken as a true description of realities. Science has to be careful when using the expressions of common language. Such expressions reveal sometimes an unexpected and even a deep truth; but they may just as easily veil some truth or distort it so much that it becomes altogether unrecognizable. In the history of the human mind there are but few ideas which are really quite new. Generally "new" ideas are old ones, appearing in a new guise. The student of history, be it the history of philosophy or of political theory or of any other side of the endeavors of human reason, wonders sometimes at the persistence of some particular set of ideas, and at their reappearance after having apparently been forgotten and discarded as obsolete for a long time. Platonism is such a complex of ideas; its influence will probably never cease. The important thing is to discern the truth in it and to beware of its fallacies. Every period of Romanticism sets in motion a new wave of Platonic conceptions.

Freud did not know anything either of Plato or of the Romanticism of past ages. He did not even know much about the ideas current at his time. He probably never cared to find out what history and sociology taught. But he belonged (cf. chap. XII) to a time and to a society of intense intellectual interests. He read a good deal, and he could not help imbibing the ideas which were discussed around him. During his lifetime, in the very years when he was building up the edifice of his theory, mass-psychology became a topic of investigation. Scipio Sighele wrote his *Psychology of Masses and of Riots*, Gustave LeBon published a work on the *Psychology of Masses* and Wilhelm Wundt made known his ideas on the *Psychology of Peoples* in three imposing volumes. Those psychologists and sociologists, however, were neither the first nor the only, nor perhaps even the most influential, authors in this field.

There was, for instance, Karl Schaeffle who tried to base a systematic and scientific sociology on the notion of the state as a living organism. There were the conceptions of the soul of a people as they had been proposed by the Romantic school of historians of the law, like Savigny, and by others who wanted to inquire into the peculiar properties of states and nations. It was the very age which saw the birth or, at least, the spread of nationalism, the age of Gobineau and his followers, the age of the nationalistic conflicts in the old Austrian monarchy, of the growth of nationalistic feeling, in spite of strong international tendencies attempting to counterbalance these forces.

The temptation to employ, without further criticism, the idea of a group-soul was doubtless very strong. The idea was received by many and taken for granted. Few indeed cared to penetrate deeper into the matter and to question the legitimacy of this popular notion. One can hardly reproach Freud for having followed the lead of many others at this time. But one cannot well spare him the reproach of having persisted in his ideas even after they had become more or less doubtful, especially after a critical attitude arose among the psychologists in regard to the notion of a group-soul.

But let us, for a moment, suppose this idea to be a true picture of reality. Are we compelled, by presuming a group-soul to exist, to accept the particular view as stated in the words of Jung which were quoted above? Is there any reason for assuming *a priori* an identity of the psychology of individuals with that of groups? Or would one have to ask first whether there is any proof of such an identity?

If a group-soul exists at all, it might of course function according to the same laws which govern the life of the individual soul. But whether this is so or not needs to be established by a special investigation. It cannot be stated as an axiom. Freud, however, treated this idea as if it were an axiom, self-evident and beyond all doubt, needing no proof. It is definitely not. Freud, therefore, is guilty of having neglected a task which was presented to him by his own theory; before applying his psychological conceptions to sociology, to ethnology, to history and the rest, he ought to have asked whether he had really established the existence of a group-soul functioning by the same laws as the individual soul to which his conceptions could be applied. A criticism of psychoanalysis on this point, the application made to social and historical facts, has to be divided into two parts.

We must first inquire into the legitimacy of the notion of a group-soul, and it will be shown that this notion has no true meaning, that such a soul not only does not but cannot exist.

Secondly, we shall have to ask whether, positing this impossible notion as justified, psychoanalysis proceeds with the requisite caution and objectivity in applying its principles to the phenomena of society and of history. In doing this, we shall have to investigate, first, the conception of an identity of the group-soul and the individual soul; this question is sensible, though the group-soul is no reality, because it had been thought of as such by Freud and is still so treated by his school. Secondly, we shall have to examine the evidence alleged by Freud and his pupils.

The whole construction of psychoanalysis, insofar as it is concerned with supra-individual phenomena, loses its meaning, once the existence of a group-soul is shown to be impossible. The demonstration of this impossibility rests on two different arguments. The notion of a group-soul is contradictory in itself; and it is in plain contradiction to the principles of sound philosophy. We put this argument second, because it will carry conviction only to those who know and accept this philosophy.

When the psychoanalysts speak of a soul as belonging to some group they probably have not in mind anything like a substantial soul. For the notion of a substantial soul they will not accept; it is to them a pure mythology, something smacking of religion, and they tell us—*vide* the next chapter—religion is but a particular kind of neurosis, an "illusion," as Freud himself called it, and not to be taken seriously. Thoroughly materialistic, the psychoanalysts do not know what to do with a substantial and spiritual soul. Their soul is merely a mind, a complex of mental states, conscious and unconscious ones, and the effect of a functioning brain. Neither Freud nor any of his pupils has ever developed a clear theory of the mind's nature; but we have seen that their way of conceiving of the mind cannot, by the principles of their theory, be other than that of pure materialism; that is, they cannot conceive the mind apart from the concrete material organ—the brain—of whose functioning the mind is an effect.

This basic position becomes, however, the first great difficulty in attributing to a group something like a mind. For a group has no material organ of which this mind might be the effect. There is no doubt that the idea of a group-soul is, to Freud, not an analogy, not a metaphorical expression or a mere illustration. It is taken quite literally. It is enough to examine his last work, *Moses and Monotheism*, to become aware of this fact. We are told that the group-mind behaves exactly as does an individual mind. Each of them possesses an "unconscious." We hear of repression of experiences made by the whole group, of these repressed experiences causing a feeling of guilt in a whole people or having other consequences. Tradition is not only likened to memory but identified with it. And so on.

The group-mind, as conceived by Freud, is a mind exactly like that of the individual, obeying the same laws, gifted with the same powers, producing the same phenomena. *But it lacks an organ.* Where does this mind reside? How does it manage to keep alive and continue to function? And what becomes of it when the group is dissolved? These are questions for the answers to which one will look in vain in psychoanalytical writings, but questions which have to be answered if the notion of a group-mind or a group-soul is to be credited with any meaning at all.

We may mention incidentally that the same difficulties beset C. G. Jung's conception of a "collective unconscious." Jung's notion is perhaps still less clear than that of the Freudian group-mind.

Perhaps this objection will be answered by declaring that the group-mind is the sum-total of all the individual minds of which the group is composed. This can be the case only in regard to functions and contents which are common to all members of the group. The group-mind has to be a unit if it is to be anything. It cannot contain things which may have a meaning for part of the members and be meaningless for the rest.

If a human mass is credited with a mass-soul, this soul can have as contents only those facts, and as its functions only those functions, which become effective in the mass. It has been pointed out by psychologists dealing with "mass-psychology" that the mental level shows, in the mass, a marked depression: intellectuality disappears; clear judgment ceases to exist; objectivity there is none; emotions and instincts, passion and primitive urges are said to rule the behavior of masses; deprived of judgment the masses become "suggestible" and apt to be led by anyone who knows how to make an impression. Solon is said to have stated that every individual citizen of Athens was a clever fox, but that in an assembly he became one of a flock of sheep. The higher a mental operation is, the more it becomes individualized and the more different from the same kind of operation in another individual. Full-grown and normal people differ very much from each other. Idiots and demented patients are very much the same.

What applies to the mentality of crowds, formed occasionally and dissolving quickly, must be true also of more stable groups. The group-soul cannot know of other things or contain other things than those which are common to all members, therefore the least differentiated, the most commonplace, the most primitive things. But this inevitable consequence seems to contradict the idea of repression taking place in the group-mind. For repression to exist, it is necessary that a conflict be established between the higher levels of the mind and the primitive levels. But when the primitive contents are the only ones of which the mass-mentality can possibly be aware, whence come the repressing forces?

We shall not go on laboring the intrinsic difficulties of this conception. Its unacceptability and its self-contradiction must obviously be evident to anyone who really examines it objectively. It is noteworthy that the notion of a group-soul, be it of nations, of races, of classes or of any group, is maintained mostly by what has been called "emotional thinking." At least, we might discover that statements of this kind are usually associated with very intense emotions: pride because of the superiority of the race; hatred because of the social position of the class; a strong antagonism, political and economic, because of competition and prestige.*

Occasionally even a psychoanalyst feels troubled by the inner improbabilities of this notion,† but it is difficult to see how it could ever be given up; it refers to points so vital that to abandon them without destroying the system is practically impossible. The majority of psychoanalysts obviously believe the group-soul to be a reality. Freud himself leaves no doubt that he is of the same opinion, especially in those parts of his last work where he deals with tradition, with historical facts which are "repressed" by a whole tribe or nation and therefore exercise

* For a critique of the notion of group-mind or group-soul see any leading sociologist or social psychologist. We might mention, for instance, among the students of social psychology, J. F. Brown, *Psychology and the Social Order,* New York, 1936, which we choose because the author holds principles very different from ours; and among the ethnologists A. A. Goldenweiser, *Early Civilization,* New York, 1922. For the history of this idea and its relations to the Romantic School, cf. Rothacker, *Einleitung in die Geisteswessenschaften,* Leipzig, 1922. Especially instructive are the *Essais de sociologie* by G. Gurvitch, Paris, 1938.

† F. Alexander, *Psychoanalysis and Social Disorganization,* Amer. Journ. Sociol., 1937, 42, 781-813.

in the unconscious of this group, throughout the generations, the same kind of influence which is ascribed to the unconscious in an individual mind. Freud is convinced that there is no essential difference between the way this hypothetical group-mind functions and the operations of the individual mind. The laws of the one are the laws of the other. Individual analysis thus becomes an instrument for historical, prehistorical, and cultural studies. Ethnological facts may be used, without any modification or interpretation, to explain facts of individual psychology.

This is amazing enough and might give rise to serious objections. It becomes still more amazing when we consider the way in which the psychoanalysts, and Freud himself, deal with ethnological data. Those findings of ethnology and comparative sociology which do not fit in with the psychoanalytic conceptions are simply discarded; those which promise some confirmation of Freudian views or which lend themselves to an interpretation in accord with psychoanalytic principles are accepted without reserve, without asking whether they be really reliable, facts or more speculations, fantastic vagaries of some ingenious imagination or statements based on solid observation. This, so far as we can discover, is the common opinion of all the leading authors in these fields. We shall quote two of them who may be safely considered as voicing the common judgment.

Freud starts with accepting the Darwin-Atkinson idea of the social structure of primitive mankind, writes A. L. Kroeber.* It is supposed that there were small communities, each headed by one man, and consisting of several females and immature individuals, the males being driven away when they became of age. This is a mere hypothesis, a mere "guess that the organization of men resembled that of the gorilla rather than that of trooping monkeys." Serious ethnologists treat it as totally unproven. But it is treated by the psychoanalysts as if no doubt could be possible, as if nothing were surer than that this kind of primitive

---

* *Totem and Taboo:* An Ethnological Psychoanalysis, Amer. Anthrop., 1920, 22, 48.

organization existed everywhere. A second basic assumption of Freud is that blood sacrifice played a central rôle in the development of primitive culture and that this custom was closely associated to totemism. The first statement, taken from the writings of Robertson Smith, is true, according to Kroeber, only of certain Mediterranean peoples and only for the last two thousand years B.C. Blood sacrifice cannot be considered as a normal element of the development of culture. The relation of blood sacrifice to totemism is "at the least problematical." Freud considers totem-abstinence and exogamy as the main and fundamental prohibitions of totemism; this is not the case. Again, the idea of the sons killing and devouring the father is mere conjecture; but the psychoanalysts argue as if no fact of ethnology were more certainly established. These are but some of the objections listed by Kroeber against Freud's ideas.

A. A. Goldenweiser* remarks that there are several minor objections against Freud's conception of totemism "which in themselves negate the possibility of the author's conception." But there are other reasons too for declaring the whole Freudian theory of primitive civilization and of the development of culture, of totemism and of the relations between the head of the tribe and his sons to be pure vagaries. The totemistic sacrifice which plays such a rôle in the argumentations of Freud is practically unknown. The "instances" of Robertson Smith on which Freud relies are all based on reconstructed material. The use made by them in psychoanalysis is characterized by Goldenweiser as a "highly arbitrary procedure on the part of Freud." The original tribe as pictured by Freud is a figment; the gerontocracy of the Melanesians, for which Freud relies on Rivers, is another purely speculative conception. The extent of cannibalism in primitive culture has been much exaggerated; the custom of devouring one's relatives exists nowhere, and the idea that sons killed and devoured their father is ludicrous.

The judgments I have quoted—and they are representative of

* *Early Civilization,* New York, 1922, p. 395ff.

serious ethnological opinion—are sufficient to show on what slender evidence are based all the ethnological analogies, so freely used by the psychoanalysts. The entire foundation on which Freud had erected the complicated edifice of his ethnological theories is fictitious. Freud's two main authorities are called, the one a dilettante—Frazer—the other a man addicted to speculations—Robertson Smith—by two authorities. But the psychoanalysts have enthusiastically taken up these ideas of their master. Many of their articles and books contain detailed analyses and "explanations" of ethnological data. There would be no reason for us to comment on these things if the Freudian school had merely proposed some theory of ethnological development; it would then be the task of the ethnologists to discuss these ideas and to prove their emptiness and this indeed they have done very convincingly. But Freud and his pupils have referred to their ethnological "discoveries" as further confirmations of their psychological theory. Because the psychological factors they believed they discovered in the individual mind offered an explanation of "facts" of ethnology, they felt justified in the use of the former and sure of understanding the latter. In the parallels they established, they saw mutual reinforcements of both their positions; ethnological interpretation was corroborated by psychology, psychology received the approval of ethnology.

As no unprejudiced observer can fail to notice, all this rests on a stupendous fallacy, a perfect vicious circle. The psychoanalysts really discovered, in the ethnological data they studied, only what they had first put there. They thus became guilty of the same habit which has been theirs and their masters from the very beginning. There might be some excuse for this, since examining one's own axioms is something of which only the truly critical and, to certain degree, the philosophical mind is capable. But in the case of "ethnological psychoanalysis," to use Kroeber's phrase, something more took place. Freud and his school became guilty of a serious and unpardonable neglect of some of the primary duties of the scholar. Freud may be forgiven for believing blindly in the statements of Robertson Smith and others when he found that they fitted so nicely into his theory. He had no means of making sure whether these statements were reliable or not. He could not help believing them since he was, of course, convinced that he had discovered the truth about the individual mind. He could have, perhaps he ought to have, inquired into the matter, sought the advice of specialists, since he was outside his own field. He did not do so, and there may have been personal reasons for his not doing so. But it is a little startling to observe how he reacted when he was told of the criticism his conception met on the part of those men who had been trained, as he had not been trained, to estimate the value and reliability of ethnological data.

Soon after the first German edition of *Totem and Taboo* had been published, the ethnologists protested against Freud's interpretations. They did not, of course, discuss Freud's psychological ideas which, they felt, were outside the field of their competence. They were even ready to take psychoanalytic conceptions seriously, provided these were based on reliable ethnological evidence. But the ethnological data on which Freud relied were not of a kind, they stated, to arouse confidence. The assumptions from which Freud started were untenable. His idea of the Oedipus-legend as a common possession of mythology was shown to be quite mistaken, his notions on totemism were wrong, and so forth.

All this could not escape Freud's attention, and it did not in truth escape it. He himself tells us that he is fully aware of all the objections and that the authorities his argumentation rests on are more than questionable. He makes this confession in so many words in his last book, *Moses and Monotheism*. But he also says that these circumstances were not sufficient to make him abandon his position or to look for other authorities, because those he had come to know previously sufficed for his desires. But they do not suffice for the exigencies of science. No scientist ever dared to assume such a position. No scholar, having been shown the unreliability of his authorities, has ever persisted in using them. This is not the way of the scholar, but the way of the fanatic.

Totem and Taboo was republished, several editions were brought out, translations in other languages appeared. But not one line was altered. It is possible that Freud did not want to retract and that he was unwilling to face a situation which in truth threatened his whole work. But we cannot understand how so many other writers continued lustily to expatiate on Freud's ethnological conception. Even if they admired him, even if they reverenced in him the initiator of a new era in psychology, they could hardly have taken him seriously as an ethnologist. They should have seen that they were pursuing ethnological chimeras, when they described—as if they had been there—how primitive tribes in prehistoric ages behaved, when they explained how man came to develop ideas on religion or to invent a way to produce fire by turning one stick of wood in another. (Man made this invention, we are told, because of his needing a sexual symbol.)

I repeat: this is not the conduct of scholars groping in the dusk of ignorance and half-knowledge for truth; this is the behavior of people who—one is tempted to say—feel that they have received a revelation of the absolute, the definite truth; of people who adopt the ways of the scholar, but who in truth feel like—prophets. We are quite willing to let them prophesy, as long as they know what they are doing and do not deceive others. But we have to expose them when, to a world anxious for truth, they offer prophecies clad in the garment of science. Some years ago, soon after the last World-War, we came across a little book by an author named Bry; the book was on "Pseudo-religions." One of the pseudo-religions listed was psychoanalysis. This man had seen more truly than many a well-trained psychologist.

Things standing as they do, it is needless to detail the various ideas of psychoanalysts on society, on culture, on history. They are, all of them, based on an all too slender evidence and, at the same time, on quite unacceptable propositions. The reason why the propositions are unacceptable is not that the average mind, fettered by the "repressed" demons of the unconscious, recoils from the truth about itself. They are unacceptable simply because they are wrong, because they are fantastic conclusions drawn from equally fantastic premises. The psychoanalysts boast of their theory being science; they even want us to believe that theirs is the only truly scientific psychology existing. But they do not obey the most elementary laws which every science and every scientist has to observe. The history of "ethnological psychoanalysis" proves better than anything else that psychoanalysis is not a science, but a creed.

Because it is a creed it is intolerant of other creeds. The more a conviction of this type develops into a sectarian attitude the less tolerant it becomes in general. The attitude of psychoanalysis in regard to religion is a striking illustration. The statements of the analysts on religion are, of course, as unreliable and based on as worthless premises as the rest of their ethnological speculations. It is not because of the strength of their arguments, but only because of the importance of the subject that a short chapter will be dedicated to this matter a little further on in this book.

CHAPTER X

Psychoanalysis and Education

PSYCHOANALYSTS talk much of education. There is, or was, a special journal for psychoanalytic education. Everywhere in pedagogical science the influence of Freudian ideas has been felt. It is inevitable that medical psychology should arrive at the making of definite statements on education. This is not due only to the natural "imperialism" of all kinds of sciences, though they all try, following an immanent law of the human mind, to extend their realm as far as possible. Physics and chemistry aspire to explain the phenomena of life, biology claims to be capable of explaining the operations of the mind, psychology to be considered as the basis of esthetics or of sociology and so on. But the special extension of psychoanalysis we are now considering was pretty well inevitable. When it had developed so far that it seemed not only to supply a theory of certain pathological phenomena but to unveil the very essence of human mentality, it could not but apply its principles to education. This was the more inevitable, since psychoanalysis had discovered—and this is one of the true advances which psychology owes to Freud—that the causes of many an undesirable development of character and also of many more or less disturbing abnormal symptoms were to be found in factors which had influenced the child and which, had one but known of them, could have been counterbalanced by reasonable education or even deprived of all harmfulness by applying the right methods of education. Psychoanalysis, or medical psychology in general, therefore pointed out certain dangers involved in education. This branch of medical activity soon found itself related to character-education in the same manner as bodily medicine was related to the prevention of malformations or to the safeguarding of the healthy development of the child's body. Insofar as psychoanalysis attempted to point out to the educators these dangers and to tell them how to avoid these pitfalls, it did but obey a necessary law. If the general statements of psychoanalysis were to any extent true, nothing could be said against their being applied to education. Since, however, we have every reason for disbelieving the principles and for rejecting the conclusions drawn therefrom by Freud we cannot feel that education will gain greatly by listening to the teachings of the psychoanalysts.

Thus all further discussion of the relations of psychoanalysis and education might seem to be utterly unnecessary. The theory is wrong, it has therefore to be rejected. Education cannot be expected to pay any attention to an essentially mistaken system. To detail every single erroneous idea that psychoanalysts thought well to apply to education would be merely a repetition of matters already discussed in the preceding chapters of this book. But the question we intend to discuss, very briefly, offers some peculiar problems, the elucidation of which is perhaps not beside the point.

First of all, there is the question whether discoveries made on *pathological* cases can properly be applied within the field of normality. This problem is of course wider than that of the relations obtaining between medical psychology and education and it has indeed been raised earlier in this book in its most general bearing. But the question of the title of pathological findings to be made the basis for propositions referring to normality is nowhere as urgent as in regard to education. Pathology has often been the way of approach to problems of normality. The study of diseases has been a powerful means for furthering our understanding of the normal functions of the body. Our knowledge especially of the functions of the nervous system owes much to the study of troubles of the brain; without the clinical and anatomical analysis of brain-troubles we would indeed be still ignorant on many aspects of brain-physiology.

But it does not follow that the same kind of relation will exist between abnormal and normal phenomena *of the mind.* A psychologist who conceives of the nature of mental operations in terms of brain-physiology is naturally inclined to assert the identity of these two sets of problems. We ought not to forget that Freud began his scientific career as a neurologist and that one of his earliest works deals with questions moving, as it were, on the borderline between brain-pathology and psychology, viz. with the speech-troubles caused by brain-lesions.

Moreover, his mentality was, as has been explained at some length above, plainly materialistic. He could not but believe in a basic identity of nervous and mental processes. Thus one understands easily how he came to make definite demands on education to prevent the development of pathological or, at least, abnormal developments of personality.

Prevention is better than cure. But prevention cannot be limited to mere negative prescriptions. Avoidance is not enough; a positive way has to be followed. Medical psychology necessarily came to make certain demands on education, to lay down certain rules to be observed in the interest of what is called today "mental hygiene." We cannot here discuss the general problem of the relations obtaining between pathology and psychology. It is however desirable that educators be aware that there is such a problem and be a little more prudent in accepting the statements of pathology. The least that can be expected is that the science of education should inquire into the legitimacy of these statements of the pathologists before adopting them as principles of its own activity.

As long as medical psychology limits its educational activity to proposing certain methods for avoiding undesirable development, or even to proposing methods for furthering desirable development, no great harm will ensue. The situation becomes more serious when the student of pathology proceeds to suggest his method, which is adapted to the study and the treatment of abnormal states, as a means to be employed in the education of normal children. But that is what psychoanalysis does. Freud's pupils not only talk of psychoanalysis of children as a means for treating certain nervous states and certain neurotic phenomena which sometimes occur in children; they believe that the very same method might be used also in the education of children who as yet have not shown any sign of abnormality. It has become clear that psychoanalytic method and psychoanalytic philosophy are in truth inseparable. Psychoanalysis in education means, therefore, the introduction of a definite philosophy. Unless education wants to drift into the current of materialism it should beware of all contact with psychoanalysis.

Freudian psychology gives its own peculiar explanation of many phenomena one observes in children. Since it is convinced that in childhood the original instincts still operate in a thinly disguised form, many behavior features in children become, according to psychoanalysis, the simple expression of instinctual longings. Thus, it is believed that the assiduous questioning which is characteristic of a certain period of childhood springs from the desire to know about sexual matters. The question which is really in the mind of a child when he goes on asking why? and whence? is that concerning childbirth and sexual relations. There are doubtless cases, in which, for some reason, a precocious curiosity has been aroused and in which questions may indeed refer ultimately to such matters. Odier has published a case of pathological curiosity in a child where the symptom could be shown to go back to such an interest. But this case too is, after all, one of abnormal behavior and cannot well be allied simply to a normal child's habit of asking questions.

The relation between curiosity in regard to childbirth and in regard to other things might be, for that matter, exactly the opposite. It is quite possible that the general desire of children to understand something of the strange world surrounding them, a desire which leads them to inquire about the cause of this or of that, may extend sometimes, perhaps often, also to the problem of the reason of the child's own existence. The interpretation given by psychoanalysis is acceptable only if the whole theory has been accepted previously. We can arrive at such an interpretation only if we believe in the libido as the one force or the one instinct enabling the human being to become interested in trans-subjective objects and if this libido is identified with sexuality. We have seen that the psychoanalytic conception of infantile sexuality rests on very arbitrary assumptions and that the so-called proofs of it are the outcome of a logical fallacy.

The main idea of psychoanalytic education seems to be the following: there is always the danger of incomplete repression and the further danger of sublimation not developing in a satisfactory manner. If we could be sure that sublimation would proceed automatically and sufficiently, there would be no need of special interference on the part of the educators. But it is not at all certain that sublimation will proceed far enough and be thorough enough to prevent the repressed material from causing some trouble which in later years may become a serious neurotic state. It seems therefore, to the psychoanalyst, better to make conscious the contents which would become repressed. The repression and sublimation will be achieved more successfully at a later age; instead of being forced to repress these things by the influence of environmental factors, education, custom, and so on, and instead of submitting unconsciously and unwillingly —that is, without clear knowledge and without an expressed consent of will—the individual child will be enabled to react against these undesirable and unpermitted instinctual desires consciously, just as it is believed that things develop during psychoanalysis.

Medicine knows of many cases in which the cure is more dangerous than the disease. The surgeon will often decline to operate because he knows that the operation might have effects likely to be more harmful to the patient than the existing trouble. One might well ask whether the risk of making the instinctual desires fully conscious—supposing the Freudian theory to be true—would not be too serious. Or in other words, it is doubtful, even from the viewpoint of the psychoanalyst himself, whether an indiscriminate use of analytical methods and principles in education might not prove too dangerous.

There is, furthermore, no guarantee that the individual in later years will be inclined to react as the psychoanalyst expects and as society and morals have a right to demand. Psychoanalysis is curiously optimistic in regard to the functioning of human nature. It is believed that the mere absence of inhibitions and obstacles will be sufficient to ensure a desirable development. This optimism is possible because psychoanalysis, on the one hand, believes in the determinism of natural forces ruling also over human personality; and because, on the other hand, it sees no reason to restrict the instinctual activity of man as long as no personal inconvenience results. Thus the law of morals is replaced by the principle of reality. The important thing is not to obey some objective, super-individual law, but to find a way to attain as much pleasure as possible at the least possible cost. No need, therefore, to explain that psychoanalysis, as a method of education, is absolutely incompatible with any philosophy of education which considers objective laws of morality.

Another point deserves attention. In discussing psychoanalysis in reference to education, its critics dwell practically always on the influence upon the child's personality. But one has to consider the educators, too. Is there not the danger of the relation between parents and children, between educator and pupils, being disturbed by the former's knowledge of the alleged instinctual forces at work? What does it mean to the parents, this belief that the behavior of their children in general, and especially their behavior toward themselves, depends on libidinous forces and on the development of the so-called Oedipus-situation? I do not mean simply that such an idea will appear shocking to many people, that they will feel that a great deal of the charm of their children's behavior is destroyed by referring it to libido, and that the love they feel for the children and the love these children manifest is not worth very much since it is merely of the rank of instinctual cravings. I do not argue from this very natural reaction, because the psychoanalysts declare this attitude of ours to be that of the unenlightened, of the prejudiced mind, the attitude of people who are still the slaves of their own repressed and unsublimated instincts; and such an argument, therefore, would carry no weight with the psychoanalysts or with people more or less willing to believe what they are told of the wonderful discoveries of this "new psychology." What I have in mind in referring to the effect upon parents and other educators is something quite different.

It is a general effect of medical psychology, of the kind of psychology Nietzsche called "unveiling," that it destroys naturalness in regard to one's own experiences and in regard to the behavior of other people. My thoughts, my feelings, my desires are no longer what they seem to be at first sight and what the unsophisticated mind still believes them to be. What I am conscious of is but the mask or the appearance of something in reality quite different. I think I am interested in science, but in truth I am seeking for satisfaction of libidinous instincts. I feel elated by some noble thought, which in truth only symbolizes some instinctual craving, and so on. It is true that neither my feelings nor my thoughts *need* be altered by this knowledge; but in fact they usually are. Man enjoys his own feelings and ideas only when he can feel sure that they are genuine, that they are neither suggested to him by another nor due to some mysterious transformation of other things.

Genuineness is a true value, and one which plays a great rôle in human life. We dislike things which pretend to be what they are not. We cannot help feeling that an interest which is really not for the object itself but for some other thing, that a sentiment of love which is really not love as we understand it but a transformation of instinctual longing, that a purpose which is directed really toward a goal different from the one which it seems to envision, are of a very inferior value. Even if it were true that all our desires, interests, and sentiments are not what they seem to be, this longing for genuineness would still exist. That it does is a fact psychoanalysis would be at a loss to explain, if this psychology ever took notice of such facts. The idea of seeking truth for truth's sake, which is the very principle of science and which is, of course, also the principle of psychoanalytic research, contradicts in fact the basic assumption of this very psychology. According to the Freudian system such a thing as love of truth cannot exist; it has to be reduced to some instinctual desire and thus loses its genuineness and its value.

The value of genuineness is too obvious to be uprooted from the human mind. No scientific explanation can ever destroy the basic tendencies of human nature. However fully educators may be convinced of the truth of psychoanalytic ideas, they cannot help being disillusioned and disappointed. If they accept those views, they become inevitably deprived of the strongest motive prompting their educational efforts. Psychoanalytic education must degenerate into an impersonal kind of relation between educator and educated, because the reality it professes to deal with is dissolved into mere instinctual elements.

Man may still enjoy the beauty of colors though science may tell him that he does not see colors but reacts only to light-waves. He may go on believing in the values of art even though he is told that he is deceived by appearances. He may continue to feel warm or cold, to see objects and to handle them, in spite of science telling him that reality consists of infra-atomic elements and their movements. Science is not impressive enough to destroy the evidence of the senses. But what we do not touch or see or hear, what is not given immediately to our sense-organization has not a consistency and reliability sufficient for resisting the destructive influence of theories. History teaches us how much the moral attitude of men may suffer when values which had been generally believed in are declared to be merely relative, to depend on cultural and economic conditions, to be not part of reality but due to man's fancy.

The more "scientific" education becomes, the less personal it becomes. Science, in the strict acceptance of the term, does not know of individuals. *Scientia est de universalibus*; the Aristotelian adage is true today as it was so many centuries ago. This does not mean that education ought not to make use of certain discoveries of science; but education can never be itself a science in the strict sense of the term. Psychoanalysis, however, proudly calling itself a science and aspiring to the ideal of an exactness like that to be found in physics, wants education to become truly "applied science"; thus it really abolishes the very essence of education and, accordingly, the true educational attitude in the educator's mind. Psychoanalysis is in fact quite incapable of understanding any truly personal relation. This is the necessary consequence of its basic attitude and its philosophy. The other ego has no real existence in psychoanalysis; it is merely one opportunity more for satisfying instinctual longings. A philosophy as subjectivistic as that of psychoanalysis can never supply a basis for education.

These objections are surely of greater importance than all the many criticisms which have been raised in the name of traditional morality and traditional pedagogics. One cannot overemphasize the fact that psychoanalysis, scientific though it believes itself to be, is infinitely far from reality. One side of reality especially is utterly beyond the grasp of Freudian psychology: the human individual and the human person. But education is of persons or it is nothing at all.

Compared with these basic difficulties created by the peculiar attitude of psychoanalysis all other objections are of minor importance. They are, moreover, so obvious that it is hardly necessary to enlarge on them.

CHAPTER XI

Psychoanalysis and Religion

NATURALISM and materialism are necessarily antagonistic to religion. A mental attitude which introduces transmundane, immaterial factors, which holds a notion like that of a spiritual soul, which believes in revelation, appears to the materialistic mind as unintelligible, strange, and dangerous. Such a mentality is the very opposite of materialism; and as long as religious attitudes exist and remain efficacious in human life, materialism feels its position threatened. The advocates of a "scientific" explanation of reality see in religion either an enemy or, at least, a rudimentary stage of evolution which has to be overcome in order to ensure the definite "progress" of the human race.

Psychoanalysis is profoundly materialistic and cannot hold any other philosophy. Materialism is its very basis. Were the follower of Freud to abandon his materialistic creed he would have to give up being a psychoanalyst. That this is the true state of things has become sufficiently clear in the foregoing discussions. There are some who imagine that they can believe in the truth of religion and the truth of psychoanalysis without becoming guilty of self-contradiction. They imagine this either because they do not know enough of both sides, or because their mind is of a kind to put up with contradictions, or perhaps because they are not critical enough to become aware of them.

Nobody who penetrates the spirit of psychoanalysis and, at the same time, is fully cognizant of the essentials of supernatural faith can believe that these two are compatible. It has been pointed out, both by Catholic and by Protestant authors, that psychoanalysis is basically anti-Christian. There is no way out of this dilemma: one either believes in Christ or in psychoanalysis. Nor have the Freudians doubted this. Religion means to them nothing more than a peculiar manifestation of the human mind, of the same rank as magical practice, totemism or witchcraft. They have even attempted to prove that religion is a product of instinctual forces and of the reaction against them.

Freud spoke of religion as an "illusion." Religious rites are likened to or even considered as identical with obsessional practices. Religion is a neurosis of groups. It is quite unnecessary to go into details. The writings of the psychoanalysts are full of remarks pointing in this direction. There is no doubt of their conviction that religion is a purely psychological fact, that it is unsound and is conditioned by the same factors as condition neurosis in individuals, that it has, for the good of mankind, to be overthrown and to be replaced by the reign of science. That is what Freud hoped for: the "illusion" will be dispelled by the light of reason; science will replace religion in culture and in life; a new blissful age will begin when science reigns supreme.

This is the mentality of a man who was born soon after the middle of the last century, who grew up in the era of materialism, "liberalism," and enthusiastic hopes for the future, and was incapable of delivering himself from the bondage of those impressions going back to his boyhood. We see today that science has failed not because it is not one of the most amazing achievements of man, or because it is incapable of further progress, but because it had been credited with the capacity to accomplish what it never can accomplish. But Freud's optimistic faith in science remained unshaken throughout the more than eight decades of his life. We can understand such an arrested development in him; but it is hard to understand how people of a later generation, who should surely be able to see how things really stand, can still proclaim a creed so clearly obsolete and so clearly defeated as scientism. To persons of this mentality religion is just one fact among other facts in the history of human culture. Nor are they prepared to admit any differences between religions. Freud's last book is a striking illustration of his inability to see even decisive points. Thus he is not aware at all of the enormous differences between Judaeo-Christian monotheism and the pagan idea of a supreme god. His conception of the monotheism of the Jews being due to their acceptance of the religion of Athon, the Egyptian sun-deity, shows that he does not recognize the essentials of true monotheism and also that he did not care to obtain reliable information on things of which he himself could not possibly have expert knowledge.*

Even a superficial acquaintance with psychoanalysis enables anyone to see the enormous gulf separating Christian mentality from that implied in the Freudian conception of man. It is accordingly rather a shock to read in an article of O. Pfister† that the teachings of Jesus in the Gospels show great analogies to the theory of psychoanalysis. But even this author—he is, as it happens, a Protestant clergyman—is compelled to add that there are great dissimilarities. We should say there are. Other Protestant theologians, for instance, Dr. Runestam of the University of Upsala, felt differently; they denounced psychoanalysis as utterly contrary to the spirit of Christianity.

A philosophy which denies free will, ignores the spirituality of the soul, and with shallow materialism, without any attempt at a proof, identifies mental and bodily phenomena, knows of no other end than pleasure, is given to a confused but neverthe-

---

* Freud adopts, in regard to the history of religion, the same method that he followed in regard to ethnology. He simply picks out of the enormous mass of available literature some few works which fit in with his preconceived ideas. Thus he makes great use of a book in which is proposed the hypothesis that Moses was murdered by the Jews. This work has been unanimously rejected by the authorities in this field: but that does not prevent Freud from basing a great part of his reasoning on this very book. His theory is indeed, according to his feelings, in no need of proof; it is rather a proof for the truth of all assertions which fit with it. This is not the procedure of a scientist. The psychoanalysts would do well to consider the obvious fact of Freud's choice of references being so remarkably unlucky. When he chooses an author, he unerringly chances on one who is held in no esteem by the authorities of the science in question.

† *Neutestamentliche Seelsorge und psychoanalytische Therapie,* Imago. Leipzig, 1934, 24, 150.

less obstinate subjectivism, is blind to the true nature of the human person—such a philosophy cannot have even one point in common with Christian thought. It is its perfect opposite. The antagonism existing between the mentality of Freudism on the one hand and the spirit of Christianity on the other is clearly felt by those who believe that religion in the modern world must be supplanted by psychology, that the analyst ought to fill the place of the clergyman, that man will find relief for his moral sufferings and answers to his personal difficulties in the office of the psychoanalyst rather than in the confessional of the Catholic priest. This idea rests on a thorough misunderstanding of religion and of psychoanalysis; indeed it wrongs both of them. There is no similarity, except perhaps a very superficial one, between the confessional and the analyst's office. Confession is a sacrament. This does not mean anything to those modern minds which regard only the psychological factors involved in confession. But even these factors are not comparable. The penitent tells in confession the things he knows, the deeds of which he feels guilty, eventually the difficulties assailing him; all he talks of is "conscious material." Nor does the confessor make any attempt at exploring the unconscious mind. Both hope that good will, deeper knowledge, and, last but not least, God's grace are going to help the penitent to overcome his sinful habits, to avoid relapses, to escape temptation, to make progress on the way of perfection.

Not so the analyst and his patient. To them the motives of which the patient is aware have but little significance. What matters is the unconscious force behind them. Neither party relies on good will, because this will is but an epiphenomenon and what is real is hidden in the depths of the unconscious. They do not refer a feeling of guilt to an infraction of an objective moral law and the rejection of a moral value, but to some constellation of instinctual drives, to the conflict between the superego and the id, and so forth. The analyst can never take the place of the priest. The priest's work has to be done by the priest alone or not at all.*

There is no need to tax the patience of the reader by reporting the ideas which the psychoanalysts have thought fit to propose in regard to religion. They are indeed mostly talking about a matter of which they have but a slight and superficial knowledge. Moreover, in this regard they rely largely on their ethnological conceptions, which we have seen to be far from trustworthy. Their conclusions in relation to religious practices, to rites, to the psychology of faith, and such matters, are therefore hardly to be taken seriously. Many of these ideas are definitely ludicrous and bespeak an incredible ignorance.

One question, however, must be faced. Why do the psychoanalysts feel such a remarkable interest in religion? There are more works and articles in psychoanalytic literature dealing with problems related directly or indirectly to religion than one would suspect. It is as if the psychoanalytic mind suffered a curious obsession and were incapable of freeing itself. Religion has played indeed an enormous rôle in history, and it continues to influence the general attitude of mankind more than science does. Science as such has hardly any influence; it is not science itself but the popular belief in science that has contributed so much to forming the mentality of today. Now the psychoanalysts do not inquire into the reasons why man came to believe in science in an exaggerated way. They take it for granted that one has to believe in science, but they try to show that every other belief, especially in the supernatural, is to be explained by psychological reasons. Their attitude is doubtless biased by their own belief in science. They are addicted to "scientism." They fervently believe in science as the panacea by which to save mankind and raise it to a higher level.

This attitude has certain roots in the history of the last sixty or a hundred years. We shall say some few words on this phe-

---

* For some further remarks on these questions, cf. my article: "Confessor and Alienist," *The Ecclesiastical Review*, 1938, 99, 401.

nomenon in the next chapter. But the phenomenon does not explain the curious fascination which religion and its allied problems apparently exercise over the psychoanalytic mind. The rôle played by religion is not sufficient for this. There must be some factor more directly connected with psychoanalysis and with the present situation of civilization in general. To see clearly on this point is the more desirable because we may hope thus to reach some further insight into the nature of Freudian psychology, or rather Freudian anthropology, and accordingly to define more clearly the policy to be observed by the Catholic, in regard to psychoanalysis.

Whoever conscientiously examines psychoanalysis and considers the facts supplied by this psychology as to its own nature, can arrive at but one conclusion. This conclusion may be stated briefly thus: psychoanalysis is a heresy. This statement may seem surprising. Christians may be tempted to reject it out of hand because they can see no relation or common ground between psychoanalysis and their faith. A heresy, they will say, is a distorted form of the true faith resulting from some of the basic articles being discarded or deformed. But surely psychoanalysis has nothing in common with Christian faith? It does not alter a fundamental article as Arianism did in regard to the Person of Christ, or as Protestantism did in regard to the nature of the Church, or as Pelagianism did in regard to the rôle of grace in man's 'salvation. The analyst will dismiss the statement as sheerly ludicrous. He feels that he has nothing at all to do with Christianity, that his activities are scientific and that science is independent of all faith. He will say that he studies religion only as one fact among others that the history of mankind has produced. He will protest that he does not think of denying or of altering any of the articles of faith because to him they mean nothing but a particular form of ignorance, or superstition, or illusion—and one does not deny an illusion or a hallucination, one studies its origin and attempts to cure the patient.

We cannot hope to convince the psychoanalyst. He will never

see himself in the rôle of heretic. No heretic throughout the centuries of Christianity ever did. Heretics either pretended to be still within the Church even though they held opinions diverging widely from the Church's teachings, or they declared that they alone were the representatives of true and unadulterated faith and that the Church had left the path of Her founder which they, the heretics, had to rediscover.

But we may hope to convince Catholics, and indeed all who believe in Christ as the Savior and Redeemer of mankind. We wish very much we could achieve this, *Deo favente*, not only because the attitude of Christians in regard to psychoanalysis would become more sharply defined and based on more than just a vague feeling of reluctance and moral offense, but also because psychoanalysis is only one instance or illustration, though a very prominent one, of a mental attitude which grew to dominate the general mentality during the last century. That attitude became very influential then, though its roots go back far into the past of Western culture. A better understanding of what psychoanalysis is and for what kind of spirit it stands might enable us more clearly to perceive traces of the same spirit in other manifestations of our modern world.

The heretical character of psychoanalysis will become plainly visible when we shall have laid bare its roots and inspected its antecedents. This will be the task of the next chapter. Here we shall refer only to the well-known fact that heresies, throughout the centuries of Christianity, always felt the need of asserting their rights over and over again. It is as if the heresiarchs suffered from a guilty conscience and in order to silence it were forced to overemphasize their alleged rights by decrying the Church against which they arose. Please note carefully that I am not here asserting my belief that the Church stands for truth, that psychoanalysis is error, that error always runs amuck when it is confronted by truth. I am not asserting all this here, because I prefer to limit this discussion to arguments based on natural logic, on the analysis of facts, on the evidence of science, without appealing to faith and the supernatural. Therefore the criticism of psychoanalysis I have tried to give here is based not on the fact that this theory implies ideas contrary to the teachings of Catholic philosophy and Catholic faith, but on the one fact that these ideas are contrary to truth. I have been careful to criticize Freudism, not because it has sprung from a non-Catholic or even an anti-Catholic philosophy, but because it has sprung from a bad philosophy. It has been my endeavor to show that, aside from all theology or faith, the theory of Freud is untenable, because it is self-contradictory, it ignores evident facts, it is incompatible with the principles of every sound philosophy.

If therefore I proceed to point out certain ideas maintained by psychoanalysis which are utterly incompatible with Catholicism, it is not to add one more argument against the conceptions of Freud, for I hope that their inconsistency has already been sufficiently demonstrated on other grounds, by an appeal not to any authority whatever, save to that logic which has to be obeyed in every scientific research and every scientific activity. I note some of the points in which the ideas of Freud and his school contradict the Catholic faith not as an argument against psychoanalysis, but as a warning directed to Catholics—and indeed to Christians generally. The Catholic mind has often been accused of being backward, reactionary, incapable of acknowledging the progress of science, unwilling to avail itself of the newest and surest discoveries—oftener than not they have proved to be rather short-lived—so that Catholics, or many of them, have become a little uncertain. They fear to be left behind, to be not "up to date," to be rather second-rate citizens, if they do not show themselves ready to accept the latest fashion in science. For there is fashion in science as there is elsewhere. Fashions in science come and go and—return. It is but a short time since the old pathology of the *humores* was held in utter contempt; the "cellular pathology" of Virchow and his contemporaries was the thing a "modern" mind had to believe in. But soon the old idea of the *humores* celebrated a triumphant restoration. It did indeed change its name, but not enough to escape being easily recognized. Instead of *humores* it talked of *hormones*; that was all. As long as a new scientific truth is the topic of the discussions of the day, it suits every intellectual and advanced mind to fall in with the rest. Otherwise one is put aside as old-fashioned, ossified, unmodern, backward and what not. This has happened several times to Catholics. They have neither forgotten nor "repressed" this experience. They have rather forgotten that they have been right more often than their adversaries care to admit.

Today, psychoanalysis is very modern. (We shall never tire of reminding the reader that modern means *modo hodierno*, "according to the fashion of today," and that the *moderni* of today may be the reactionaries of tomorrow.) Psychoanalysis pretends to be thoroughly "scientific." It claims to have definite proofs for its assertions. Few people are capable of looking into the matter sufficiently to form a judgment of their own; not to be reckoned with the dull, ignorant, trailing-behind followers of ideas which have become obsolete, they rather prefer to be enthusiastic about all that is presented to them as new and scientific.

But Catholics know also, notwithstanding their being a little scared by the idea of unmodernity, that whatever really contradicts the teachings of their faith cannot be true. They know for certain that a philosophy or a science which disregards fundamental conceptions of Catholicism will ultimately disappear, however great its success may be for the present time. I hold that psychoanalysis is an enormous and a dangerous error. I desire to prevent as many people as possible—and primarily of course as many Christians as possible—from falling a prey to this error.

There is one fundamental conception in the Christian religion which is not only neglected but simply denied by psychoanalysis. This is the conception of sin. In psychoanalysis there is no sin. Its philosophy is definitely deterministic and the notion of sin presupposes free will. Also there is no place for the notion of sin in this system, because human behavior does not depend, according to the principles of Freudian anthropology, on conscious but on unconscious forces. It is but a logical consequence that psychoanalysis interprets conscience not as an awareness of conformity or non-conformity with eternal laws of morals or of values, but as the expression of a restored or a disturbed equilibrium of instinctual forces. Psychoanalysis necessarily sees in conscience merely a psychological phenomenon. Nor can this conception of human nature acknowledge anything like responsibility.

It is a matter of course that psychoanalysis has no use whatever for any notions referring to the supernatural. This complete denial of the supernatural is not proper to empirical science which wisely limits its researches to the fields accessible to human reason. The true scientist has too great a reverence for facts to pass judgment on things simply because he cannot grasp them by his methods. He carefully avoids pronouncements concerning matters with which natural unaided human reason is not competent to deal. But the psychoanalyst tells us that all belief in the supernatural, be it in the grace of God, be it in God Himself, be it in the efficacy of the sacraments, or in the immortality of the soul—that all these ideas are the natural offspring of instinctual factors which this psychology boasts of having uncovered and thus deprived of their impressiveness. Psychoanalysis sees no difference between the Catholic religion and its uses, its rites and its sacraments on the one hand, and the most primitive and most fantastic customs of the aborigines of Australia or Central Africa, on the other. There is hardly one article of faith which has not been subjected to analysis and made the object of a psychoanalytic "explanation." These so-called explanations would be rather a shock to a Catholic mind, if they were not so patently based on an absolute failure to understand the doctrine that is being explained.

We have considered in the foregoing paragraphs only the

relations of psychoanalysis to Catholic faith; we have said nothing on Catholic morals. Some few words on this topic are desirable.

Psychoanalysis as such has nothing to say on morals. It calls itself a science, and science can make statements only on what is, never on what ought to be. This is true of science as such. It is not true of scientists and of the actual use they make of science for propagating some "reform" of morals and for declaring that this or that attitude in regard to morals is right or some other attitude wrong. Such statements made in the name of science are, of course, not the expression of conclusions forced upon the mind by facts, but the expression of convictions which have quite a different origin. Science can only tell us what means we might use to realize some aim; but it does not know anything of aims. Medicine does not state that health has to be preserved; medicine only tells us how we may manage to preserve it. The often heard expression, "scientific education," either means that we may learn from science how best to achieve our ends, or it means nothing at all. Anyone who believes science capable of making any statement on *why* people have to be educated knows nothing of the true nature of education. It is the same with morals. "Scientific ethics" is simply a nonsensical term.

But even the scientist is a human being. He cannot help having convictions and ideals and wishes. It is but natural, though not right, that he should attempt, be it "unconsciously," to present his personal ideas and ideals as if they followed from sciences. Sciences which deal with man are particularly in danger of trespassing on a field where they have no competence. Because health is a good which is naturally desired by man, medicine easily comes to believe that its statements on hygienic measures are of the nature of moral precepts. Because psychology knows that a normally functioning mind is a value to be desired, the psychologist believes himself to be entitled to enunciate rules on education. Medical psychology is even more inclined to commit this error than any other kind of psychology. The medical psychologist has too often observed the disastrous effects which mistaken education may have upon the development of character and personality. He therefore simply declares that such or such a method of education "has" to be adopted. Thus it becomes more necessary to examine carefully the spirit of a psychology which proclaims its rights to prescribe to education its methods and its goals.

Education is more than instruction. It is primarily the building up of a moral personality. Ethics and education are therefore closely interrelated. And education does not end after high-school or after college. It practically never ends. We are educated by facts, by environmental influences, by ideas, and we have to educate ourselves.

A psychology born of a definitely anti-Christian spirit cannot but be exceedingly dangerous. Even if a psychoanalyst tries to avoid all wounding of the moral or religious feelings and ideas of a patient, he cannot do so in fact. His method, his interpretations, his whole mentality is of a type hostile to the Christian spirit. This mentality creeps in, as it were, at every moment; it is implied in every most trivial remark. Even if he is resolved to abstain from all influence on the patient's faith or morals, his resolve is ineffective; the psychoanalyst cannot help transmitting to his patient the contagion of an anti-Christian spirit.

There is something profoundly wrong with this spirit. And what is wrong is perhaps best perceived if one considers the ideas which psychoanalysis has of the normal man. Freud's theory was, and to a great extent still is, an approach to the cure of neurotic patients. Every treatment has to refer to some idea of normality, because the attainment of normality is the sign by which a treatment is known to have been successful. Freud said more than once that a man is normal if he is capable of working and of enjoying his life. There is nothing else in the psychoanalytic conception of normal human nature. Enjoying implies,

of course, adaptation to reality, since without this, unpleasantness would be greater than pleasantness.

This conception is stated anew, for instance, by Hendricks,*
who declares that the culmination of the ego-development consists in the individual becoming capable of maintaining his
existence and securing adequate gratification of libidinous and
aggressive instincts in a socialized environment of adults. These
definitions are, as everyone sees, very incomplete; moral factors
are absolutely ignored, or rather are included in the notion of
adjustment to the social environment. It is a widespread error
to believe morality to be limited to the relation to one's neighbor; duties toward one's own person are neglected, as are, of
course, duties toward God.

It follows naturally that psychoanalysis proves incapable of
evaluating adequately phenomena like consciousness of guilt or
conscience. Conscience originates, one author remarks, in a hostile identification;† no glimpse of the true nature of this phenomenon entered the mind of the author referred to. Another tells us that the desire to confess a sin committed—it
need not be in the confessional, because this desire belongs to
human nature—results from a disclosure-impulse related to the
"partial instinct" of exhibitionism.‡ By still a third we are informed that the need of confession is related to oral eroticism.
There is no need to multiply instances. The three mentioned
here reveal an absolute ignorance regarding religious as well as
general psychology.

The naturalistic conception of human nature colors every
statement on morals. True commandments, eternal laws, do not
exist according to this view. This mentality cannot but have a
destructive influence on any person who holds different convictions. It is probable that à psychoanalytic treatment of such a

* *Ego-development and certain Character Problems*, Psychoana. Quart., 1936,
3, 320.
† H. Nunberg, *The Feeling of Guilt*, Psychoana. Quart., 1934, 3, 589.
‡ D. T. Burlingham, *Mitteilungsdrang und Gestaendniszwang*, Imago, Leip.,
1934, 20, 130.

person either will prove a failure, if the convictions are strong enough and if the difference between them and those of the analyst is perceived with sufficient clearness; or else will lead to gradual undermining of the convictions which will give way under the continuous pressure of the hostile spirit of psychoanalysis.

The danger of non-naturalistic morals being destroyed by analysis, even if the psychoanalyst has no intention of doing so, is all the greater, because the morality or amorality of Freudism may become a very strong temptation. The psychotherapist soon becomes for the patient a person of authority; call it transference, if you like; the name does not matter here. A conception of life which appeals to the instinctual side of man exercises a natural seduction; if this seduction becomes strengthened by authority it may easily prove to be irresistible.

It is hardly true that psychoanalysts in general preconize laxity in morals. But they conceive of morals in a manner which is just the opposite of what a Catholic knows moral law to imply. This refers primarily to sexuality, but it is the same with every other side of behavior too. One has to conclude that a Catholic ought to beware of getting too close a contact with Freudian ideas. If he is fully acquainted with them, he will avoid such a contact by himself. If he is not, he ought to be warned away.

Some adversaries of psychoanalysis have stressed the "immorality" of the theory and also of the practical attitude in regard to certain moral problems. The analyst, they say, is bound to hold views incompatible with Christian morality; and therefore he cannot but have a destructive influence on the moral behavior of individuals and on the moral ideas of the public. The point deserves elucidation.

The conception Freud and his school have formed of human nature is doubtless different from the conception underlying Christian, especially Catholic morality. The "pleasure principle," even after its transformation into the "reality principle," is not the kind of motivation Christian morality supposes to be at the bottom of moral behavior. The idea that human nature is in order and "normal" when the individual is capable of work and of enjoyment is not an idea acceptable to Catholic ethics. These features of psychoanalysis are more important, for answering the question, than is Freud's emphasis on sexuality. However wrong this notion of an all-pervading libido might be, it need not be immoral.

The fact that psychoanalysis is a purely naturalistic system and quite incapable of evaluating religion and religious behavior according to their true worth, is of course a serious drawback. Some analysts hold that one need not endanger a person's religious beliefs as long as these beliefs are not either the outcome of pathological factors or an obstacle for the regaining of mental health. It is, however, difficult to see how the analyst can, hard though he may try, avoid endangering the religious attitude. Any patient, even of medium intelligence, cannot help perceiving that the general spirit of the theory with which he is made acquainted during treatment is hostile to religious beliefs. Whether the patient reflects on this or not, makes hardly any difference.

The antagonism between psychoanalysis and Catholic morals, insofar as this antagonism is implied in the system of Freudian philosophy and psychology is one thing; the eventual conscious and direct influence by advising the patient to act against the principles of Catholic morals is another. If it were known that many or that some psychoanalysts advised their patients in a manner as to suggest a behavior contrary to morality, the danger of this system would become very great indeed.

Some of the ideas held by the psychoanalysts are contrary to Catholic conceptions without being exclusively characteristic of Freudism. It is a matter of course that an analyst, finding a person hopelessly entangled in domestic difficulties and incapable of getting along with her husband or his wife, will advise this person to divorce. This may be as such no bad advice; but it implies, in the mind of the analyst, that after the divorce this person ought to marry someone more suitable. But the advice might be given by any non-Catholic physician; the convictions prompting it are not specifically Freudian, they belong to a set of ideas common to all "liberal-minded" people. The same might be said of the suggestion to seek prematrimonial sexual satisfaction. It would be different, if it were suggested that a married persòn should seek extra-matrimonial sexual relations for some reason or other.

It is very difficult to know what the average attitude of the analysts is in regard to such problems. It is also very difficult to make sure whether some reports received are quite trustworthy. Psychoanalytic treatment may, in some cases, especially if it has been unsuccessful, leave a definite resentment in the mind of the patient; such a mental state may well falsify, even without any conscious intention of calumny or of prevarication, the memory of things mentioned during the hours of analysis. A certain disregard for objective truth is, moreover, not uncommon with some types of neurotic personality. Reports one gets from neurotic patients have, therefore, to be considered with a good deal of precaution.

Some psychoanalysts may have professed a too "liberal" attitude in regard to certain moral laws. But it is still questionable whether this attitude results from their being followers of Freud or from their general mentality. One has not to forget that many definitely anti-Catholic ideas on morals have been proposed by people who were no psychoanalysts. The opinions advocated by the Bolshevists on marriage, on sexual relations, etc., at least in the first part of their reign, depended not on any influence on the part of psychoanalysis. Freud's views indeed contributed to the spreading of the discussions on sexual matters; the emphasis he laid on sexuality and his apparently scientific proofs for the basic importance of sexual factors in human nature strengthened the position of those who attacked the system of Christian morality. But one cannot well say that Freud himself taught directly an anti-Catholic morality. He taught it, however, implicitly.

So far as reports may be relied upon, one indeed gets the impression that some psychoanalysts do not feel any reluctance against advising definitely immoral acts, especially and even exclusively in regard to sexual behavior. In a paper read some years ago at a meeting of the French psychiatrists, Dr. Genil-Perrin referred to numerous cases he and others had come across which seemed to show that such advice was not infrequent. But it is impossible to lay hold on any reliable figures. We can neither know how many of the psychoanalysts would, eventually, consider advising immoral behavior, nor how often they would feel moved to do so. The only thing we know for sure is that the system of psychoanalysis contains no factor which would disallow such an advice being given. We know also that a good many reports exist telling of such an attitude on the part of some psychoanalysts. It is to be presumed that not all these reports are false or exaggerated. But justice demands that we limit our judgment to the facts we may prove. And the only thing we can prove is the essential antagonism existing between the general spirit of Freudism and Catholic mentality. This, however, should be sufficient for making Catholics avoid as best they can any contact with psychoanalytic psychology and surely any situation which might give to the analyst, even against the will of the person seeking the psychoanalyst's advice, any influence on his visitor's ideas.

The list of the statements made by the Freudian school which are utterly incompatible with Christian faith could be continued for a good while. We think that we have said enough. No Catholic can ever feel tempted to make his own these ideas— *e.g.* of religion as a compulsory neurosis, of God as father-image, of communion going back to the totemistic meal—ideas, which he cannot but feel to be wrong, not to say sacrilegious. But there is always one objection. Is it not possible to disengage the method from the unacceptable philosophy? Can we not, though Christians, make use of the instrument supplied by psychoanalysis? Can we not leave aside the naturalistic conceptions, the nonsensical ideas on religion, the denial of freedom, the exaggerated emphasis on instincts, and "baptize," as it were, psychoanalysis, more or less as St. Augustine is said to have "christianized" Neo-Platonism or St. Thomas Aquinas to have baptized Aristotle? These pagan philosophers, too, had taught things which Christian philosophy could never accept; but they had taught also other things which were true or which, at least, allowed of some modification to make them true. If Christian philosophy had behaved in regard to pagan philosophy, as we want the Catholic to behave in regard to psychoanalysis, it would have meant an enormous loss to humanity and would perhaps have barred the growth of a true Christian philosophy. Why then this radicalism in face of psychoanalysis, a radicalism of which the Church has never been guilty in the past?

The answer is that the analogy does not hold. We have tried to show, in the eighth chapter, that one cannot separate the philosophy from the method, that he who adopts the latter needs must accept the former. But there is another reason for the intransigeance we recommend. Psychoanalysis does not stand to Catholicism in the same relation as pagan philosophy stood, in the first centuries of Christianity, to Catholic philosophy. Psychoanalysis is more like Manicheism or any other of the great heresies than like the philosophy of Plotinus or Aristotle. And the Church has never compromised, however little, with any heresy.

One might call the spirit of psychoanalysis, and with good reason, a pagan spirit. But it is not the paganism of pre-Christian times; it is a paganism that follows after centuries of Christianity. And this is quite a different spirit. The paganism of old is dead, at least in the countries of occidental civilization. There is no chance of revival. That spirit cannot become alive again, because the alterations the human mind has undergone by the influence of the two thousand years of Christianity cannot be eradicated. Neo-paganism is not a relapse into the paganism of the age of Plato or even Seneca. It is not a relapse but a revolt.

To understand the nature of this spirit we have to examine the origin of psychoanalysis and the forces which contributed to its making. We have also to inquire into the conditions which made possible the amazing success of Freudian conceptions. By doing this we shall, at least that is our hope, arrive at a still better understanding of the true nature of this theory.

CHAPTER XII

The Place of Psychoanalysis in the History of Human Thought

A SYSTEM of philosophy, a theory of biology, a conception of some problem in psychology or sociology is primarily what it is by its particular nature and the content of its propositions. But such a complex of ideas depends also to a great extent on historical conditions. It is, and sometimes very much so, a child of its age, and it bears, therefore, the imprint of the characteristics of the general mentality reigning at the time of its birth. One cannot do justice to the philosophy, for instance, of St. Anselm of Canterbury or to that of Immanuel Kant without taking account of the peculiarities of their times, the political, social, economic and generally speaking, cultural conditions. Certain defects we may notice in such a system are caused by these conditions; certain misstatements are due either to knowledge not sufficiently advanced or the influence of certain prejudices of which not even the greatest mind can free itself totally.

We should err in attributing to the system itself defects due to such factors. A great conception proves its greatness precisely by still being of value to us after the time-bound elements have been eliminated. Aristotle's notions on the soul have not been disproved by the advances of modern biology and psychology, though some of his statements are evidently false. The ideas of Aquinas on certain phenomena of physics are definitely mistaken, but their being wrong does not diminish the validity of his philosophical views. By discovering the main and basic ideas which are dependent on historical factors we are enabled to understand better why a theory was bound to go astray. A theory which in its very foundations proves itself to be wholly the product of a particular mentality, one which existed and could exist only in a particular historical situation, cannot aspire to the noble name of lasting truth.

Even the greatest errors of the human mind contain some truth. There are utterly mistaken views which, in spite of their picturing facts in a distorted manner, have grasped some essential truth which later became disengaged from the mass of falsehood and emerged as a valuable possession of the human mind. A wrong idea, however, does not become right because it contains some elements of truth. Our knowledge of the working of the mind, our understanding of human personality and character may have been furthered, to some extent, by psychoanalysis. We have to ask, however, whether this progress is not paid for too dearly by our having to put up with such a mass of manifestly wrong statements. Nor is it true that psychology had to wander in the maze of these falsehoods in order to become aware of these few truths. It may well have been that psychoanalysis, though it got hold of some true ideas, was as a whole more of an obstacle to the advance of psychology and the conception of human nature than a furthering factor.

The foregoing chapters have tried to show that psychoanalysis misconstrues human nature and the operations of the human mind. They have tried to prove that psychoanalysis is greatly mistaken as well in its basic principles as in its particular statements, be it on psychology, or on ethnology, or on education. It has been pointed out that we in fact are not compelled to apply the principles or use the methods of psychoanalysis for achieving what Freud's theory originally was meant to achieve, viz., the cure of neurotic troubles. How then did such a theory, whose errors are so very patent, achieve such a success? Clearly psychoanalysis must have satisfied some deeply felt need of its time. A brief study of the general conditions reigning when psychoanalysis was born and developed will show the factors which helped psychoanalysis to achieve a success so far beyond its deserts.

There have been other wrong ideas in the past which became exceedingly successful, though their triumph was perhaps not as impressive as that of psychoanalysis. There was, for instance, the theory of evolution, as taught by Lamarck and still more as taught by Darwin. The theory of evolution, though upheld in modified form by many biologists today, is definitely on the decline. The notion of natural selection which holds a pivotal place in Darwinian theory is no longer considered to be the basis of a "scientific" theory enabling us to understand the relation of the various species of living beings. Many biologists today feel these views to be unsatisfactory and contradictory to facts. Yet some few decades ago evolution was hailed as the final solution of the problems of life. The theory of evolution satisfied a profound desire of the general mentality of those days; it apparently offered a means for linking together the phenomena of life and those of mechanics, since natural selection and similar notions gave the impression of being mere mechanical factors. The theory was also in perfect accordance with another deeply ingrained tendency of nineteenth-century mentality; it supplied not only a link—though it was still but a "missing link"—between animals and man, but it introduced also the notion of continuity in biology.

It was Linnaeus, the famous botanist of the eighteenth century, who said *natura non facit saltus* (nature makes no leaps). This is not, as many apparently believe, a proposition belonging to Scholastic philosophy, to which it stands, in truth, in absolute contradiction. Scholasticism indeed conceived of the totality of being as consisting of a series of separate levels of existence between which no transition did or could exist. This notion, originally derived from Neo-Platonic philosophy, was held to be so basic that St. Anselm of Canterbury, for instance, declared that anyone incapable of being aware of this fact did not deserve to be called a human being.

At the time of Linnaeus, however, the idea of continuity had gained an enormous importance. The genius of Newton and of Leibniz had devised methods of considering continuous phenomena as if they were discontinuous and, on the other hand, of uniting single and discontinuous data in such a way as to make them points of a continuous process—infinitesimal calculus. Mathematics and physics making use of mathematical methods and notions had, at this time, become the ideal of science. Kant denied the name of science to every arrangement of facts which would not lend itself to mathematical treatment. The late eighteenth and the whole nineteenth century believed in physics almost as if it were a new faith. It was but an inevitable result of this attitude, to attempt to introduce the idea of continuity even in fields where, at first sight, it seemed to have no right at all.

The theory of evolution is simply the result of applying the idea of continuity to the varieties of living organisms. It does not matter that neither Lamarck nor Darwin conceived of their theories in this light. It is indeed not necessary at all that the inventor of some theory be aware of the conditions which fashion his mind and which mold his outlook on reality. It is only a subsequent analysis of the general cultural situation, the *geistesgeschichtliche* retrospection, which discovers the factors which had been at work. One may look at the theory of evolution as at an attempt at applying the notion of continuity to the realm of life. But one might also consider this theory as a compromise between the apparent discontinuity of the species and the general idea of continuity as a principle of science. To become "scientific," biology had to introduce somehow the notion of continuity. One may look in the same manner also on psychoanalysis.

The first preliminary note on psychoanalysis, a name which had not as yet been invented, was published, in the *Neurologisches Centralblatt*, by Joseph Breuer and Sigmund Freud in 1894. The title of this article read: *"On the Mechanism of*

Hysterical Symptoms." We may well take note of the fact that this title contains the term "Mechanism"; this little fact reveals something of the attitude of the authors. We shall see that the retention of this expression is not without a deeper significance. In 1895 followed the volume, by the same two authors, *Studies on Hysteria.* Its publication coincided with the end of the collaboration; from this time the work was carried on by Freud alone.

It is noteworthy, and we have pointed out this circumstance already on various occasions, that by a curious coincidence the same year 1894 saw also the publication of another paper which, though it inaugurated another movement in psychology, a movement which, though it does not strike the eye of the onlooker as much as does psychoanalysis, is perhaps not of less importance. In that year Wilhelm Dilthey, then professor of Philosophy at the University of Berlin, delivered a speech in the Academy of Science; the title read: *"On Explaining and Understanding in Psychology."* The famous philosopher complained, in this speech, of the nature of psychological research and psychological theory. He reproached the psychologists of his time for neglecting the nature of mental phenomena, for following slavishly the ideals of physics and for overlooking the essential differences of mental and physical facts. Dilthey then coined the phrase which later on became, so to say, the program of a new school of psychologists: "We explain nature, but we understand the mind." The idea he meant to convey was that psychology, to be really a science of the mind, has to free itself from the bondage of "exact" science, to develop methods of its own, and to take account of the properties of its object.

The objections Dilthey raised against the then current psychology need not be detailed here. One fact, however, is of interest for our purpose. Dilthey was voicing what was evidently a general feeling of dissatisfaction caused by the attitude of psychology. Psychology, as it was cultivated in the laboratories and taught in the classrooms and explained in treatises, proved to be insufficient to the needs of many other branches of knowledge which needed psychology. Interesting though the statements were on the psychology of sensation, on elementary laws of memory, on the range of apperception, on the minimum time of perception, and so on, they did not do a great deal to satisfy the needs of education, or sociology, or history, or even psychiatry. Education wanted to know how to deal with its proper problems; it wanted psychology to reveal methods of teaching with greater efficiency, how to devise ways of instruction, how to influence the moral development of its pupils. Sociology wanted to be told what the psychological conditions are which mold this or that form of society, what are the differences of general mentality in primitive and in advanced culture, by what mental operations men get in touch with each other and influence their mutual relations. History had desires much of the same kind. And psychiatry, of course, expected psychology to supply a knowledge of the normal mental functions, in the same manner as physiology supplied such a knowledge of bodily functions.

All these sciences were disappointed by psychology, psychiatry no less than the other disciplines. The psychologists, true to their ideal of science, were unwilling, and in fact did not believe themselves able, to approach the complex phenomena on which these other sciences sought information. The psychologists felt that they had first to acquire a more complete knowledge of what they termed "elementary facts," before they could dare to approach the study of complex phenomena. Accordingly, they answered the urgent demands of the others: you will have to wait; psychology is but beginning; we cannot as yet make reliable statements on complex phenomena; you are asking too much.

Whether it was too much to ask or not, education, sociology, psychiatry, had to have some answer, because otherwise their work was condemned to an absolute standstill. The result was the development of many psychologies independently of the laboratories. There are indeed many problems of a nature more or less psychological which might be studied without the help of the laboratory and its apparatus. Such a study, however, was not countenanced by "official" psychology. Science—and psychology had to be a science in the very strictest sense of the term—uses experiment; no experiment, no science; no measurement, no science.

The various attempts by those who needed psychology and were left without answer were not controlled by any recognized conception. Each of the individual scholars was left more or less to himself. He devised notions on psychology as they suited his particular problems. The psychiatrists wrote introductions dealing with normal psychology to their treatises on psychopathology; but this normal psychology was not based on any other than prescientific knowledge. It was in many cases mere speculation or a compound of elements, taken from writings of philosophers, psychologists, and from a more or less limited personal experience. The way these *membra disjecta* were combined was dictated, oftener than not, by the needs of the moment and by the particular problem the psychiatrist desired to clarify. The whole situation was definitely unsatisfactory.

The disadvantages of this situation became even more impressive when psychiatry discovered troubles which could not be considered as due to organic lesions of the brain. In France a new psychiatry began to develop. The heads of the new movement were on the one hand Charcot at Paris, on the other Liébault and Bernheim at Nancy. Freud had gone to Paris, in the early eighties of the nineteenth century, to study under Charcot and had worked also for some time with the masters at Nancy. The latter made large use of hypnosis for the investigation of mental phenomena and for the treatment of certain mental troubles.

The observations of Charcot and the data gathered at Nancy proved that purely mental causes were capable of producing far-reaching bodily and mental symptoms. In these cases, which

were subsequently known by the name of neuroses, or psycho-
neuroses, no brain physiology was of any avail. Symptoms which
could be provoked by suggestion or made to disappear by it,
did not allow for any explanation based on the physiology of
the nerve centers. Thus a good knowledge of the functioning
of the normal mind became all the more necessary. But if Freud
turned at all to psychology for enlightment on the problems
which occupied his mind, he surely did not feel that he got
any help. Psychology had nothing to say on such complicated
facts.

The fathers of psychoanalysis were, therefore, left very much
to themselves. They had to construct their own theory of the
way in which the mind functions. In doing this they had to
rely, of course, on the ideas then current and with which they
had become imbued in the earlier years. The first theoretical
conceptions seem to have been mostly or even exclusively
Breuer's. He wrote the chapter on theory in the *Studies on
Hysteria* and he apparently supplied the concepts needed for
dealing with the new problems.

It is necessary, to understand the nature of these conceptions,
to consider the antecedents of psychoanalysis. In doing this we
are very much helped by a complete and competent study which
Dr. M. Dorer published, in 1932, with the title: *Historische
Grundlagen der Psychoanalyse* (Historical Foundations of Psychoanalysis).*

Freud himself has more than once denied having been influenced by any writer on philosophy or psychology in developing
his theory and its basic notions. He asserts that he has read
neither Nietzsche nor Schopenhauer and that he is ignorant of
the ideas of Herbart or of any other man who, in the last third
of the nineteenth century, played a prominent rôle in the fields
mentioned. There is no reason not to believe him. But so far as
we know, he does not assert the same ignorance on behalf of
Breuer. The latter had a definite interest in philosophy; he was

* Felix Meiner, Leipzig.

a member of the Philosophical Society at the University of Vienna and once delivered there a speech on evolutionism and the teleological principle, besides taking part in several discussions. I happen to know by personal information that Breuer had read Herbart and that he was well acquainted with certain contemporary philosophers, among whom H. Taine deserves perhaps to be mentioned in particular. It is quite possible that several of the notions Freud used in erecting his system stemmed originally from Breuer, notwithstanding that the two authors had separated at the time of the publication of the *Studies*; we may assume that this book contains but a part of what the two discussed.

In any event a man need not have actually read the writings of those authors who are influential in molding the general mentality of his time. Many of their ideas penetrate, and quickly too, into wider circles. Often we are not even aware of the strength and extension of such influences. We may think we have kept our original ideas untouched, and yet we may have been subjected to many influences which gradually and insensibly have changed them. This possibility is very real especially in a highly intellectual environment, enthusiastic for all new and striking ideas, loving witty formulations, admiring the genius of a man even when opposing it. This was indeed the atmosphere in which Freud could not help moving in the Vienna of the eighties and nineties.

It is therefore more than probable that he drank in, without noticing it, many ideas which were then much discussed. That was a time when to have read Schopenhauer was considered necessary for everyone who aspired to the name of a cultured person. It has been said that the society women of those days had a volume of Schopenhauer at hand, to peruse while the maid did their hair. Newspapers of a high standard used to report meetings of scientific and philosophical associations and the newest publications in all fields of human knowledge and endeavor. Intellectual and artistic achievements played a greater rôle then in the conversations of certain circles than did politics or economics. A new theory in physics was deemed to be of interest for every cultured individual. A new book by a famous author, however difficult, was expected to be known at least to the leading minds. Society prided itself on remaining in touch with intellectuality. Lectures given by the famous teachers of the university or from outside had crowded audiences. Philosophers, physicians, scientists, took part in all kinds of social "events." Intellect was held in high esteem, and achievements in its field were regarded as exceedingly important; they were recognized also by the government, since decorations and the membership of the Upper House were bestowed on many a famous professor. It was not a bad time, this age, in old Vienna, nor was Vienna itself a bad place to live in.

This highstrung intellectuality had its drawbacks. It was doubtless partly snobbish. It was exceedingly "liberal," in the specific sense this term was given then. It was mainly antireligious, though it was not in any sense intolerant. Religion was recognized not only as a need of the masses, but as a personal attitude, hardly compatible indeed with true philosophy— unless it had dwindled down to some vague and pale deism; but retaining one's faith was not made a reproach to anyone. There was even a marked interest in religious problems, though rather as pertaining to ethnology and the history of culture than as having any actual bearing on individual life.

It is unthinkable that Freud should not have been influenced by this intellectual atmosphere or should not have become acquainted with many of the ideas which were of interest to the circles in which he was moving. He was, of course, in touch with many of his colleagues whose intellectual curiosity was not at all limited to facts and discoveries in the field of medicine. The mentality of the more prominent physicians of his time was a definitely broad one. The famous surgeon, Billroth, had a fine understanding of music—he was an intimate friend of the composer Brahms—and a general appreciation of art; Freud's teacher, the physiologist Bruecke, had written on problems of speech and of painting, and had a philosophical trend of mind. So had another of his teachers, Rokitansky, who was one of the fathers of modern pathology.

Thus, in unraveling the threads interwoven in the fabric of Freud's system, we need not wonder at there being many which cannot easily be traced back to some immediate influence. It is only by looking at things afterwards and from a different angle that an individual scholar may detect all the factors which contributed to building up his mind. Many never arrive at such an objective view, either because they do not feel interested or because they lack the necessary critical ability.

For a complete study of all the historical factors which molded Freud's ideas one would have to consider not only those which were active in the Vienna of his time but also those which might have been of influence during his stay at Paris. We have referred incidentally to Ribot and his knowledge of English philosophy. There is also the figure of Taine, though the latter probably was better known to Breuer than to Freud. We cannot attempt here a truly detailed analysis of the whole mental atmosphere which surrounded Freud and surely exercised a formative influence upon him. But some of the more important factors must be noted.

The psychology of Freud uses terms which were originally Herbart's. This philosopher made a curious attempt at developing a mathematical psychology which was definitely dynamic in its principles. The contents of consciousness were conceived as due to the interplay of forces adhering to ideas. The notion of cathexis is indeed already implied in Herbartian psychology, as are those of repression and inhibition, of the threshold of consciousness and of ideas pushing upwards from the unconsciousness into the consciousness. Herbartian is also the notion of quantities of energy and of the relation of emotional states to the forces at work in the mind. The ideas of Herbart reached Freud through two channels. Breuer was well acquainted with them, and contemporary psychiatry contained many traces of these ideas, especially in the works of Griesinger. The latter, however, transferred the dynamism, which in Herbart was of the mind, into the physiological substructures; the forces, which with the philosopher were of ideas, became in the mind of the more materialistic alienist expressive of brain processes. This development progressed farther in the psychiatry of Meynert who conceived of mental processes as the result of "mechanics of the brain." Griesinger as well as Meynert knew much of Fechner's ideas; the latter was anything but a materialist at heart, but by becoming the founder of "psychophysics" he furthered the impact of materialism on psychology. The psychologists of those days—those at least who did not go the whole length of a complete materialism—adopted the conception of "psychophysical parallelism." This view goes back to Descartes' conception of absolute dualism. This philosopher severed the mind from the body, crediting the latter with an existence by itself and with becoming united to the soul, or spiritual substance, only accidentally. This was in truth a revival of old Platonic conceptions. As in Platonism, so in Cartesianism the problem arose of how to explain the relations between mental and bodily phenomena. Since the unity of matter and soul, as it had been established by the philosophy of Aristotle and Aquinas, had been dissolved, some kind of relation between the two substances had to be stated. But Cartesianism did not admit the idea of an immediate action of mind on body and vice versa. The impossibility of such a conception had been seen clearly by Spinoza. He overcame the difficulty by making spirit and matter two sides of one substance. Leibniz, on the other hand, in his Monadology, introduced the notion of "pre-established harmony" between otherwise independent elements of reality. From these sources sprang the idea of psychophysical parallelism, which was used as a principle of explanation by Fechner in 1852 and later. The series of bodily and of mental phenomena run parallel to each other without influencing each other. To every mental phenomenon belongs a bodily change, to every bodily alteration corresponds a mental phenomenon. But never is a phenomenon of the bodily series caused by one of the mental series, nor does ever a bodily change cause a mental state. By adopting this view they apparently tried to achieve two things: the absence of a causal relation between mental and physical phenomena allowed them to safeguard the existence of psychology as a science in its own right, and it allowed them at the same time to be as physiological as the fashion of the age demanded and thus to escape the reproach of being "unscientific." It has, however, been perhaps not sufficiently noticed how close this theory of parallelism is to materialistic monism. Parallelism denies to the mind any direct influence on the body; the chain of mental phenomena goes on parallel to that of the bodily changes, both correspond to each other perfectly, not because of a relation of mutual causality but because of a pre-ordained parallelism. The mind becomes, by this interpretation, a mere epiphenomenon. It can be left out altogether without the behavior of the individual becoming altered. Nothing is then easier, given a certain type of general mentality, than to deprive the mind of all independent existence and to make it a mere manifestation of somatic functions. Modern materialism may boast Plato or at least Descartes among its ancestors.

The mind of the nineteenth-century scientist was a curious mixture of all kinds of elements which existed side by side, often in spite of their being originally hostile to each other. This does but mirror in the individual mind the tendencies of the general mentality and civilization as then existing. The capacity for synthesis has diminished very much; instead of synthesis we observe eclecticism. It is not astonishing that this age felt suspicious in regard to syntheses since the last attempt in this direction, Hegel's, had lost credit shortly after having been acclaimed as the highest achievement of the human mind. Eclecticism as such is not to be despised, provided that there be a principle of choice. But such a principle was missing. It can be found indeed only in philosophy, and at philosophy this age of science and "progress" looked askance.

No wonder, therefore, that in Freud's mind there were many tendencies which cooperated though they were not at all of the same spirit. Herbart's psychology had been dynamic, but that dynamism was only of ideas. His conception reappears, as has been remarked before, in psychoanalysis in the shape of cathexis. Ideas as such did not appear as depending immediately on bodily processes; but strivings or instincts seemed to be related more closely to the functions of the body. Instincts were also observed in animals, and the success of evolutionarism made it desirable that psychology should place man as close to the animal as possible. A shifting of emphasis from ideas to instincts offered a way out. This appealed greatly to Freud's mind since his master Meynert, for whom he professed even in his later years a deep admiration, had been influenced by the philosophy of Schopenhauer, as had Griesinger before him. The voluntarism of Schopenhauer is the other root of the Freudian conception of instincts. Schopenhauer conceived reality as consisting mainly of will. Will, unconscious in nature, conscious in man, is the essence of reality. The parallel to the place allotted to instincts in psychoanalysis is easily recognized. Perhaps one might go one step farther. Schopenhauer's will is an impersonal and cosmic power; it is at least supra-individual. It seems as if traces of this conception were discoverable also in Freud's way of considering the group-mind, though the influence is definitely more visible in Jung's notion of a "collective unconscious."

The philosophies of Herbart, of Schopenhauer, of Fechner, were still metaphysics of a more or less idealistic kind. They were certainly not materialistic. But materialism was the last word of the nineteenth century, the answer science had to give to the mind inquiring for the essence of reality and the nature of man, though science had no right to make any statements of this kind. Materialistic and scientific views had come to be identified. Freud could hardly be expected to have ideas different from those held by the leading minds of his day. His intention was, in regard to psychology, the same as Fechner's. He wanted to build up the science of the mind, taking the term "science" in its strictest sense. The categories of science became those of his psychology: efficient causality, energy, quantity, measurement, and so forth. His ideas were dominated by the principles of elementarism—that is, the idea that science necessitates the establishing of ultimate elements which form, by combination, more complex phenomena.

Elementarism has another side too. This view believes that truth can be found only in the invisible, in what is inaccessible to immediate observation. Atoms or infra-atomic elements are the true reality; what is perceived is but a manifestation of these hidden factors. In other words the immediate experience of the senses is misleading. The age had forgotten the essential differences of mind and matter; it was self-evident to the scientists, physiologists, psychologists, that the same categories applied to both these realms. Just as the immediate experience of the senses was misleading, so also was the immediate experience of inner life, of mental states. (The historian of ideas wonders how far this attitude was dependent on Kantian principles. Kant states that not even our mind perceives itself "as such" and that here too we have but "appearance." Freud refers approvingly to a similar remark he found in Lipps, who then taught at the University of Munich.) This manner of looking at reality doubtless contributed to Freud's conceiving of the instincts as the only "true reality" in mental life.

Much could be added to the characterization of the intellectual situation of the last third of the nineteenth century and to the analysis of the influences to which Freud was exposed. We cannot indulge in a further study of this side of the question. But there is another side which deserves the utmost attention.

Freud was a physician. So was Breuer. Both had been trained in the spirit of medicine as it reigned then in the medical schools. We have already referred incidentally to some of the leading ideas of this spirit and to some of its most discussed problems. This was the time of Virchow who proclaimed the reign of anatomy in pathology—*Der Anatomische Gedanke in der Medicin*—a viewpoint which was indeed not altogether new. Morgagni in the eighteenth century had given to his famous treatise the title: *De sedibus et causis morborum,* and the institute of pathology at Vienna, founded by Freud's teacher, Rokitansky, bore the inscription: *Indagandis sedibus et causis morborum.* But it was a view which could only come fully to the fore after the invention of the methods of microscopical examination of tissues. Pathology had come to be almost identified with anatomy. Diseases were conceived as troubles of single organs or of functions. Analysis had become the only method which scientific medicine recognized as legitimate.

Physicians used to boast of this new spirit as an achievement of science and empiricism. They did not know that their colleagues who first consciously introduced this methodological principle in medicine did so under the influence of a philosopher. J. F. Pinel, the famous French alienist—who first "broke the chains of the insane"—wrote his treatise on *Nosologie philosophique* after having become acquainted with the works of Condillac. The elementaristic idea, being alone recognized as scientific, contributed to strengthening this attitude of the physicians. To state it in a somewhat exaggerated manner: for scientific medicine at least the patient had disappeared, there were only diseases.

The case observed by Breuer and the facts Freud had come to know in France did not lend themselves to such an outlook. Here the physicians were faced with problems which were definitely of the person and not of an organ. Personal fate and experience, personal attitudes and feelings were revealed as determining the appearance and the form of symptoms. Breuer and Freud became aware—and this is part of their historical achievement—of a new set of problems not previously taken into account by the medical world. These new problems demanded a new viewpoint as well as a new method. It is the merit of the two Viennese physicians to have been fully aware of the novelty of the problem. They did not try to cope with it by applying the old categories of pathology, helped along by more or less fantastic speculations. But they were, at the same time, incapable of really freeing themselves from the bondage of materialistic, elementaristic, anatomical medicine. It is the tragedy of psychoanalysis to have set out to discover the whole and to have ended with smashing it to pieces.

We have commented before on the fact that Freud retained as a name of his *system* of psychology the name he had originally devised for his *method*. It is the fate of psychoanalysis to have remained but—analysis. The spirit of elementarism proved too powerful, the ideal of science too impressive, the notion of analysis too tenacious to permit a real progress beyond the medical mentality of the nineties of the last century. Psychoanalysis thus appears as a compromise. It attempts to do justice to the new facts of which its founders had become aware and, at the same time, to retain the form of science which was then alone recognized. The discrepancy of aim and of method is the reason for the inconsistencies in psychoanalysis and for its being built on unacceptable and badly construed axioms. Its being of the nature of a compromise is also the reason of its success.

The first publications by Breuer and Freud and later by Freud alone did not attract much attention. But as soon as the psychiatrists and psychologists became aware of the true implications of psychoanalysis they made a stand against it. So did some moralists, though at this time psychoanalysis was mostly an affair of medicine and psychopathology and had not yet made known its claim to be a theory of human nature in general. The opposition of the moralists and of the general public came mainly from their resenting the over-emphasized sexuality. The opposition of the psychiatrists had other reasons, the foremost of which was that Freud's ideas were "unscientific," that he introduced factors unknown to medicine and biology, that he indulged in fantastic speculation not at all corroborated nor capable of corroboration by the acknowledged methods of medicine.

Though these critics did not in truth see clearly in this matter, and they hardly could be expected to do so, they nevertheless were moved by a vague awareness of something new trying to break into the field of medicine and psychology. They resented this, and they reacted to it in the only way they could be expected to react. Since the new thing was not to be combatted by the methods used in medicine, the defenders of tradition resorted to the usual anathema: they declared that psychoanalysis was unscientific, that it applied notions alien to true science, that it was mere speculation. We know that they were right in a sense, but not in the way they imagined.

Psychoanalysis, however, continued to develop. The number of those who followed Freud's lead increased. The new psychology began to attract attention outside the circles of psychopathologists, physicians and, of course, people suffering from neurotic trouble and hoping for deliverance. The notions of psychoanalysis became part of the vocabulary of psychology and psychiatry even with those who still refused to accept Freudian ideas. Repression, complexes, instincts, analysis, and so forth, were spoken of as well-known things. To have read Freud became a necessary accomplishment and not only for the psychologist. The new doctrine spread from Vienna to Germany and to the English-speaking nations. It was less well received in Latin countries, nor has it yet met in them the success achieved elsewhere. There are indeed psychoanalysts in France, in Italy, in Spain; there is a French *Journal de Psychanalyse*. But the number of periodicals and of adherents Freudism possesses in Anglo-Saxon countries and possessed until recent times in Germany has not been paralleled in the Latin countries. It would be worth while to inquire into the reasons of these differences; but this is not a problem that calls for discussion here.

The tremendous success of psychoanalysis naturally created some reaction. But the point of attack changed. Psychoanalysis was no longer criticized for not being scientific enough, but for being too much so, that is, for applying the categories and modes of thought which are suited in science to psychology and other fields—*e.g.,* ethnology or the interpretation of art—where these categories are definitely out of place. This change of front on the part of those adversaries of psychoanalysis who argued from the point of view of psychology and the study of cultural phenomena has a very curious parallel in the attitude of the official Russian psychology and science of education. Immediately· after the last World War, when the Bolshevist régime, was established, psychoanalysis enjoyed a great success in that country. It had been well received there before; but now, if not actually made the official basis of education, it was at least taken very much into consideration. But recently it has been condemned as being an altogether "bourgeois" kind of psychology and has been practically suppressed. Here too one observes this peculiar change of front.

Psychoanalysis, seen from the outside, seems as if it should be quite acceptable to the followers of Marx and Lenin. There is quite a similarity between psychoanalysis and Marxist conceptions. The latter conceive of civilization, of art, of science, of all that is called the higher achievements of culture as a "superstructure" erected upon and conditioned by the economic forces which alone represent the reality of social and historical evolution. In psychoanalysis we observe the same relation obtaining between the instinctual forces and the "superstructure" of the ego and the super-ego; the instincts are the true reality, every other phenomenon is built on them and conditioned by them. However this may be, the fact is that official Bolshevism has anathematized psychoanalysis. (At least the reports say so.)

All this is rather remarkable. It seems to indicate that psychoanalysis presents openings for attack from two opposite sides. The acknowledgment it received from the Bolshevists at first is of course equivalent to a condemnation by all non-Marxist philosophy, and the disapproval it meets now amounts to an acknowledgment by the representatives of a "bourgeois" ideology. These facts become explicable if we assume that psychoanalysis contains two sets of ideas which are in truth incompatible with each other and which allow for criticism from one side or the other.

The psychoanalysts react differently to the fact just mentioned. They are incapable of understanding it. Their interpretation is dictated by their extreme subjectivism and the blindness for objective facts correlated to it. Instead of asking for the objective reasons they simply declare that there are none but that the critical attitude in regard to psychoanalysis is exclusively determined by the "resistance" its opponents feel. The critics are the victims of their unconscious which does not allow them to become aware of the truth. They do not criticize psychoanalysis because they have any objective reasons, but because they are urged towards resistance by unconscious and repressed factors at work in their personalities. The shifting of the point of attack is declared by the psychoanalysts to be the result merely of these subjective attitudes. The adversaries, having become aware of the success psychoanalysis achieved in spite of their declaring it unscientific, have to assume another position and therefore combat this theory now for being too scientific.

The psychoanalysts are indeed so much blinded by their subjectivistic attitude that they have never even inquired whether there might not be objective reasons for this shifting of the attack. They overlook the obvious fact that the general mentality has undergone deep changes since the years when Freud was criticized because of unscientific methods. The psychoanalysts act as if the world were still at 1900. Perhaps they themselves are; the world is not. They seem to have overlooked all the evolution in intellectual and general cultural life which set in even before the last World War and has proceeded rapidly since then.

The true reason for the phenomenon under discussion is the compromise-character of psychoanalysis. Because this doctrine is a compromise and not a uniform whole, not a true synthesis, it presents to the observer various sides open to attack. Which side the observer sees depends upon where he himself stands. The scientism of the nineties and of the beginning of the present century was most alive to the differences between psychoanalytical ideas and those accepted by and fundamental to science. Modern times have become much more alive to the essentials of psychology and accordingly have perceived that Freud's ideas are still fettered by too much scientism. The reason for the change of criticism is not the "resistance" of the critics, but the development of the general mentality.

A close study of psychoanalysis reveals that this doctrine contains divergent factors. It started because it was born out of the desire and the necessity of understanding mental troubles with an attempt at truly psychological consideration, at grasping man's life and personality in their concrete wholeness. It deviated from its original direction because its fathers could not free themselves from the old ways of thought. Nobody will blame the founders of psychoanalysis for that. When the new spirit asserted itself, when it had become clear that the methods of science were not adaptable to the needs of psychology or the science of character, Freud had probably become too old to change again. But his younger followers should be able to open their eyes to reality.

It is because psychoanalysis is a compromise that it became so remarkably successful. After the first reluctance or astonishment caused by the novelty of its assertions had been overcome, it became acceptable and appealed to the scientific spirit because it still contained a good deal of that very spirit. And at the same time it seemed to take account of a development in culture which even the scientist could not fail to notice.

The human mind does not like absolute novelty. What is quite new has a disquieting quality. Man prefers to be left undisturbed. Repeatedly in history compromises have met with success. Compromise is indeed the one great tool of the politician, of the social reformer, of the man with new ideas. If such people prove to be intransigent, they fail. The great masses do not want to be thrown out of the accustomed track altogether. They very much prefer to move in the same direction, repeating the same things, hearing the same things. They need at least some point at which to connect the new thing with the old habits. They welcome compromise. It is only exceptionally that an idea or a doctrine which involves a total break with tradition becomes successful without having to compromise after all.

Psychoanalysis was admirably suited to a period of transition. It retained enough of the old spirit and it was sufficiently modern. The beloved and accustomed ways of thought had not to be given up and replaced by the new doctrine. By accepting the new views one became nevertheless exceedingly modern. We repeat: we have no fault to find with Freud himself or with his first pupil⁵. But why do so many people today embrace these self-contradictory ideas? There are of course several reasons for this.

First, the spirit of scientism is not dead. There are still many who believe in science as the faithful believe in God. But they cannot ignore the fact that science has failed on many points and that it has shown itself especially incapable of coping with the problems of the mind. But psychoanalysis is a "science of the mind."

Secondly, psychoanalysis claims to have explained the very nature of man and to have solved many riddles which are insoluble by other psychologies. Man has become more of a problem to himself today than for many centuries. There has perhaps been no age which has been as anxious as ours to know the truth about man. Psychoanalysis declares it knows the answer.

Thirdly, there is a certain factor which makes psychoanalysis acceptable to many, which factor indeed is more due to a misunderstanding of this theory than to an understanding of its true intentions. Psychoanalysis seems to procure a legitimation, by science, for the passions, the sensuous desires, and the illicit longings of human nature. It is easier to indulge in licentiousness if one may refer to the danger of repressing one's instincts.

Fourthly, psychoanalysis meets the tendency towards irrationalism which is very widespread to-day. Freud's doctrine is in fact very rational, over-rational indeed. But the matter which is rationalized in this system is in itself irrational, the instincts, the dark urges of human nature, which arise out of the unconscious, out of the id where the light of conscious reason does not penetrate, even out of prehistoric times the traces of which are still active in the depths of the modern mind.

Fifthly, psychoanalysis speaks an esoteric language. Its followers use certain terms which the uninitiated person does not understand. They nod at each other knowingly, possessors of secrets which the world in general does not share. They write and publish indeed; they make known their ideas; they discuss with others. But all this has but little importance. The important thing is that to understand psychoanalysis fully you have to be analyzed. Analysis takes the place of a rite of initiation. Only those who have passed through the ordeal of analysis know the thing really and from the inside. They are, to use a similarity taken from gnostic ideology, the only *pneumatikoi.* In them the pneuma of truth lives; the others are outside.

It will be remembered that I called psychoanalysis a heresy. The adherents of this school behave, in a way, as do the members of any more or less secret sect. A sect has to be secret as long as it fears the opposition of official public mentality, either because the defenders of tradition and custom may use violence, or because the sectarians themselves fear and feel that they might be offenders against truth. The outward behavior and the demand for initiation are, of course, no sufficient proof of the character of heresy. The statement needs further elucidation.

First of all, we have to define heresy. I feel that we will do this best by adopting the definition given by Hilaire Belloc.* "Heresy is the dislocation of some complete and self-supporting scheme by the introduction of the novel denial of some essential part therein. We mean by 'a complete and self-supporting scheme' any system of affirmation in physics or mathematics or philosophy or what-not, the various parts of which are coherent and sustain each other. . . . It is of the essence of a heresy that it leaves standing a great part of the structure it attacks. On this account it can appeal to believers and continues to affect their lives through deflecting them from their original characters. Wherefore it is said of heresies that 'they survive by the truths they retain.' "

In this definition the name of heresy is not restricted to attitudes regarding faith or the Church. There are philosophical or even mathematical heresies. There are heresies in medicine. There are heresies also in psychoanalysis, and the attitude of the "orthodox" in regard to dissenters is in accordance with this view. The "orthodox" psychoanalysis anathematizes everyone who, after having belonged to the initiated, ventures to have ideas different from those recognized by the school. Jung met this fate and so did Stekel, to mention but two names. A heresy exists only by declaring itself to be the true conception and by declaring the one from which it separates itself to be wrong. The history of religious heresies contains many a striking example of the fact that the heresies themselves acted against their dissenters in the same way as the group which they left had acted in regard to themselves.

Every system attempting to compromise between two antagonistic and incompatible sets of ideas is heretical. It is a heresy in regard to each of the two—eventually there are even more—original ideologies. We could call psychoanalysis thus

* *The Great Heresies,* New York, 1938, p. 4.

a heresy in regard to the spirit of biology on the one hand and the spirit of psychology or philosophical anthropology on the other. But this is not what we have in mind, though the compromise-character has something to do with our calling Freudism a heresy. Nor shall we make use of the fact alluded to above, viz., that the psychoanalysts behave in a way we know from the history of heresies and that Freud himself behaved very much as a heresiarch. We believe that there are still deeper reasons for our view.

It has been pointed out by many authors and at many times that even an utterly mistaken idea has to contain some little truth, else it could not exist at all and could not meet any approval. I have never denied that there are some truths in Freudism. In the concluding pages of this book I shall refer to what I believe to be the lasting achievements of psychoanalysis. It is necessary to ask where the truths, however disfigured and often hardly recognizable, which are contained in psychoanalysis have their origin.

To answer this question we have to go back farther than the 90's of the last century, and also farther away from psychoanalysis than we have done until now. Psychoanalysis—this much has become clear, we think, by the discussion in the present chapter—cannot be evaluated if it is not seen against the whole historical background of the age which gave it birth, if it is not understood as a phenomenon which expresses and, as it were, mirrors certain fundamental traits of general mentality and general culture. An attempt of this kind was made, rather inadequately, years ago by A. Hoche, a German psychiatrist, in a discussion with E. Bleuler.* But since then many things have become more sharply outlined and the changes which have been

* At the meeting of the German Association of Psychiatrists at Breslau, 1912, Hoche emphasized that psychoanalysis is a cultural phenomenon. "I understand perfectly," he said answering his opponent, "that Dr. Bleuler resents being evaluated from the point of view of culture." But Hoche's analysis did not go deep enough. He believed psychoanalysis to be related to what one used to call the laxity of morals and the decline of the true scientific spirit. This is but touching the surface of the problem.

going on in the last twenty years have made it easier to see things as they are.

Heresy, according to Belloc, consists, in taking out one part of a system and replacing it either by some other things or by leaving its place unfilled. It is therefore necessary to define the system out of which psychoanalysis took away not indeed one part but several parts. Freud, of course, did not consciously proceed in this way. He had no intention of becoming a heresiarch. He did not even know that his ideas were a partial acceptance and a partial denial of some definite system. But a historical evaluation regards not what a man intended or what he was conscious of, but the factual results of his activity. Not even when he stated his intention in a program, and then acted differently from that statement, did Freud's intention mean much to a historical judgment on facts of culture. That a man should have an intention and then be led or forced to act differently is sometimes an interesting feature of biography; it may stamp the man as a tragic hero, but it is of no importance to objective history. Just as it does not matter for the unraveling of factors which contributed to some structure whether such factors were clearly known to the founder, even so the founder's intention is of no importance. Facts alone decide.

We have spoken before of the "intention" which prompted the founders of psychoanalysis, of their feeling dissatisfied with the then existing psychology and with the means medicine proffered for the study of neurosis; but they were hardly conscious of these feelings and intentions. They did not know in fact that they were opposing to the elementaristic views of their time an indeed rudimentary but nevertheless definite idea. The "intention" of which mention has been made is not a conscious one; it is, to say the truth, not an individual intention but a general tendency of cultural evolution.

If, therefore, it is objected that nothing is known of Freud having ever had any intention of replacing some parts of a system by other things and of thus founding a system of his own,

I would admit that the statement is true but I would definitely deny it the weight of an objection.

The great and true conception underlying Freud's system is that of the unity of human nature. Psychoanalysis rests on the conception of man, his bodily constitution, his personal history, his character and his mental troubles—be they symptoms of a pathological disturbance or difficulties in his everyday life—as being essentially of a whole, as being manifestations or sides of man seen as an indissoluble unit. One will have to count among the real merits of Freud his having grasped this truth however vaguely. Even though he was not aware of this idea, even though it became in his hands disfigured and distorted, it nevertheless was brought to the consciousness of subsequent decades by psychoanalysis; if not by psychoanalysis alone, at least to a certain extent by it.

This idea of unity had been lost, mainly owing to the influence of elementarism and dualism as they had been born of the spirit of Cartesian philosophy. No need to explain that the Cartesian dualism was much more pronounced and much more disastrous in its consequences than the original Platonic conception had been. Since the time of Descartes the knowledge that man is a unit and not simply an aggregate gradually disappeared. Monism of the kind that had been fashionable during the second half of the nineteenth century was incapable of restoring this idea, because its notion of unity rested on a total disregard of the essential features of human nature.

Freud's philosophy is indeed a materialistic monism. And his awareness of the necessity of safeguarding the unity of human nature is incompatible with this philosophy. By introducing the philosophy of materialistic monism into a system of ideas where the notion of unity has its legitimate place, psychoanalysis acquires the nature of a heresy.

Psychoanalysis is mostly kept alive by its retaining or even reviving the idea of unity. But neither Freud himself nor any of his followers have been capable of understanding the implications of this idea. Because they do not understand it, they fail whenever they approach the problem of person. They are not even able to see this problem in its true light. They are impersonalists, though the fundamental tendency which stood godfather to psychoanalysis is definitely personalistic.

The idea of person is an offspring of Christianity. None of the philosophers of antiquity, not even Plato or Aristotle, was capable of conceiving a true idea of person. This idea could be discovered only after Christianity had taught mankind the dignity and responsibility of the individual person. By emphasizing the free will of man and its bearing on his eternal fate, by making every individual responsible for his fate in the next life, by proclaiming the infinite superiority of the spiritual, immortal soul over all creatures of this sublunar world, Christianity opened the eyes of man to a true understanding of himself, his dignity, his destiny, his responsibility. Outside of a Christian philosophy no possibility can be found of demonstrating and of safeguarding the human person. All philosophies which, while not Christian, state and try to demonstrate the dignity and the peculiar position of the human person do this because they retain some little—in many cases it is more than a little— of Christian philosophy.

This is not tantamount to saying that what is good in psychoanalysis is old and what is new therein is bad. The little truth which psychoanalysis contains does not regard only the dignity and unity of the human person. But the attraction which psychoanalysis exercises on not a few people who hold metaphysical convictions of quite another kind, is due mostly to the vestige of Christian philosophy which still lives in psychoanalysis.

One may justly wonder whence this fragment of Christian philosophy came. One can hardly allude to the intellectual atmosphere of Vienna; notwithstanding the fact that Austria was a Catholic country, Vienna was not at all penetrated by a Christian spirit. It was very "liberal," it was rather anti-Christian, though not in an aggressive manner; and the circles in which Freud may be supposed to have moved were surely not of a kind to bring him in touch with the Christian philosophy. It is true that at this time Brentano was teaching philosophy and that, having been a Catholic priest until the Vatican Council, he had a good knowledge of Christian philosophy; it is true too that Brentano might have moved in much the same circles as Freud did. But there is no trace of either Freud or of Breuer having been influenced by Brentano's philosophy. Nor did the Christian or Neo-Scholastic side of his teachings impress very much larger circles. Thus the origin of the Christian element in psychoanalysis has to be sought for elsewhere.

We may suppose the Catholic philosophers to have been of even less influence than Brentano. Catholic philosophy and the history of Scholasticism had a quite remarkable representative in Werner who did much to make known Scholastic, and especially Thomistic philosophy. But one may doubt whether Freud had so much as heard Werner's name. Physicians bothered but little about philosophy, and surely least of all about Scholasticism.

In 1879 however, the renaissance of Scholasticism had been inaugurated by Leo XIII in the encyclical *Aeterni Patris*. The Neo-Scholastic movement which had already set in thereupon gained enormously in vigor. But even the time of promulgation of a papal encyclical depends on the general situation and the general mentality. Pope Leo XIII would hardly have issued this famous encyclical had he not known that the time was ripe for it. The time had come, because the world, not only Catholics but intellectuals at large, began to be more and more dissatisfied with the philosophy they knew. The time had come, because mankind began to feel utterly at a loss. Men felt hopelessly exposed to relativism. They had nothing upon which to get a hold. They were drifting without knowing where and without knowing what made them drift.

The problems to which Scholastic, that is Christian philosophy, gives the solutions—so far as the human mind is capable

at all of discovering them—were felt, vaguely, dimly, unconsciously, even outside Catholic circles. The steadily growing
interest in things medieval which we witness today is a proof
thereof. A short time before the Leonine encyclical appeared, a
scholar of a tremendous range of knowledge had published
a book in four volumes: *The History of Occidental Logic.*
K. von Prantl, the author, had undertaken this stupendous
work with the intention of demonstrating, once and for all, the
utter unimportance of medieval philosophy. Scholasticism was
to him a meaningless repetition of formulas and what was good
in it was but the heritage of antiquity. Prantl indeed knew
more in this field than anyone, but he understood less of it than
anyone too. A few years after Prantl thought he had done away
with Scholasticism and the study of medieval philosophy, the
books and articles dealing with these subjects had grown to be
so numerous that it was practically impossible for anybody to
read all of them. And, I repeat, it was not the Catholic scholarly
world alone which contributed to these studies.

We refer to these facts in order to make clear our idea that
there was, in the times we are envisioning, a dumb, unconscious, unrecognized tendency moving toward a return to a
sound philosophy. It was not the study of this philosopher's
works or of that system, not a clear knowledge of what was
amiss with the age, that urged man toward a new conception.
It was simply a general longing of the age.

Freud wrote in his later years a little treatise on the *Unrest in
Culture.* He analyzes, of course according to the principles of
his theory, the phenomena he observed around him. In doing
this he commits the very same mistakes we had to call attention
to when reporting on "ethnological psychoanalysis." But one
might surmise that Freud had always been alive to this unrest.
It had existed long before the war of 1914 and before the post-
war crisis convulsed Europe. It had existed in fact for centuries.
A keen mind, capable of observation, with a sharp feeling for
problems, as the mind of Freud doubtless was, could not fail to
be impressed by this general situation. In his earlier years he

might have been utterly unaware of this impression. He might have been deluded, as many were, by the apparent security of the times. With an unshakable faith he might have believed in the future of science and in its becoming the means for saving mankind. But, no less than many others, he was somehow aware that mankind needed to be saved.

That he hoped for redemption by science is part of his heretical attitude. But it becomes heretical, because he was, unwillingly, an exponent of the general unrest and the general need for security. Not economic security, necessary though it had become even then. Not political security, which a great majority believed to be assured. But intellectual, mental security in face of a world which was in danger of drowning in a sea of relativism. And Freud became also an exponent of one very intense longing, though this too was hardly expressed then with any clarity, the longing for a true understanding of man's nature. No man in modern times, even if he chooses to renounce Christianity altogether, can think and feel and study without relying on the great truths Christianity has given to the world; nor could Freud.

The problem of person is the one where psychoanalysis is most dependent on the principles of a sound philosophy and where it betrays these principles most. It is a problem which cannot be thought of without arousing immediately all the questions bearing on man's ultimate destiny, the true nature of his being, his origin, his place within reality—without feeling that behind all these questions looms God.

The intense preoccupation with religious things which the psychoanalysts manifest, the curiously embittered way they talk of religion, is a sign of their being aware—in their unconscious, of course—of these burning questions as being somehow very near to their own problems. In Freud's last book, *Moses and Monotheism,* there is a passage where the author confesses that he envies those who believe, but that he himself feels unable to follow them.

A Summary and a Challenge

IT IS hardly necessary to repeat the principal objections which have to be raised against psychoanalysis in the name of sound reason, of philosophical truth, of psychological and ethnological fact. It is not that psychoanalysis flatly contradicts a philosophy we believe to be the true one; this argument will make no impression on anyone who either clings to another philosophy or sincerely believes he has none at all. To convince the man who holds a different philosophy it would be necessary to prove to him that the fundamentals of his own philosophy are mistaken. This is extremely difficult because philosophical attitudes are mixed up, very often, too often indeed, with emotional attitudes and also because too many people are not aware at all of the foundations of their philosophical ideas. To convince the man who despises philosophy and boasts of having none at all, it would be necessary to make him see that even the denial of philosophy is a particular philosophical position, worse in fact than any "fantastic" speculation, because it is ignorant of its own nature. This also is difficult because hatred of philosophy is an obstacle one can hardly expect to surmount. An appeal to sound reason or commonsense does not impress the average believer in science and scientific methods—be it real science or only the parody of science, masked in the dress of science and couching unscientific notions in the impressive terms of science—since commonsense lost its credit with the true scientist ages ago.

Even before Kant in a well known passage of his *Prolegomena* spoke so contemptuously of "commonsense," simple reason had come to be disregarded; reality was believed to be at bottom what physics showed it to be and no longer what the senses led man to believe. Neither an appeal to philosophy nor to reason is likely to shatter any of the convictions of the psychoanalysts. The only thing these admirers of science and despisers of reason and philosophy respect are facts and the self-consistency of a system. They all are likely to believe that a statement is true when it squares with all known facts, and that a system deserves to be called true when it is self-consistent and does not, even in its ultimate consequences, lead to any contradictions.

Though we, for our own part, are prepared to give more credit to philosophical principles and to trust reason more than the scientific mind today generally does, we shall not stress considerations either of philosophy or of reason. The incompatibility we have shown to exist between psychoanalysis and the principles of sound philosophy may serve as a warning to those who still believe that some synthesis may be brought about. As we have already pointed out, there are some who try to disengage the psychoanalytical method of investigation and treatment from the philosophy which is at the back of the whole Freudian system. We have endeavored to demonstrate that the bond between these is necessary and indestructible; the very moment the philosophy on which psychoanalysis rests is abandoned, the whole theory becomes impossible and self-contradictory. The psychoanalysts who will not allow that such a separation may be possible are right in this and show a better understanding of their ideas and their fundamental positions than do those critics who bow before the method and reject the philosophy.

We hope to have shown by conclusive arguments that Catholic philosophy and psychoanalysis exclude each other. The admirers of Freud and the advocates of "modern science" will, of course, conceive of this demonstration only as a new proof of the unmodernity of Scholastic philosophy. They cannot be expected to feel differently. They are, however, wrong. But it is not for these pages to point out the basic mistakes made by an ultramodern conception of science and of philosophy. Moreover,

Scholasticism had for centuries grown accustomed to being considered obsolete and unmodern; for being so it has a remarkable vitality. But a person who has neither a sufficient knowledge of Scholastic philosophy nor the capacity or the inclination to become acquainted with it will be in no way impressed by being told of this incompatibility.

But, as we have tried to prove, there are facts with which psychoanalysis not only is incapable of coping, but which this theory simply disregards and which have to be taken at their full value. And there are in Freud's system contradictions and logical fallacies which an objective mind cannot put aside as unimportant. As long as psychoanalysis does not give a clear and satisfactory answer to the challenge of such facts and as long as it fails to justify itself against the reproach of logical inconsistency, its demand to be recognized as a true science, even as The Science of the human mind, remains unfounded, a mere pretension.

As a rule the psychoanalysts refuse to consider any criticism raised against their ideas. It was Freud's habit to disregard all criticism, and this procedure has been followed by his pupils. The father of psychoanalysis rarely and incidentally referred to any critical remarks; and his pupils have generally but one answer: the critic's statements are contrary to those of Freud. We remember being answered, many years ago, by one of Freud's most prominent pupils to the effect that, whenever asked why this or that statement is true, he would refer the critic to the works of Freud.

The psychoanalysts have, as we saw, another weapon of which they make extensive use. Inability to accept their ideas is not credited to objective reasons nor to rational arguments, but to the irrational forces which are at work, they say, in the minds of the critics. During the discussion referred to in the preceding paragraph we were told by another prominent representative of psychoanalysis that our unwillingness to accept the Freudian conception of "resistance" was due to—resistance and therefore a striking proof of this fact being real. Unless you have been analysed and unless analysis has taken from you the resistance against some general truths, a resistance conditioned by "unconscious" factors, you are incapable of evaluating psychoanalysis. For that reason the Psychoanalytical Association refuses to receive anyone who has not undergone complete analytical treatment.

This demand is unique in the history of science. It is true, of course, that a physicist will not take seriously the criticism of a person whom he knows to be ignorant of the principles of physics. The mere statement that this or that "cannot be true" has no weight with the scientist, if such an objection is not based on a full knowledge of the principles and the methods of science. But there are no principles and no method which permit and legitimatize the ignoring of facts or the sinning against the fundamental rules of logic.

We may concede to the psychoanalysts that many of the objections raised against their theory, especially in the first years when psychoanalysis began to be widely known, were based on prejudices or were urged with arguments which certainly lacked objectivity. Moral resentment, the feeling of being shocked by certain statements, and so forth, are not valid arguments in a discussion of scientific ideas. Psychoanalysis is indeed, as we have been at pains to demonstrate, contrary to morals; but it is not so because it lays such stress on sex or because it draws certain consequences, but simply because of its basic principles and because of the philosophy on which it rests and from which it cannot be separated. Earlier critics may have had some inkling of this, but they failed to penetrate sufficiently into the ideological background so as to become fully aware of it. We may hold them excused, because these fundamental ideas were not so visible in the first publications as they have become now. Today we are able to detect these basic principles in the early writings of Freud and of his school because we look back after having been made aware of them by the study of later books and articles.

But let us, for one moment, suppose as true that this idea of "resistance" is the only cause of so many rejecting the teachings of Freud. Even if this supposition were really the case, the answer of the psychoanalysts would still be quite insufficient. We believe that the position taken by the Freudian school is another striking proof of their tendency to disregard objectivity and to seek reasons and causes exclusively in the subjectivity of the individual mind. But, assuming the position of the psychoanalysts to be justified, what would they have to do? Is it really enough to dismiss all criticism by referring it to subjective and individual factors? We do not think so.

Psychoanalysis boasts of being a thorough, all-comprising explanation of mental facts. Inability to accept the psychoanalytical theory is such a fact. It has therefore to be explained. The psychoanalyst says that he explains the fact by referring it to the working of resistance. But this explanation is merely a formal one. It takes no account of the particular reasons alleged against the propositions of psychoanalysis. To refer to resistance might be a sufficient explanation in those cases in which the critic without basing his judgment on any definite reasons simply declares psychoanalysis to be wrong and unacceptable. Mere resistance might have many ways of expressing itself. Why does it, when opposing psychoanalysis, take on just this form? By what peculiar trick does resistance condition the objections based on facts of psychology, of ethnology or on the logical fallacies contained in the Freudian system?

We have remarked that psychoanalysis shows an amazing disregard for the material contents of mental states and of their phenomenological peculiarities. The theory is really interested only in genesis. The only question it asks and desires to answer is where some mental fact had its origin. The particular nature of the mental state is of no importance. It is noteworthy that psychoanalysts, though they have collected probably a greater mass of material than any other psychologists on this matter, have not contributed anything essential to the descriptive psychology, for instance, of dreams.

This disregard makes the psychoanalysts an easy prey to rash generalizations. As soon as they form the idea of some attitude as being conditioned by certain of the factors they are accustomed to emphasize, they will have it that these conditions obtain in every case they observe. They do not think it possible that the deplorable resistance shown by their adversaries could have several reasons, least of all that there could be objective reasons, derived not from attitudes or complexes, but resulting from the objective structure of their own theory and its incompatibility with facts. They do not, therefore, even trouble to look at the arguments brought forth; these arguments are against. psychoanalysis, *ergo* against the becoming conscious of repressed material, *ergo* due to resistance. Not worth while considering them. But that is no way of arguing. The only sensible reaction would be a carefully objective consideration of the arguments of their adversaries.

The way in which the psychoanalysts respond to criticism has to be abandoned. As long as they continue to answer by merely repeating that they are right and by referring to their own ideas, their defense is not worth anything, because it does not take account of the things of which they are accused. Logical fallacies are not eliminated by committing them a second and a third time. Nor have the psychoanalysts ever answered in a satisfactory manner the reproach of neglecting essential facts of ethnology and of relying on bad evidence. Asserting that these things have to be true because they fit in with Freud's ideas is not an acceptable answer.

Some authors have tried to prove that the statements of psychoanalysts might be confirmed by experimental research in psychology. They have referred to phenomena like retroactive inhibition as being in accordance with Freud's conception of repression. Such and similar statements are based, however, more on analogies than on identities. S. Rosenzweig indeed predicts that the opposition against psychoanalysis will be overcome by experimental research.* Until today little has been done to make his assertion probable. His thesis is indeed more of a program than of an achievement. There is one experiment, however, which ought to be made and which would, we feel sure, possibly shatter some of the psychoanalytic positions, because it has to be done with the very method of Freud. This decisive experiment has not been made, so far as we know, by any psychoanalyst.

It has sometimes been urged against the interpretation of dreams that a patient or some other person might, during analysis, tell the analyst a dream which was not dreamt at all but invented. The results of analysis, it was surmised, would then become misleading. To this the psychoanalysts answered, and they were quite right, that the fact of a dream having been invented does not matter since nobody can invent anything not belonging to and not expressive of his own mentality. But one might suggest this experiment: take a dream out of a book, for instance one of the prophetic dreams recorded in history or one of those told in some biography or even one of the experimenter himself. These dreams cannot contain any material belonging to the analyzed person. But the psychoanalysts might refer to the common knowledge of mankind, to ethnical symbols, to the persistence of prehistoric influences. It is therefore better to devise another experiment. Show a picture to the person to be analyzed. Let him look at it long enough to get a complete idea of it. Let him describe this picture while he still has it before his eyes. Thus even the selective influence of personal attitudes will be excluded. And proceed then as if this description were a dream of this person. Use the procedure of free association, starting from the various elements of the description the subject has given.

Many years ago I made some experiments of this kind. The

* *The experimental study of psychoanalysis*, Charact. a. Personal., 1937, 6, 61.

analysis of this "dream" brings forth very much the same unconscious material as does the analysis of a real dream. The experiment is indeed not devised for disproving the statements on the unconscious material. But what it does definitely disprove is, the idea of the causal relation between the mental fact or element which is made the starting-point of analysis, and the material which is brought forth. It destroys also the notion of symbolization. How could anything in the life of the analyzed person ever condition his having seen and reported the things he has been shown in a picture? This becomes especially impressive if one uses a picture which has nothing to do with the common situations of life, *e.g.*, a more or less schematical illustration of an apparatus for metabolism experiments.

It is up to the psychoanalysts to make such experiments and to discuss their bearing on Freudian psychology. Just as it is up to the psychoanalysts to answer the various criticisms many authors propose. And, to repeat this once more, the answer cannot be given by referring to the alleged results of psychoanalytical investigation, because it is the method itself whose reliability is doubted. Nor, as we endeavored to show, is practical success any proof of the truth of the theoretical statements.

The psychoanalysts must give a clear answer to the contention that their psychology rests on a materialistic basis. If they want their psychology to be what they believe and say it is, then its propositions ought to be independent of any philosophy. We are fully convinced that there is no psychology at all which could be independent of the philosophy which the psychologist consciously or unconsciously adopts. Accordingly, we do not feel that psychology ever can become a science molded on the ideal of physics or even of biology. But the psychoanalysts think such a psychology possible. Let them prove then that their psychology is truly independent of materialistic metaphysics and of hedonistic ethics, and that it is not necessarily subjectivistic and not incapable of incorporating in its system the idea of person.

To cope with these demands the psychoanalysts would have

to become philosophers. It is to be hoped that, had they but acquired a little knowledge in philosophy and some capacity of perceiving the kind of logic they use, they would see a good deal of the truth regarding their psychology. But it is much more to be feared that not one of them will attempt to acquire the necessary knowledge in philosophy. They will not attempt it, first, because they are too sure of possessing the whole truth on human nature; secondly, because they despise philosophy—though without knowing much of it; and thirdly, because they believe they already know enough of this despised subject. It has been often the misfortune of philosophy that too many people believed themselves to be capable of passing judgment on metaphysical or other assertions without troubling to get reliable information and without bothering to learn how to deal with these problems. It is always much easier to deny the existence of a problem than to attempt to solve it. No wonder that there is a close friendship between psychoanalysis and positivism, since there is no "philosophy" so full of negations as positivism is.

Let us look again briefly at the criticism which we have seen to be demanded by the factual statements and the theoretical assumptions of psychoanalysis.

Psychoanalysis is a thoroughly materialistic conception. It stands and falls with its materialism. Whosoever feels incapable of accepting the philosophy of materialism cannot but reject psychoanalysis. Because of its materialism, the philosophy of Freud and his school is, in what regards ethics, a simple hedonism. It is addicted to an extreme subjectivism which even blinds the eyes of the psychoanalyst to obvious objective facts and truths. Because of its subjectivism it is impersonalistic and ignores the essence of the human person. Its philosophy, therefore, is based on ideas which not only a Catholic, but every man believing in a higher principle existing above matter and dominating it, cannot but reject.

As a theory, psychoanalysis rests on several serious logical fallacies. It is guilty of more than one *petitio principii*. It commits the same fault also in regard to facts, especially when applying its notions to ethnology or the study of religion. The alleged proofs to which the psychoanalysts refer their critics are no proofs at all, because they imply all the logical fallacies which invalidate the theory and the method.

The method is so closely linked to the theory and to its philosophy that no one rejecting these can adopt the method, unless it be that he understands by psychoanalytic method merely the production of free associations. But if a method is to bear the name of Freud, it must be more than the production of free associations—it must necessarily include certain interpretations which become meaningless outside of a purely naturalistic conception of man's nature.

The "axiomatic" propositions which pervade the theory and on which the latter is based imply several notions which are either self-contradictory or disproved by facts.

Psychoanalysis disregards the observations of experimental and otherwise empirical psychology, because it does not itself take account of obvious facts of introspective psychology. Thus it persists in identifying all kinds of pleasure with that arising from gratification of the instincts and it reaches accordingly mistaken ideas on the ends of strivings, conations and volitions. Its conceptions of the mental development of children are also characterized by a total disregard of the facts ascertained by immediate observation.

Nor is the contention that all mental phenomena ultimately derive from instincts and their representations without its serious drawbacks. Psychoanalysis can explain, at best, that at a given moment of a person's life some mental state arises and why; it can never give a satisfactory explanation of the existence of such mental states and of their peculiar qualities.

The ideas many psychoanalysts maintain in regard to facts of physiology are partly preposterous, partly, to say the least, arbitrary and lacking any reliable proof. Interpretation and fantastic speculation take the place of observation and experimental analysis. As a theory of neurosis the system of Freud is unsatisfactory, because many of its assertions rest exclusively on the interpretation suggested by this very same theory, illustrating thus the logical fallacy of which psychoanalysis becomes guilty. The successes obtained by this mode of treatment are no more convincing proof of its truth. Psychoanalysis, claiming to be the only reliable and truly scientific psychotherapy, fails to explain why results as good as its own may be achieved also by methods which retain no element of psychoanalysis, whether of the method or of the theory. There is no proof that psychoanalysis is necessary for the treatment of neurotic disturbances.

The applications to ethnology, of which the psychoanalysts are evidently rather proud and which they consider as one of Freud's greatest achievements, are absolutely erroneous, since the evidence to which they appeal is quite unreliable. Freud and his followers have neglected to make sure of the reliability of the authorities they quote and of the validity of the facts to which they allude. Their conceptions of primitive society, of the development of rituals, of totemism, and so forth, are contrary to the findings of ethnology and prehistoric research.

Neither Freud nor any of his followers has a true idea of what religion is or of the essential characteristics of the various religious forms. They are especially in the dark in regard to all facts referring to Christianity. Hasty generalization, arbitrary assertions, ignorance and imagination replace exactitude of analysis and critical appreciation of data in these vagaries.

The alleged confirmation of Freudist conceptions to be gained from the study of prehistory, of ethnology, of religion does not exist at all. It is the result not of two independent lines of research leading to the same conclusion—which alone would amount to a confirmation—but of a vicious circle in argumentation, the interpretation of ethnological and other facts presupposing already the truth of the psychoanalytical theory.

Psychoanalysis appears thus as an immense error. Its success in the modern world is caused by its being a compromise of divergent and even contradictory sets of ideas. Indeed psycho-analysis is a characteristic feature of the period of transition from the late nineteenth century to the present day or rather to the periods which are going to evolve out of the chaos of our days.

Psychoanalysis, as we see it, is indeed what I have called it in the title of this book: a "successful error." I have tried to show what Freud's error or errors were and why his system, in spite of its immanent falsity, came to achieve its success. But no system of ideas exists without containing some truth. There must be truth also in psychoanalysis.

We must be on our guard against the notion that the error of a gifted mind, let us say a genius, is better than the truth stated by an average personality. The error of a great mind does not become better by being associated with a remarkable effort of the intellect. An error is forever an error. It is measured by its relation to truth and is not altered, in its nature, by any factor of subjectivity. Freud may have been a genius; that makes things worse, not better. If we try now to state the merits of psycho-analysis and of its founder it is not because of any feeling of admiration for the person of Freud. I have said more than once, in the foregoing pages, that mine is not the biographer's atti-tude. We are studying the history of ideas and not of persons. Everyone of course is free to admire a man who for many years, in spite of great opposition, pursued what he believed to be the truth. But this admiration of a personal quality has nothing to do with our judgment on ideas and on their truth.

There may be more truths concealed in psychoanalysis than will be mentioned here. But these truths, if they exist, are hid-den under such a mass of misconceptions, of mechanistic, ma-terialistic imagery, and are so thoroughly disfigured by being clad in the vestments of a theory which disregards the essential features of human nature, that it would take a long time and much strenuous effort to clear away all the useless and utterly mistaken paraphernalia. Psychoanalysis has discovered this or that fact in psychology; but these discoveries would have been made anyhow because of the general tendencies in psychology, which we detect now as having been active in the past. All these things are of minor importance compared with Freud's two or three greater achievements.

Freud inaugurated the movement of medical psychology. Psychoanalysis was the first attempt at discovering the nature of neurosis and at devising means to help a group of sufferers who are more numerous than one might think at first and who are becoming steadily more numerous.

Freud's theory was the first to emphasize the enormous importance the experiences of the child have for the future development of personality. His views intensified the sense of responsibility of educators who have thus become conscious of their duty not only to impart knowledge and to teach morals but to observe with the utmost care the personality of the child and to avoid all influences which might threaten his further development. The vulnerability of the personality of children has thus been emphasized and brought to the attention of psychologists, physicians and educators.

One may call it a merit of psychoanalysis that, in an age of unduly exaggerated intellectualism, it has made visible the influence of non-intellectual factors within human personality. Though the relation of these factors to personality and to the faculties of the mind was misinterpreted by Freud, he nevertheless restored in a way the old and nearly forgotten knowledge that man is not pure reason or pure spirit, but a being composed of matter and soul.

Behind this, however, is hidden what is Freud's greatest and most unexpected achievement. He restored the knowledge of the leading rôle of the mind, the knowledge of the dominating place held by the soul in human nature. To do this was not his intention. He did not know that he was serving the rebirth of a truer conception of man's nature than he himself was ever capable of imagining. We do not here allude to his discoveries regarding the influence mental factors have on bodily phenomena, nor to his unveiling of the mental origin of so many troubles, nor to his having demonstrated the curative influence of mental attitudes. All this is but the peripheral manifestation of things much deeper and much more important. Freud's real achievement is: This discovery that mental treatment is capable of healing certain bodily troubles, that it may result in a total change of attitudes, has delivered mankind from the bondage of biologism. Not every thing is due to heredity, to bodily constitution, to an immutable set-up of personality, decreed by blind fate. The dominion of the mind is reestablished.

It is an irony of history that this was, we will not say achieved but started, by a man whose whole mentality and whose training made him a materialist. The rebirth of a better understanding of the dignity of the mind and of the place it holds in human nature has been partly the work of a scholar who endeavored more than many others to drag down the mind to the level of mere biological function. To have opened the road to such an understanding is not Freud's personal merit, nor can this be credited to psychoanalysis, the spirit of which is in fact contrary to a development which cannot end but by bringing back something of the truths of old to the general consciousness.

Freud and his school are, in regard to this fact, and to several others, but the exponents of a deeply hidden undercurrent which had started even before psychoanalysis came to exist and has gone on all these years, insensibly though steadily gaining in strength. But we may be grateful for a peripheral manifestation if by it we are led to become aware of some great truth, of some high value, of some enlivening.

Balaam *redivivus*. Freud, a disciple of materialism, a believer in science, a man to whom words like objective value or moral law had no meaning, a mind whose analyzing power tended towards the dissolution of human person, this very same man appears as a servant of higher plans and wider scopes. Ignorant of this fact himself, he prepared the way for views which are destined to overthrow his own, as falsehood will be always overthrown by truth.

Psychoanalysis lived and still lives by strength of the little truth it contains and of the greater truth of which it is the foreboding. Where it has sinned against truth lies its weakness and the germ of its end. Falsehood cannot survive forever. Truth lives eternally.

Index

Book Order Form

Please send me the following books:

Quantity	Title	Price per book	Total
	What's Wrong With Freud?	$ 24.95	

Shipping/Handling charges: $2.95 for the first book, 75 cents for each additional book. Please allow 3 to 4 weeks for delivery	Postage/ Handling _____
	TOTAL _____

Enclosed is my [ ] check or [ ] money order (in U.S. Dollars) made payable to **Roman Catholic Books.**

[ ] Yes, please place me on your mailing list to receive your full catalog of books.

Please print:

Name: _____

Address: _____

City/State/Zip: _____

Telephone #: _____

Mail your order to:

Roman Catholic Books
A Division of Catholic Media Apostolate
Post Office Box 2286, Fort Collins, CO 80522